SHANE SPALL is from a large Midlands family. Her mother called her Number Five and her father after a character in a Western, played by Alan Ladd.

As a teenager in the 70s she worked in a Quaker hotel in Birmingham and on her day off would sit in New Street station and wonder where everyone was going. She now knows they were mostly going to work or coming home. The day that the young actor Timothy Spall arrived at New Street in 1981 she was in a council flat a few miles away. They could have been ships that had passed in the night but he sought her out because he had fallen passionately in love with her when he had accidentally touched her arm one evening. The young actor now gets to play parts called 'old man' but is considered to be a 'national treasure'. He's a bit of a show off, but his wife doesn't mind, she keeps his feet on the ground. They have three children and used to have a bulldog that couldn't swim and a goldfish but they fostered it out as it got lonely staying home on its own.

THE VOYAGES OF THE PRINCESS MATILDA

OF THE

SHANE SPALL

EBURY
PRESS

1 3 5 7 9 10 8 6 4 2

This edition published 2013
First published in 2012 by Ebury Press, an imprint of Ebury Publishing
A Random House Group company

The Random House Group Limited Reg. No. 954009

Addresses for companies within the Random House Group can be found
at www.randomhouse.co.uk

A CIP catalogue record for this book is available from the British Library

The Random House Group Limited supports the Forest
Stewardship Council® (FSC®), the leading international forest-
certification organisation. Our books carrying the FSC label are printed
on FSC®-certified paper. FSC is the only forest-certification scheme
supported by the leading environmental organisations, including
Greenpeace. Our paper procurement policy can be found at
www.randomhouse.co.uk/environment

MIX
Paper from
responsible sources
FSC® C016897

Designed and set by seagulls.net

Printed and bound by CPI Group (UK) Ltd, Croydon, CR0 4YY

ISBN 9780091941819

To buy books by your favourite authors and register for offers visit
www.randomhouse.co.uk

For the boy Tim who phoned me from the Holiday Inn, and our extraordinary children, Pascale, Rafie and Sadie.

And Dr Jonny Gaynor, Professor Tony Goldstone, Dr Panos Kottardis and the Haematology Department at University College London Hospital.

Contents

Introduction

A gale is blowing as I look out of the porthole and our ropes all groan in protest. The wind blows one way and a fast current pushes *The Princess Matilda* the other. It is springtime but so cold and I have asked Tim to fill the coal bucket once he has finished checking our mooring lines. With this nor'easterly blowing I am tempted to light the fire in the saloon, but I suspect the wind would puff acrid clouds of smoke down the chimney. We are moored in a sheltered lagoon yet, even in our safe haven, the water slip slops under our bow and it is bucketing down with rain. Tim is now soaked to the skin, but still he and I can't think of any other place we would rather be.

Across the lagoon is an impressive piece of Scandinavian architecture. The Norwegian white weatherboard church was built in 1868 to make the Norse sailors feel more at home. Roald Dahl, coincidentally the author of a book called *Matilda*, was baptised in this church shortly after my own father was born. Cargo ships crossed the North Sea and travelled down the west coast of Britain carrying Norwegian timber to shore up the Welsh coalmines. But Tim and I have come all this way by sea too. No mean feat for two people without any seafaring experience. When he was growing up, the closest Tim came to water was the boating pond in Battersea Park. He had a Saturday job at the funfair. For me, it was a filthy canal just off the A5.

*

My earliest memory is sitting on Dad's shoulders as he walked along the towpath. He told me stories of his childhood, when the cut was teeming with horse-drawn barges laden with coal.

'I used to chuck stones at the boats and the bargees would aim great lumps of coal at my head!'

My father's granddad had been a boatbuilder, and had probably helped to build the narrowboats my dad used as pelting targets. He did his stone throwing more out of necessity than spite because my grandma could not afford to buy fuel. Her 12 children were feral and occasionally hunted in packs. Dad was the swimmer in the family, so his brothers would shout names at the barge helmsman, who would wave his fist at them. With him distracted, my father swam alongside the boat, grabbing one huge lump of coal after another. Once it was in his slippery hand, he would gently lower the fuel into the cut without making a splash.

'But Dad, why?' I asked him. 'What was the point of dropping the coal in the canal?'

He stroked his chin and looked around just in case there was anyone eavesdropping. 'We used to get 20 to 30 boats a week, so when it was dark I'd dive down and get the coal out. There was more than enough for Mother and I'd flog the rest.'

He was always a dodgy entrepreneur, my dad.

Shortly before he died, I asked him if he remembered his granddad.

'No me love, he died before I was born, but Mother used to have an old photograph of him. He looked like a genial man, served his apprenticeship as a journeyman engineer and travelled all over the country.'

'And he ended up building boats in the Midlands?'

My dad nodded.

'Did he ever build sea-going boats?' I asked.

He thought for a little while and replied. 'Who knows what he built before he settled down. Mother said he was a master craftsman, he might have gone out to sea for all I know.'

My dad ran his veined hands through his hair and laughed. 'I always fancied I had a bit of Jolly Jack Tar in me.'

Then it was my turn to laugh. 'Do you remember that third engineering officer, Dad? The one on that cruise you and Momma took me on?'

My dad raised an eyebrow. 'I wanted to break his neck.'

I had my first love affair aboard an ocean liner. That was what gave my dad murderous thoughts and me my sea legs. The day Dad found out, a sou'easterly gale was blowing a Force Ten and the propeller came out of the water, sending a momentous vibration all the way through the ship. I was down below the waterline when it happened, looking for my third engineer to tell him to keep out of my father's way. It was tempestuous down there.

*

Our tempest is dying down and Tim has got his sea-charts spread out on the floor. Some of the passages we have made on *The Princess Matilda* are amongst the most treacherous and challenging waters in the world. Together we have navigated many nautical miles as we journey around the British Isles. But we are hardly in Dame Ellen MacArthur's league; we have to keep leaving the boat. Tim has to earn the mooring fees and that often takes him out of the country. Since we left the salty end of the Thames in 2005, Tim has worked on location in Los Angeles, New York, New Mexico, Canada, South Africa, Spain, Ireland, Germany, Italy and Watford, and I have travelled with him, so we have to find a secure mooring while we are away. The other limitation is the weather. We are fair-weather sailors and can only cruise between April and, if we are lucky, October. Mooring up before the bad weather sets in means we have had a new winter home every year since 2006. We love seaside towns out of season, when all the fairground rides and beach huts are mothballed and the tourists have gone home. There is nothing quite like an empty beach, even if you are being knocked off your feet by the force of the wind. In the winter we keep our fire alight and, after a day out, eagerly head back to our boat to be thawed out.

Tim and I consider ourselves to be pretty lucky people. Tim, as an actor, does not have a 9-to-5 job, and as his PA neither do I. But I am a PA who also does the dirty washing as well as wrestling with filthy wet ropes while hanging on to a boathook to secure a mooring buoy, often in torrential rain. Sometimes it is impossible to get off our boat. We have run aground once or twice. Other times we have anchored in the middle of nowhere or moored on a branch of a tree. Tim and I are very self-contained. Even though we have been married for almost 30 years, we still enjoy each other's company. We can measure our married life together in two ways: before we had a boat and after we had a boat.

Back in 1997, we got our first boat, *Cassien*. She was past her prime, an old rust bucket otherwise known as a narrowboat. I think my dad and his grandfather, the journeyman, would have recognised *Cassien* as a coal barge with a roof and windows. We bought this particular boat because our youngest daughter, Sadie, thought the red upholstery was pretty and our son, Rafe, was excited about the bunk bed in the back cabin. Tim and I loved the little saloon with the L-shaped fitted sofa that pulled out to make a double bed. Our eldest daughter, Pascale, was a teenager and had other fish to fry. We cherished that boat for it helped my husband in his long, slow journey back to health. It was a very slow boat because four miles an hour is the speed limit on a canal. So in a way, Tim's recovery mirrored its sluggish progress up and down the Grand Union Canal, the main artery of Britain's inland waterways. I suppose we can also measure our married life together another way: before and after Tim being diagnosed with acute myelogenous leukaemia.

8 May 1996 is a date seared into my brain. This was when Tim was told he had days to live. That is what 'acute' means. Leukaemia is a blood disorder and he spent over three months in protective isolation. While he was being treated with aggressive chemotherapy, many of his arteries collapsed. When he was recovering, we had to be close to a hospital, just in case of any complications.

*

Our slow old rust bucket was the perfect weekend getaway from London. Every Friday after picking our two youngest kids up from school, we would drive through rush-hour traffic to get on to the M1. *Cassien* was moored just off Junction 16. This might not sound appealing, but as soon as we got onboard we would move the boat and 20 minutes later our little home-from-home would be situated in stunning countryside. That is the beauty of having a boat: you can always change the view. Tim was still very weak when we bought *Cassien*. He had had major surgery a week before our first outing.

Cassien brought back so many memories for Tim and me, as our first holiday together had been on a narrowboat. Tim said he would take me anywhere I wanted to go, and he expected me to say Spain or Italy. At the time my eldest sister, Jack, ran a pub on the old A5, the last but one in England on the Llangollen Canal. We spent a week on a hire boat discovering this bucolic waterway. Three decades later, I looked at my south London boy, still weak from his illness, standing on the back deck of our own boat, *Cassien*, with a smile on his face. It was worth every traffic jam we encountered on the M1. For the first few weekends Tim was unable to pull in a rope or knock in a mooring pin or operate a lock. The kids and I did it. Rafe would wield the mallet as I positioned the huge metal pin. Sadie, a little scrap of a thing, would open the lock gate.

There is something incredibly healing and soothing about being near water – most of the time. Tim fell through an old wooden jetty on our second weekend aboard, and we had not even left the marina. His ankle and foot swelled up like a balloon. His platelets were still very low; they are what control clotting and bleeding. The following weekend he slipped down a bank and grazed his hand very badly. A healthy person can take small accidents, but a recovering cancer patient cannot. But it did not put us off. It made us even more determined to make the most of every single day.

Tim's mantra is *'don't let fear hold you back'*, and he has faced some hugely scary choices, both in his illness and his career. But some of the choices we make on our trip around the coast are pretty scary too. The sea is a dangerous place, full of peril. That is why our coastline is dotted with lighthouses and lifeboat stations. It is also littered with shipwrecks. Tim has skippered our boat around hazardous headlands known as 'the graveyards of ships'. The captain of any vessel has to get the weather, tides and timing right. Split-second decisions are the difference between life and death. The first officer on the *Titanic* gave the order, 'Hard-a-starboard!' a few moments too late and an iceberg sank the unsinkable.

So, these are *The Voyages of The Princess Matilda*. This book tells two stories, and I make no apologies for combining them, as they seem to me to be inextricably linked. The first is how Timothy and I took charge of our new boat and valiantly (or stupidly) attempted to sail her to Wales, another country! That, as you will see, was something of a gargantuan effort. The other story is how Tim beat his illness. When he was dreadfully sick, my laptop was my constant companion as I sat vigil by his hospital bed. I would type for hours, putting all my emotions into the hard drive. Tim thought I was writing my thesis. But I also kept a notebook where I scribbled my thoughts before I went to sleep. I called these my 'midnight notes' and I hope you will forgive me for using some of them in this book.

As you shall see, this book is about being alive. It's also very much about family, old friends and about the loved ones we have lost along the way. They say that travel broadens the mind. In my experience it does so much more than that.

*

The wind has dropped. If Tim and I were alone on our boat we would probably leave this mooring, but we have a VIP in our spare cabin. Well, actually, she thinks the cabin, if not the whole boat, belongs to her, for it was named in her honour. Our granddaughter, Matilda, is five years old and is spending part of her school holidays with us. We shall take no chances while she is aboard. Tim and I shall wait patiently for a perfect day, when the sea ripples gently like a silk handkerchief. There will be no clouds in the sky and just a hint of a balmy wind that will beckon us to continue our journey. We were not always this sensible. What follows is how a couple of novices went out to sea.

Chapter One
The Top End of the Salty Thames

'How on earth are we going to get all of our stuff down there, Tim?'

We had just carried half a dozen boxes, two large blue IKEA bags and four black bin liners out of the car. That in itself was a marathon task. The car park was in Brentford, a five-minute walk from the river. And the river was way down below us at the bottom of a long ladder.

'Let's just concentrate on getting you down there first shall we?' Tim replied.

We peered over the wall with anticipation. There she was. *The Princess Matilda*, our brand new barge, sparkling blue and black, was moored on the Thames. She called out to us to come and claim her, but first we had to get down to the bugger.

*

Peter Nicholls, the very likeable, mildly eccentric and irascible boatbuilder, had delivered *The Princess Matilda* to Brentford. In many ways, Peter reminded me of my dad, standing for no nonsense and prepared to get his hands dirty. He had brought our boat 90 miles down the Grand Union Canal from Braunston where she had been built. They had passed through Northamptonshire and Buckinghamshire without any incidents. Then, a few miles north of Brentford lock, a queen-sized mattress had become tangled around the propeller of our *Princess*. It had stopped her in her stride.

Some people still use the canals as a fly tip. We have seen all sorts since our canal boating days began, including a dead sheep, a live calf and three television sets in a flotilla of suburban debris. We once saw a headless dog inside a supermarket trolley. That was not very nice. On one occasion, on an unattractive Midlands canal very close to where my dad used to swim for coal, we had to stop while Tim removed from the propeller a man's shirt, a pair of stained white Speedos and, rather interestingly, a size 48 double F cup brassiere. One can only hope that the dog-decapitating, supermarket-trolley-chucking, incontinent transvestite who created all this carnage has been rehabilitated. I prefer the coconuts that are put into the canal by Hindus living around Southall, who hope their offerings will end up drifting out to sea via the Thames to the River Ganges.

Knowing what the cut can throw up, the news of the mattress came as no surprise to us. But it was not as easy to detach a mattress as a bra, even one sized double F. Peter had to put *The Princess Matilda* into a dry dock to get it removed. While he was wrestling with bolt cutters, Tim and I were in America. We had flown to northern California to attend the wedding of Alicia Silverstone and Christopher Jarecki. Tim had worked with Alicia on *Love's Labour's Lost* and they had become firm friends. When Tim makes a new friend our whole family does too. On our return to London, we phoned Peter.

'Yes, she's all ready for you, no damage, but she's moored on a pontoon outside the marina. I couldn't get her in, the tide was too low,' he said.

Tim and I didn't think this would be a problem. We had been looking forward to taking charge of our new sea-going boat for months, and actively involved with this project from the beginning, more than a year before. Peter used to send us photographs of the work in progress. From the drawing up of the plans to the modifications of the design, the barge was our baby. It was a happy coincidence when we discovered we were expecting our first grandchild as the first plans were being drawn up. We were in West Hollywood at the time. Tim was making *Lemony Snicket's A Series of Unfortunate Events*, with Meryl Streep and Jim Carrey. I had screamed when I'd heard the news about our eldest daughter's pregnancy. And finally at last we were going to see our new boat in all her glory.

*

My husband climbed over the wall, shouting instructions as he manoeuvred himself on to the metal ladder. 'All right, darlin', take your time, don't look down, I'm right here,' he assured me.

I peered over the wall. It might have been only 12 feet but to me it was the Eiffel Tower. I turned around and grasped the rails on top of the ladder with clammy hands. I stepped down to the first rung, my left foot searching blindly for the next and accidentally kicking Tim in the head. He swore and hurried down the ladder out of my way. Our new boat was moored against a narrow holding pontoon that had been pulled away from the ladder by the momentum of the tide.

Tim told me to hang on while he made a leap for it. 'OK, go down one more rung and give me your hand,' he instructed me.

'Are you sure?' I asked him.

'Yes, hurry up, I don't know how much longer I can hold it.'

Uncharacteristically, I did what I was told. I don't like doing that. I took one step down, turned, stretched out my hand and noticed the tide was swirling and coming in rapidly. Tim had pulled the pontoon as near as he could to the ladder with a boathook, and with his other hand he pulled me on.

The pontoon felt less than safe as it rocked up and down and from side to side. It was only designed to have boats moored against it while waiting to use the lock into the marina.

It felt like we were on a cakewalk, an old-fashioned fairground ride designed to make you fall over in the most humiliating way possible. This was intensified every time a boat passed or one of us moved. And over the next couple of hours, we had many passing boats and I had to move about a great deal. We still had to get all of the bags and boxes down the ladder too.

Tim found a spare rope in a box on the back deck and jumped off the bucking pontoon and back on to the ladder. He disappeared over the wall. His head reappeared moments later and he shouted down to me. 'I'm glad we decided to leave the dog at home. OK are you ready?'

He lowered the first of the IKEA bags down to me, shouting, 'Go on grab it! Grab it!'

'I can't, lower, lower.'

It was like a ridiculous competition from a reality show. I clutched the bag, trying not to fall in the river as my weight made the pontoon tilt. I quickly took three steps back. Tim let out more slack. I undid the rope and Tim pulled it back up and disappeared once again. I dragged the bag to the boat and tipped new sheets, towels, tea lights and the rest of the IKEA booty on to the back deck, then rushed back to my kamikaze post. For the next hour or so the IKEA bag kept going up the wall empty. It came back filled with our worldly goods swinging from side to side.

The last bag was filled with essential groceries, bottles and a bag of ice. I put these next to the galley window while I waited for Tim to come down the ladder. We stood expectantly by the wheelhouse door, each waiting for the other to get out the keys. Tim held out his hand.

'You have them.'

'No, you have them.'

'No, Tim, you have them! Check your pockets again,' I said as he searched frantically, patting all of his pockets.

He shook his head, 'Maybe they fell out while I was up there?'

Once more he climbed the ladder and was gone a few minutes, by which time I remembered Peter had said he had left a spare set in a secret hiding place. Tim came back down the ladder looking very forlorn. I rattled the spare keys. With a huge smile on his face, he put the key in the lock and we entered the wheelhouse. The wheelhouse is a very large space, with two doors on either side and a concertina door to the back deck. After he unlocked all of these, Tim undid the door that leads to the steps down into our boat. We moved inside. It was beautiful. Over our solid fuel stove was the small figurehead we had bought in West Hollywood just after we had discovered we were to be grandparents. It has dark hair, brown eyes and little wings. We had had to wait several months before we gave the figurehead a name. She is now called Matilda, named after our granddaughter, who also has dark hair and brown eyes, but has yet to grow wings.

We put a great deal of thought into the design of this boat. Our last two had been narrowboats so this time we wanted something wider and seaworthy. It had taken a few years for Tim to persuade me we should get a sea-going boat. What I like about the canals is you can touch the bottom if you fall in. Eventually he talked me around. I had done my research and whittled it down to two boatbuilders. The first one I telephoned told me that his vessels started at a quarter of a million pounds, could we afford him? I hung up, patronising sod. I then gave Peter Nicholls a call. He answered all my questions and I arranged to pay his boatyard a visit. I was shown around a new build that was almost completed. I liked it and more importantly I liked and trusted Peter. I reported back to Tim. We gave Peter the commission to build us a boat. And here at last, over a year later, we were aboard her.

The Princess Matilda has two cabins, central heating and two bathrooms. She can sleep six. Tim and I have a large family and we like to have visitors when we are afloat. Our sofa in the saloon converts into a double bed. Tim was the interior designer, and all the furniture was handmade in walnut. The walls are clad in cherrywood, which gives *Matilda* a very '30s retro feel. The master cabin is reminiscent of a stateroom in the old *Queen Mary*. We both chose the solid fuel stove. There is nothing better than a roaring fire on a frosty night. In the galley we have a huge slab of marble as a worktop, as I enjoy cooking and it makes a handy ironing board.

That first afternoon, I filled the sink full of water while Tim searched for the ice in the bag of groceries and we plunged a bottle of champagne to chill while we brought everything down from the back deck. We then spent a busy couple of hours unpacking and stopping every now and then to take a look at the continually changing view out of the windows and commenting on the speed of passing boats. The wake left us bobbing up and down.

I complained to Tim, 'I thought there was an 8 mile an hour limit around here.'

'Apparently not,' he said as he tried to tune the television aerial. 'This is a dreadful picture. Maybe it will improve as the tide comes in. So darlin' what are our plans?'

'Dunno, let's get our maiden voyage with Peter out of the way first shall we?' I replied. 'Have you found BBC Two?'

It is easy to forget that the River Thames is part of the sea. Its waters are a mix of salty and fresh; the depth and the speed of its currents are ruled by the pull of the moon. We watched and felt the tide's gathering force. The river level rose as the afternoon drew on, quickly submerging the mud on the opposite bank and lifting up the groaning flimsy pontoon. Our ladder got shorter and shorter. I was sorting out clean sheets as Tim took the chilled Moët out of the sink.

'We should have put everything onboard at high tide,' he said.

I laughed, 'Next time. Pour me a glass darling, please, then help me make the bed.'

'Give me a chance. It's gone everywhere! This bottle must have been bashed on the wall, where are the dishcloths?'

I passed him one and shook out a brand new duvet.

'I've been up and down that ladder more times than a demented budgerigar and now you want me to wrestle with a duvet cover,' he complained as he passed me a glass.

After everything was shipshape, we surveyed our second home.

'Sorry for being tetchy,' Tim said. 'Let's sit on the roof darlin'.'

We made a toast and Tim put the glasses and bottle out through the open window. I followed him up the steps with two brand new IKEA cushions. Then, holding on to the handrail, we walked along the narrow deck that runs around the boat. Tim retrieved our drinks and I threw up the cushions. *The Princess Matilda*'s flat roof is enormous. We could almost play a game of tennis up there. Tim can step up from the deck to the roof, but I have to scramble up on my hands and knees. Not an elegant manoeuvre but it is worth the effort. The last of the flood tide brought out the rowers making the most of the slack water. We waved to them but they ignored us. Rowers are the cyclists of the water. They always look like they are having a terrible time.

The River Thames is a magical place to be on a summer's evening. The only noise was the odd splash and grunt from the rowers. In the space of a few hours, the whole energy of the river had changed. That afternoon Tim and I had unpacked piles of books, so I knew what I was looking for as I disappeared down below. I climbed back on the roof with a set of binoculars and one of our many tomes about the river.

I flicked through the book. 'Ah, Tim, I think we're moored near the spot where Julius Caesar crossed the Thames.'

We then spent 20 minutes arguing about who played Caesar in the movie. Tim was adamant it was Sir John Gielgud and I was quite sure it was Marlon Brando.

'No Brando played Mark Antony.'

My husband does a pretty good impersonation of them both, but Brando is his best. His shoulders rise, as he slightly juts out his chin. He speaks through his teeth from the back of his throat. It takes him forever to deliver the line. '*I could'a been a contender Julius, I could'a been somebody!*'

It was a beautiful evening, and a trip boat passed us by on its way back to Westminster Pier. The passengers all returned our wave.

We watched the trip boat as it disappeared around the bend of the river. The rowers had all vanished too, retreating to their boathouses with the last of the daylight. We felt we were the only people on the river.

We took it in turns looking through the binoculars, fascinated by the changes in the landscape brought about by the shifting tide. We pointed out old jetties that emerged as the tide ebbed, leaving behind the relics of past times. When it was too dark to see much, we lay on our backs, Tim's arm around me. It was a new moon and we watched the clouds moving across the sky. Then the clouds disappeared too, and as the night drew on the first of the stars appeared.

'Isn't that the Plough, Jupiter, Mars?'

Neither of us spoke for a while, satisfied and happy to be lying together looking up into the heavens. Then the silence was broken, and we both sat up.

'Did you see it?!'

In the west a shooting star had crossed the cobalt blue of the night sky. Silently we both made our shooting star wish.

We knew without saying a word, watching that shooting star, that it heralded a new chapter of our life.

*

I was looking for greenfly on the elderberry bush in our garden. You walked down the path and stood in front of me. You had fear in your eyes. You opened your mouth and said, 'Look at these.' I told you to go to the chemist to ask advice about the ulcers, but then they weren't just mouth ulcers, were they? Horrible purple red patches on the inside of your mouth. The chemist told you to consult a doctor. 'Phone Dr Gaynor,' I said. 'He'll sort you out, give you some vitamins, a tonic, maybe an injection to give you a boost. You're run down darling and have been working too hard. You've done three jobs back to back. You're not superman.'

Chapter Two
London Bridges

We went to our bed that evening, burrowing down under our brand new duvet in our brand new cabin. Both of us were tired, but not that tired. Later we discussed the prospect of taking the barge downstream into central London. Peter, the boat-builder, was going to join us the next day to show us the ropes, metaphorically and literally.

Tim took the helm in the wheelhouse the following morning. Peter advised him about the controls and we set out on our maiden voyage down to Limehouse. It was a stunning journey into the centre of London, passing countless familiar places: Richmond, the Royal Botanic Gardens at Kew, Battersea Power Station, the Houses of Parliament, the London Eye and the Tower of London.

We headed towards Kew Bridge, the first of London's famous road bridges. These are each incredibly distinctive. Some are arched, others cantilevered and a couple are suspended over the river. Tim and I know them off by heart now. After Kew comes Chiswick, Hammersmith, Putney, Wandsworth and Battersea. We have crossed Battersea on a red Routemaster many times without knowing anything about the hidden cast iron arches below. And we often sat in a traffic jam on the Albert suspension bridge, intrigued by the road sign instructing troops from Chelsea Barracks to break step. Going under the bridges is a different experience altogether. Most of them have a red or green disc to show which part of the bridge is navigable. And just in case, some have a bale of straw that hangs from chains, which I suppose means *mind your head*.

Tim slowed down between Wandsworth and Battersea Bridges. He wanted to point out to the irascible Peter, who was greedy to get his hands back on the steering wheel, the three tower blocks of the Winstanley and York Road council estates. Tim's family was re-housed to one of the blocks, Chesterton House, in 1968. Shortly afterwards, the house in which he and generations of his family had been born was knocked down. Some called it 'slum clearance', but Tim's mother hates her old family home to be called a slum.

Peter was handed the binoculars and Tim pointed, 'That's where I grew up.'

I visited Chesterton House shortly after Tim and I met. The flat was on the sixth floor, and the lift was broken. My boyfriend said this was often the case, so we began our climb up the concrete stairwell. He said it would be worth it when we got there, and he was right. It was a huge stylishly furnished and beautifully decorated flat. Enormous picture windows showed us views across the rooftops of south-west London. Tim's mother Sylvia made lunch along with her mother Beatrice.

'Call her Little Nan,' Tim said. She was so tiny. Tim told me later that Little Nan had watched both of her parents die of TB.

As we ate, Sylvia and Little Nan told me all about their old home and about bath night. Sylvia was louder than anyone else. 'We had one once a week whether we needed one or not. I would go first, the tin bath filled from the gas Ascot in the scullery. Tim and his brother Nicky would get in next, then their dad Joe would tip the bath-water down a drain in the backyard and refill it for himself.'

Tim laughed and said, 'Sounds like a Hovis advert, Mum.'

Peter took the wheel as we neared Chelsea, as Tim wanted to take photographs.

'I used to fantasise about living on a houseboat on Cheyne Walk,' he said.

I interrupted, 'And now look at us. We have a boat of our own. And it moves – those are all stuck there.' I regally waved my hand as we passed the houseboats on Chelsea embankment.

Tim took the helm again as our boat approached Westminster. It was Peter's turn to take out his camera. He was keen to photograph the Palace of Westminster and Big Ben. I kept watch for the trip boats picking up passengers on Westminster and Charing Cross Piers. A recreational boat like ours has to keep out of the way of working boats. The tide was running really fast and the trip boats and ferries left a scar on the water behind them. The river was silt brown, frothy, confused and angry, fighting against the wake of the riverboats. When you approach a bridge you can see and feel the might and force of the tide swilling and swirling through the arches. As we came through Waterloo and Blackfriars Bridges large waves broke against us broadside and splashed the windows in the wheelhouse. Peter suggested Tim put on the window wipers to clean away the spray. The waves and turbulence got more vigorous as we came under Southwark heading towards London Bridge. This bridge is arguably the most famous and the most boring of all London's bridges. It is rather an anticlimax when you travel beneath it, but one's eyes are drawn immediately to the more stately Tower Bridge ahead.

On the Thames we learnt we had to keep a look out for what was ahead, but also what was coming behind. There were numerous craft to look out for on this busy part of the river: tugs towing rubbish barges, police and harbour master launches, rowing boats, speedboats, trip boats, ferries, yachts and narrowboats. We had navigated the tidal Thames on both our narrowboats. It was not much fun. In fact it was terrifying, the wake from the bigger craft almost swamping *Cassien* on one occasion. Our narrowboats didn't have any protection and Tim and I were often soaked to the skin. But today on *The Princess Matilda*, we stayed dry in the haven of our wheelhouse. We also had more power and speed to get out of the way of the trip boats.

The last trip boat had come exceedingly close to us and slowed right down for the tourists to take photographs of the Tower of London. We could hear the commentary over the PA.

'To your right ladies and gentlemen is the infamous water-gate entrance to the Tower. It has been known as the Traitors Gate for over 400 years. Through the gate Anne Boleyn, the second wife of Henry VIII, was taken by barge to be tried and executed...'

We missed the rest because the trip boat was motoring upstream and we were being taken by the tide, at a furious rate, downstream. All I could think was that the barge taking Anne Boleyn to meet her fate must have done so on a slack high tide. I hoped we would enter into Limehouse, our final destination, on a gentle tide too.

The Princess Matilda passed under Tower Bridge. It is a wonderful sight when it opens. Tim and I have sat in a restaurant on Butler's Wharf, which used to be a bonded warehouse, and seen *HMS Belfast* going through. The old navy ship weighs almost 12,000 tons and is 69 feet high. *The Princess Matilda* weighs a little less than that and is only eight feet high out of the water, so we had plenty of headroom.

Tower Bridge was specifically designed to let sailing ships with tall masts into the Port of London. The Port of London is also known as 'the Pool', for on a calm flood tide this is what it looks like. Anne Boleyn's last view of the river would have been a shimmering flat lagoon. The Lower Pool of London is downstream of Tower Bridge, where the deeper drafted ships used to lie. Tim and I have never navigated the Lower Pool when it has been calm. It has always reminded us more of a bubbling jacuzzi. And here again on the day of *The Princess Matilda's* maiden voyage we encountered another whirlpool as we pushed onwards towards Wapping Pier. Our last challenge was the wide expanse of river known as 'the Fairway' in front of Limehouse lock. It was obvious that this was going to be quite a challenge. Flotsam and jetsam hurtled past us at a furious pace.

Peter told Tim to push the boat at full throttle because we had to cross the river. This was easier said than done. Our boat can do 7.5 knots and the tide was doing 4. We had our destination in sight but we were on a swift outgoing tide. *The Princess Matilda* travelled sideways as she crossed the Fairway. We overshot the lock, so Tim turned the boat head-on to meet the force of the ebb tide.

My knuckles were white and I whispered under my breath, 'Come on *Matilda*, come on *Matilda*...'

To get in to the slack water of the lock cutting, a boat needs a great deal of power and *The Princess Matilda* didn't let us down. Nor did Tim, my skipper. We all cheered as we came into the shelter of Limehouse pier head. Tim and I hugged and kissed, and shook Peter's hand.

'We love her, Peter,' I said. 'You've given us a great boat, thank you.'

Peter replied, 'Thank you, I'm pretty fond of her myself.'

All we had to do then was wait for the green light to indicate the lock was prepared for entry. While we waited I nipped below and checked how our lunch was doing. I had just put a pan of new potatoes on to boil when Tim gave me a yell to come back up top.

Someone waved to us and indicated which side of the lock

we should tie up. The lock-keeper had opened the sluices and prepared it for us. Once we were in, Tim climbed on to the roof and threw a rope up to the assistant keeper. I tied my bowline around a cable, so it would rise with the water. Peter took care of the sternline. Limehouse is a large lock and three other boats joined us to pen through. The last boat in was a small cruiser and the skipper got his timing wrong. The vessel was bashed by the force of the tide against the brick wall of the pier head. The crew entered the lock behind us pretending they didn't care about the angry looking dent on their bow. There was a great deal of overwrought issuing of instructions as they tried to secure themselves in the lock.

'Fenders portside … PORTSIDE! Throw the line. THROW THE LINE!'

From my own experience I know that whenever anyone shouts 'throw me the line', it will invariably end up in the water. And sure enough, this is what happened. The cruiser began to drift away from the lock side, so there was more yelling.

'Stern to! STERN TO!'

There was a yacht tied up on the other side and the crew were running backwards and forwards, all of them yelling, 'FEND OFF!' The cruiser was heading their way.

'Fenders to starboard! FENDERS TO STARBOARD!'

I decided I had time to check how the Jersey Royals and roast were doing.

A lock is like a bath: you fill it until it is the same level as the bath above, or pull the plug if you need to go down. But on tidal locks the bath water level changes rapidly. The lock filled fairly quickly and it was quite turbulent, so Tim and I hung on to our ropes to keep the boat against the wall. The damaged cruiser was rafted against the yacht and its crew looked at us with accusing eyes, as if it had been our fault they messed up. When our boat was level with the lock side Peter hopped off and waved us goodbye.

'Hey Peter,' I said, 'aren't you staying for lunch? I've got a chicken in the oven and some potatoes on the hob.'

Peter laughed and came back on board and helped Tim moor on a water point in Limehouse Basin. While they messed about with hoses to fill up our two fresh water tanks, I drained the potatoes and made a salad. They were still both faffing about, so I sat on the roof and surveyed our new mooring. Hardly anything remains of the old dock. The name Limehouse speaks for itself. It comes from the limekilns, established along the river in the fourteenth century. In the nineteenth century, seaborne cargo used to be unloaded in the Pool of London and transferred on to barges that entered the basin much the same way as we had. The barges travelled from the basin and through the Regent's Park Canal to the inland waterways. The old ware-houses around the dock have now been replaced with waterside 'lifestyle' apartments.

Limehouse was the gateway between the tidal and manmade waterways of Great Britain, but Tim and I were more interested in its association with Charles Dickens. After lunch we said goodbye to Peter, who appeared to be reluctant to leave *The Princess Matilda*, his latest creation. But the ship was now ours, so we carefully locked up the doors and set out to explore the back streets and old wharves off Narrow Street, which crosses the basin. One of the first jobs Tim did after he was ill was *Our Mutual Friend*. The villain, Rogue Riderhood, 'dwelt deep and dark in Limehouse Hole'. He also drank in The Grapes in Narrow Street. Dickens describes the pub as being 'a tavern of dropsical appearance … [with] corpulent windows in diminishing piles'. It has not changed one little bit. Walking back to our boat, after a couple of gins in The Grapes, Tim and I found a few deep, dark wharves that we thought could be Limehouse Hole. Tim would say, 'This must be it.' Then we would find another and I would say, 'No this must be it.'

Something else we could not agree on was where we should go next on *The Princess Matilda*. When we commissioned Peter to build this boat we had vague plans to go around the British Isles. Frankly, I had never been convinced that this was a good idea. Tim suggested a compromise. We could go downstream as far as the Thames Barrier and if I was not happy, we could turn around and come back. The lady lock-keeper at Limehouse was very helpful and suggested the best tide to get us down to the barrier.

'You don't want to be pushing too strong a flow, nor do you want to be going too fast so you can't change your mind.'

The Thames Barrier protects London from flood tides and is an astounding feat of engineering. In the 1920s a surging storm tide caused Chelsea Embankment to collapse. Thousands of people were made homeless. The barrier was built during the 1970s. At this time, I was living in London and used the underground most days. I remember the signs warning commuters what to do if they heard the flood alert siren. Tim and I watched the news when the Thames Barrier was opened in 1984 and used to drive down to Greenwich when a storm surge was forecast. We would have a pint in The Anchor and Hope, a pub with an extraordinary view of the barrier. When the ten steel gates are raised against the might of a surging tide, we could see waves crashing and complaining at the huge barricade. As far as I am concerned, the river ends at the Thames Barrier and the sea begins.

As Tim and I cruised towards the Thames Barrier, we felt very small. The barrier spans 520 metres, which in my book is a third of a mile. It is wide. Extremely wide. I began to miss the narrowness of a manmade canal. I knew then that I was not ready to take on the sea yet, so Tim turned the boat around and we went back upstream. We agreed that we would go through the barrier in the autumn, once we were more used to the boat. In the meantime, we would spend the summer on the upper Thames.

A short time later I was down in the galley plugging in my laptop to charge and heating soup on the stove. Tim shouted for me to come up into the wheelhouse.

'I've got something to show you.'

I poured the soup into cups and hurried up the three steps to join him. He used his cup to point out an old wharf as we headed back up the river.

'That's Convoy's Wharf. Do you know what's behind there?' I shook my head.

He looked at me and said, 'Deptford.'

Then I understood. I took Tim's cup off him and gave him a hug. He knew what the hug meant. It meant I am so fucking glad you are alive.

*

'See you tonight, chicken. Love you, bye.' You tucked me in and put my alarm on for an hour later. I took the kids to school, I sorted the ironing out ready to pack for Cannes, and I missed the doctor's phone call because I was dropping your evening suit off at the dry cleaners. I tried to get you on your mobile, but it was switched off. You attempted to catch me at home but you finally got hold of me by leaving a message at my gym. 'Tell Shane to phone, it is impor-

tant.' *I had to get some change for the public phone. You must have had your mobile in your hand.*

'Can you come?'

I knew, but I didn't say anything. I let you speak.

'I've got a serious blood disorder!'

'Where are you?'

'Deptford.'

I heard your voice, the fear, and I told you to put me on to somebody to give me directions. And I shouted at God as I climbed into the car. 'You bastard! You fucking bastard!'

Chapter Three
The Upper Thames

Tim and I held hands as we sailed on the Thames beneath Waterloo Bridge, heading upstream now. We were happy to be side by side, delighted to be doing what we had planned and dreamed of in the dark times. For that is when we made our plans for the future.

'If and when I get better, we're going to get two things: a Rolls Royce and a boat,' Tim had told me. And that's just what we did. The old electric-blue Rolls Royce kept breaking down and, come to think of it, so did our first crumbling narrowboat, *Cassien*.

The non-tidal Thames begins at Teddington Lock. This is where the tidal stream ends. Tim and I love the Thames because it is a river of mystery. Its source is barely a bubble that rises in the Cotswolds near Cirencester. We don't know how that insignificant bubble ends up swelling to the much larger river that spills over Teddington weir. The fact of the matter is that billions of gallons of fresh water cascade over this controlled waterfall every day. Tim and I had moored near there on both our narrowboats and heard it crashing over the top and through the sluices, and watched kayaks white-water rafting in the torrent.

Teddington has three locks. You have to wait for a green light to show you which one to go into. Once through the lock, our first stop has always been a mooring below Hampton Court Palace. Henry VIII spent three honeymoons here. The Royal barge would have discharged the King and his new Queens very close to where we now moored our brand new *Princess*. When the trip boats finally stop picking up tourists from Hampton Court and the night draws in, the river becomes still.

After mooring, Tim and I walked to a nearby pub. It was a scary walk on a dark night. The Palace was sinister in the gloom and an owl began to hoot. We heard a fox screech as if it had been caught in a trap. The riverside pub was very close and so we both began to run. Was that the ghost of Katherine Howard pleading for her life or the night fishermen on the other bank? One night at Hampton Court was enough for us. We left the next morning for Runnymede, the reach above Bell Weir.

Runnymede is where King John signed the Magna Carta in 1215. In fact, there is a small island on the Thames named 'Magna Carta' after the document that changed the face of English rule. A friend used to have a house on the island. Tim and I had Sunday lunch there once. Our youngest, Sadie, was three and she and I stayed by the swimming pool after lunch while everyone else went to explore the island. Sadie was a little chatterbox and I could easily keep track of where she was by the sound of her constant talking, so I lay on a sunbed and closed my eyes. But after a few minutes I leapt to my feet: the chatter had stopped. She was in the pool, face down in the water. I grabbed her and shook her and she squealed in anger, spluttering like a newborn baby. Her water wings had been discarded at the top of the steps. It had been a close shave.

We left our narrowboats on the weir moorings below Magna Carta Island countless times. The lock-keeper is a gruff bear of a man with a huge beard. He tells us all the gossip. The river- and canal-boating community is a captive audience. He has lived in the Bell Weir lock house for years and knows everyone. But it is not the quietest spot to have a mooring. On a warm summer's evening when you sit out on the deck, you can hear the traffic on the M25, which straddles the river a stone's throw away. The lock is also right underneath the Heathrow flight path. All the long-haul flights going out to the Middle East and Australia go over at about 11pm. But I tell myself, if the millionaires on Magna Carta Island don't mind being under the flight path, why should I?

We have lots of happy memories of this mooring, despite the noise. If you block out the cars and the aeroplanes, the river is a thriving natural habitat for fish and birds. Wild salmon jump up the weir and kingfishers skim the water. Coots, moorhens and Canada geese fight for the breadcrumbs thrown out of our galley window. One summer's afternoon when the heat was shimmering in the air, Tim dived into the river and reappeared between two swans.

I yelled at him, 'For God's sake Timmy, they'll break your arm!'

'As long as they don't want to mate with me for life, I'll be fine,' he said, doing backstroke and pulling up his trunks. But they ignored him and he swam back to the bank. It was hard to believe London is so close.

Beyond Magna Carta, the river runs past Windsor Home Park, one of the very few places where the Thames Path has to leave the river. This has always felt very unfair to me. There are endless *No Mooring* signs. Mind you, if I were the Queen, I would not like boats moored down the end of the garden either.

Every time we pass the signs I say to Tim, 'Did I ever tell you about that festival I went to?' And he always replies, 'What the one where the coppers told you to clear off? No, you've never told me!'

I have an old photograph of me at one of the illegal festivals held in Windsor Great Park in the 1970s. There were half a dozen sound stages and loads of hippies smoking grass and getting stoned. The police turned up by the coach load and used truncheons to politely encourage everyone to leave. That photo was taken shortly afterwards. I look at this picture and want to write this girl a note: 'You have seven years to wait for your true love.' But she would have answered, 'Fuck off, my true love lives in Wales!' I had no idea there was a spotty 17-year-old south Londoner living in a council high-rise who would become the love of my life.

Our Windsor mooring is a special place, known to us as Rat Island. You will not find the name on any map, but it is the second little island under the Eton Bridge. Years ago Tim and I moored there on *Cassien*. I remember sitting on the deck one evening as the sun went down. Out of the corner of my eye I saw something moving. I thought it was a squirrel so ignored it. A few minutes later, it appeared the whole of the grass was wriggling. I shone a torch, and discovered the island was swarming with rats. We always pull up the gangplank now. What we like about this island is that it is very private. Windsor is a very touristy place and if you moor below the castle, people sometimes stop and peer into your window. Not many tourists know about Rat Island.

The Thames is a magical river with backwaters, eyots and hidden islands. We are still convinced we are the only people who have ever moored in these secret places. Every time we go up the Thames, I re-read *Three Men in a Boat*, and read sections out loud to Tim. He is not always receptive, but I can picture every island, pub and lock that Jerome K Jerome writes about. The book still makes me laugh out loud, the silly men and the dog, Montmorency, lurching from one mishap to the next. At the time we first set sail on *The Princess Matilda*, we had a dog of our own, a lovely-natured bulldog whose name was Nelly. She couldn't swim, poor Nelly.

The first time Nelly fell in she was a puppy and we were on our second narrowboat, *The Colleen Bawn*. We were moored above a lock and I had let her out on to the grass for a wee. I went back inside to make some tea, keeping my eye on her through the galley window, which was level with the grass. Then I heard a splash. Tim was in the shower but, hearing my screams, he rushed out to see what was going on. Nelly had dropped like a brick and had briefly disappeared from sight. Tim had grabbed a towel to wrap about his waist when he came barefoot to the rescue. He slipped on the wet grass as he ran, and I hurried to his aid.

'Oh God Timmy, she's going under again!' I screamed.

Tim managed to get to his feet once again and slid to the bank, still grasping the towel. He lay down on the wet grass and reached down into the water. He could see bubbles rising to the surface. Nelly reappeared two more times before he managed to snatch her by the nose and drag her out. Meanwhile the towel had slipped off and Tim was stark naked. A convoy of boats had watched the drama with great interest. Nelly trembled for 10 minutes and then puked. The third time she fell in, we got her measured up for a life jacket. She hated wearing it and gave us a pathetic and beseeching look every time we strapped her in.

Shiplake, just above Henley, is bulldog-friendly and calm. Nelly could paddle in and out of the river there. Shiplake Island has a beautiful camping site with huge ridge tents that are put up in the spring and taken down in the autumn. The lock island plots are highly coveted and are passed down through generations of the same families. It could be a picture on a biscuit tin from the 1950s or from an old Scout manual. The antithesis of Shiplake is Oxford. The towpath becomes dusty from all the bikes tearing along beside it. Our boats always become showered with dust and grit when we moor there. When we visited on *The Princess Matilda*, it made us want to turn around and head back downstream, back to the peace and quiet of Shiplake, Henley and the eyots.

The day before we left Oxford, Tim heard the desperate screams of a drowning boy. 'Help! Help!' the lad shouted. His drunken mates were laughing from the bank, but he really was in danger. They carried on laughing and guzzling from cans. Tim stripped down to his socks and underpants and dived off *The Princess Matilda*, into the river. He managed to get hold of the panicking boy before he went under for the fourth time. With the help of a passing punt, the lad was pulled to the river-bank. I called for an ambulance.

After the boy was taken to hospital I realised Tim could have broken his neck diving into the murky waters. God knows there could have been a supermarket trolley lurking below, but it was me that shouted, 'You'll have to go in Tim!' He had almost died nine years before and there I was telling him to risk his life.

*

Our daughters, Pascale and Sadie, joined us in Henley in late July. It was so splendid to have them onboard. Pascale, our eldest daughter, was over for a brief visit from Melbourne, where she lived. Moreover, with her she had her brown-eyed, dark-haired baby girl. We all looked at the little figurehead above the stove. It looked like our grandchild. We had first seen her just moments after she was born. Pascale had pulled back the towel, still bloody from the birth, and said, 'Meet Matilda.' I phoned Peter Nicholls the next day to tell him what to christen our new barge.

Tim and I were so excited to have Matilda on board. We had bought her a life jacket in Abingdon-on-Thames while on the phone to Pascale. 'How heavy is she? Measure her, weigh her again,' we'd said. And now, in Henley-on-Thames, we strapped her into it. It had a collar to keep her head out of the water, should she fall in. Pascale, Sadie and I could not make up our minds who looked cuter wearing their life jacket, Matilda or Nelly. Or who out of the two hated wearing one most.

Nelly always drew a crowd of admirers as we went through the busier Thames locks. She was not always happy to be the centre of attention, and even less so if there was laughter involved. A bulldog is a sensitive creature and one wearing a life jacket can be an object of fun, so ours would often turn her back on her audience. Nelly's number one fan, Alicia Silverstone, joined us on *The Princess Matilda* at Maidenhead. She and her husband Christopher had caught the train down to spend the day with us and our daughters and granddaughter. They had come to the UK on a second honeymoon.

That evening we stopped above Bell Weir lock again. It is a great place to moor if you want to party and make noise because no other boats moor there. There is a reason for this. The bank is overgrown with weeds, brambles and nettles so it needs patience and a death-defying leap from our boat to the bank. Tim gets the bow as close as he can without running aground so I can get ashore. To secure us I will tie a rope around a branch, ripping my arms to shreds on the brambles. Then Tim can get off with his mallet and mooring pins. We heave and pull, each with our own rope until the boat is secured. Heaving and cursing is nothing new on the Thames.

We have always kept a scythe onboard our boats to slash away the nettles and weeds so Tim can see where to put down the gangplank. There is nothing worse than laying down a gangplank that isn't on terra firma. A scythe helps to pinpoint the bank. This whole operation takes about 20 minutes with both of us swearing. Ingenuity, teamwork and bloody mindedness are all Tim and I require to moor. Regrettably, on this occasion aboard *The Princess Matilda* we had guests who were unaware of the hazards of this particular mooring.

Alicia and the dog appeared on the deck before we had used the scythe or set down the gangplank. Before we could shout 'NO!' the dog, minus her life jacket, jumped and fell through the nettles and into the river. It was not very deep, but Alicia was not to know that. She made a grab for Nelly's collar, but it came off in her hands. A bulldog does not have a neck.

'Oh my God, oh my God!' Alicia's Californian twang rang out.

She was half on and half off the boat. Christopher jumped over the side to the rescue and was standing waist high in the water. He grabbed the dog first: he had no choice, his wife was so insistent.

'GET NELLY OUT! OH MY GOD SHE'S DROWNING!'

It was like a scene from *Three Men in a Boat*. Christopher scooped the dog out and threw her to Tim on the bank. The dog weighs over three stone, so it was quite a throw and quite a catch. He then went to help Alicia, who by this time was thrashing about. 'OUCH! OUCH! IT'S POISON IVY!'

She had her backside and bare legs stuck in the nettles. I would like to say Pascale and Sadie helped me look for dock leaves, but they just chucked me a torch. It was dark now and they had more sense. Baby Matilda slept through the whole thing.

*

Saturday
You came back from Dorset where you'd been shooting the first part of the NatWest advert. You'd filmed on the moors. You said, 'It was freezing cold, I felt like I was going to get pneumonia. I got back to the hotel at 7:30 and didn't even make it to the bar. I fell straight to sleep.' 'That's not like you Tim.' We picked Sadie up from her riding lesson and took the kids for lunch at the Harvester. You then slept for three hours. You poured a glass of wine as soon as we got home. You took a sip then it sat there untouched.

Sunday
We went to the Cast and Crew showing of Secrets and Lies. *At the party afterwards in Blacks, you sat and chatted to Jane Horrocks. I thought this was odd, usually it's me that sits and you are the butterfly. You don't like to miss anything. I stood. You sat. Then we went home and you slept.*

Monday
Had lunch with Miriam and wrote a note to Brenda Blethyn to thank her for letting us use the Folkestone flat.

Tuesday
I shopped for a pair of red gloves to go with the evening purse that Pascale brought back from LA for me to wear at Cannes. We fly tomorrow evening after you finish filming the ad. I ordered a new sofa.

*

Tim and I took the boat back to Limehouse the following week and left Nelly with my sister Jack. The dog's boating days were over. We could not risk her falling in again. She was getting too long in the tooth. *The Princess Matilda* needed a new home too. We had serious decisions to make about finding a winter mooring for the boat. When we had first thought about getting a sea-going boat, Tim was excited about the prospect of getting to the Isle of Thanet in Kent. On a road map it doesn't look too far. We thought it would be a short hop by sea. When Tim was a child, he and his family used to holiday on Thanet, which is separated from the mainland by the River Wantsum. Margate is Thanet's premier seaside town and his mother Sylvia has a retirement flat there. Nicky, one of Tim's two older brothers, lives near Ramsgate harbour. Tim thought we should see if we could get a mooring there. I made some phone calls. Yes, they had space but not until the end of October. It is possible to get to Ramsgate in one go, but we had time to spare and thought we would take the opportunity to have a look at the Medway towns – Rochester, Strood, Cooling and Chatham. Our guide was a road atlas. The Medway comes off the Thames and we used it to point out villages and towns.

'Cooling sounds cool, maybe we can moor there?'

It didn't occur to us to do it any other way.

The beginning of autumn induced a blanket of melancholia that seeped into my soul. Pascale and Matilda had gone back to Australia and seeing them off at Heathrow was torture. I experienced a feeling of complete bereavement. The nights were swiftly drawing in, the leaves changing colour, the dew heavy on the grass. When Tim and I took our early morning walks along Narrow Street, the mist hid the river from view. Tim always snaps me out of my depression. In fact he says, 'Snap out of it!' And on this occasion he reminded me we had a son about to open in a play at the Barbican. The play was *The Knight of the Burning Pestle*. This play has a special place in our hearts.

Chapter Four
The Play's the Thing

When I first met Tim in 1981, he was performing in a production of *The Knight of the Burning Pestle*. He played Ralph, a grocer's apprentice, who over the course of the play-within-a-play becomes Rafe, the Knight of the Burning Pestle. It is a satire on chivalric romance. It was to set in motion another kind of romance too. Tim at the time was sharing a flat with Paul Sands, a mutual friend, who took me to see the show.

I saw Tim before he saw me and I thought his performance was hilarious. He lit up the theatre with his energy and anarchy. The audience loved him. He made us laugh then made us cry. I don't know about anyone else in the auditorium, but I fancied the pants off him. Paul put the damper on that when he told me Tim had a serious girlfriend, so I didn't even try to flirt with him when I met him later. Tim remembers coming up to Paul's room and sitting next to me. He says he touched my arm and that it felt very soft. He phoned me a few weeks later. I was living in Wolverhampton at the time. I answered my phone and a voice said, 'Hello, this is Tim, Tim Spall. Do you remember me? I'm in Birmingham. Do you fancy dinner this evening?'

Of course I remembered him. How could I forget that amazing performance? He told me he was rehearsing at Pebble Mill in Birmingham, which was 20 minutes by train from where I was living with my four-year-old daughter Pascale. I explained to him that I didn't have a babysitter but he was welcome to come around to my flat. He said that would be great, so I rushed around to the off-licence and got a bottle of gin.

I really liked him. He turned up with the contents of the Holiday Inn minibar. We listened to Billie Holiday and talked; I was very impressed that he didn't try to sleep with me. We just danced and talked all night. At about 5:30am he looked at me as we sat across the room from each other.

'Can I kiss you?'

Before I could reply, he crawled across the carpet on his knees and kissed me just below my left ear. We both laughed.

'Wait here,' I said.

I picked Pascale up out of her bed – she was fast asleep – and carried her into the sitting room.

'This is my daughter.'

He touched her cheek and I put her back to bed. Three months later we were married and setting up home together. Tim adopted Pascale, and he and I enthusiastically set about extending our family.

*

Wednesday
Swallowing panic, I followed the signs and parked the car, for once not caring if I was going into shot. You were in your trailer. Someone pointed it out to me and I walked in. You cried and I held you. 'Dr Gaynor phoned, he said I must go and see him straight away, and I said, "I can't, I'm working, I can't leave the set, tell me what's wrong?"' There was a knock on the door. 'Five minutes Tim.' 'OK!' Your voice giving nothing away. We cried and phoned the doctor. He was seeing a patient, so you did your scene and I waited, walking up and down the trailer. Unable to be alone, I went to the car and sat watching you, my hand redialling the surgery. I could not get a signal. I got through just as you finished and Dr Gaynor told me the name of the hospital I should take you to. 'What, today?' 'Yes, as soon as possible!' I wrote down the address. Unit PPW4, University College London Hospital.

How could we take anything in? We were supposed to get a plane tonight. I have to pick your suit up from the dry-cleaners, and I have to pack for the Cannes Film Festival. I have to pack things for the hospital. This can't be happening.

Gaynor says to get you to the hospital NOW, but you won't let the crew down. You say, 'I'll be finished in a couple of hours, go home and pack me a bag, I'll only be in overnight, we can always go to Cannes tomorrow right?' I leave you in the trailer and go home. I have to make arrangements.

Deep down my first instinct is to get in the car and just drive. I want to escape. I want to run away. I want this not to be happening. I want to be alone, yes truly. I don't want any of this. As I walk through the front door of our home I see the answer machine is blinking. I press play. 'Hello this is Dr Gaynor, I need to speak to Timothy, I'll try his mobile!' Beep Beep. 'Shane, call me!' Beep Beep. 'Darlin' call me!' Beep Beep. 'I'll try you at the gym!' Beep Beep. 'I've left a message at the gym, please call me!' Beep Beep. 'Hello, are you in?' Beep Beep. 'Call me!' Beep Beep. 'Call me it's important!'

And now I know what was so important, but it can't be true. Beep Beep. 'I'm wrapping in half an hour, bring my phone charger please darlin'.' You want to finish the day before you go to the hospital. You find out you have a life-threatening disease and you want to finish the job first. I want to bolt, I want to hide, I want it to be yesterday again. Rafe and Sadie squabbling, Pascale sulking. I wander around the house. There are the clean piles of clothes ready to pack. My premiere frock is wrapped in silky white tissue paper and I won't be able to collect the kids from school. I panic. My mind will not work. I cannot focus. My kids, who can pick them up? I phone Kellie Jackson – we were at Goldsmith's together. She says, 'Is there anything wrong?' I tell her and get in the car. I hit every red light, take wrong turns and my brain says it's a mistake. I take one look at you when I get back to the set. Your face is grey and I know it's not a mistake. We grab everything from your trailer: your watch, book. Someone shouts, 'Have a good time in Cannes!'

I drove, what did we talk about?

The kids, what we would tell them, what we would tell your mum, what we would tell the advertising agency? Keep it secret, keep it out of the papers. Phone your agent. Pippa's just out of hospital herself. She says to leave it all to her, yes, leave it all to Pippa. We can't find a ticket machine to pay for the parking. I got the stuff out of the car while you wandered around with pound coins clasped in your hands. What a ridiculous situation. They were waiting for you, your name was already up on the board, and the nurses smiled at us both and said come this way Mr Spall, this is your room and we looked in to the bathroom as you do in a hotel and I said, 'This is OK isn't it?' 'There's a minibar in here too!' and we laughed.

*

Pascale's new baby brother, Rafe, was named after the character Tim had played when we fell in love, and 24 years later Rafe was cast in the same show. Both Tim and I were so excited and rather anxious about going to see our son perform in this very special play. And, as predicted, it snapped me out of my autumnal melancholia.

We went to see Rafe's show the night before we left our Limehouse mooring. My sister Jen had flown down from Scotland to see her favourite nephew perform and she commented that it was such a bonus to have the boat moored so close to the Barbican. This was a first for us: getting dressed onboard to go to see a play, and not just any play. We all walked along the embankment past the Tower of London and then through the City to the theatre. Our seats were on the front row, so we swapped them with people sitting a few seats behind us. We didn't want to put Rafe off. Tim and I were so very proud of our boy. His performance was just as funny and as physical as his father's had been.

Afterwards, we all had dinner and congratulated him, but when we were leaving, Rafe said, 'Mum, Dad, don't you think you're being a bit foolhardy taking the boat to Ramsgate?'

Tim assured him everything would be fine. 'We'll get down the estuary no problem, the weather forecast's good.'

'And we're stopping off in Rochester first, aren't we Tim?'

'Yes, it is on the Medway. We're going to have a literary odyssey, read some more Dickens. *Great Expectations*: Miss Havisham's house is in Rochester. We're leaving early in the morning. The lock-keeper said the tide should turn about halfway. We'll get down there in no time,' Tim said.

We locked out on to the Thames just as dawn was breaking. Jen climbed over the barrier to wave us off, but there was a mist hovering inches above the silent river. This was the highway of London's hidden city.

Tim drew my attention to the huge cranes rising above the mist along Canary Wharf. 'They look like they're telling us to go back. "Go home, you do not belong on the river!"'

We both laughed nervously. The sun, barely risen, was a hazy red.

'Red sky at night shepherd's delight…'

Tim interrupted, 'Red sky in the morning shepherd's warning, red sky in the afternoon, shepherd's house on fire!' He guffawed at his own joke with fear in his eyes.

There were no other boats on the river, just us. Tim and I felt we were the first people ever to have gone down the Thames – or up the Amazon. We were intrepid but terrified in case the lock-keeper had got the timing of the tides wrong.

I kept telling Tim to stop worrying. 'This is their job, and they know what they're doing.'

I didn't let on that I was worried too.

The sun rose over the Isle of Dogs. The river was soundless, the only noise, our engine and the swoosh of our bow pushing against the tide.

'Look Tim, look!'

We could see the mast of the Cutty Sark and Christopher Wren's twin domes on the Old Naval College in Greenwich. A gap between the two parts of the College exposes the Queen's House set back in Greenwich Park. Queen Anne didn't want her view of the river ruined. There was still a riverside beach in front of the embankment as we passed.

'The tide will be covering that beach soon, Shane.'

We have walked on that beach many times at low tide. The last time we had shared a bottle of Bass Blue pale ale. We drank it as we poured my dad's ashes into the Thames. The wind was blowing in the right direction and they remained visible for a while, forming a thin film on the water. I tipped the remains of the pale ale, his favourite beer, mixed with the residue of his ashes, into the water and Tim handed me a yellow rose, keeping one for himself. We both threw our roses into the river. The tide took them, gathering speed towards the Isle of Dogs.

When Tim was recovering from cancer he used to drive to Greenwich and sit in the bay window of the Trafalgar Tavern, just by the Old Naval College. He would come home and tell me how work on the Millennium Dome was progressing. You can see the Dome from the Trafalgar. Now we could see the Dome from the deck of *The Princess Matilda*. It was odd seeing the embankment and the pub empty. Usually it is teeming with tourists but now we had no one to wave at us. I held two yellow roses in my hand. I gave one to Tim, just as he had passed one to me on the day we scattered my father's ashes. We threw the flowers into the river – for me that feels much better than leaving them by a gravestone.

'I miss my dad,' I said.

'I know you do, love.'

The huge elbow of the Isle of Dogs nudges out towards the Greenwich Peninsula. Ahead of our boat was the white helmet of the Dome. It looked like it had been speared with giant cocktail sticks awaiting lumps of cheese. But in front of us was my nemesis, the Thames Barrier. The dawn sun was behind us as we approached. The last of the mist had been burnt away and so had my fear. Now, so much more than four months ago, I had a real curiosity about what lay on the other side. Maybe it was because the strong rays of the hazy sun had coloured the river a yellowy red. The waterway beyond the barrier was glowing and still, the same colour as the sky. We glided through the cathedral-sized concrete pier heads. The piers are topped with silver, housing the engines that raise the barriers lying on the riverbed. The river was bathed in gold and the sunlight shimmering on the water entreated us to go on. It suddenly occurred to me that I loved our boat.

We passed a psychological and physical line that morning. There would be no turning back this time. Just as the lock-keeper predicted, the incoming tide slowed as we cleared the Thames Barrier. But *The Princess Matilda* now had to share the river as London awakened. Just beyond the barrier, the Wool-wich Ferry links the North and South Circular roads across the Thames. The ferry was midway across and crammed with commuter traffic as we approached. Tim slowed right down and waited for the ferry to dock. We sped through the narrow channel as the ferry took on cars and lorries. Jets were taking off from City Airport. It reminded us we were still part of London's metropolis.

This part of east London is the home of the Dagenham Motor Works. We had no idea the cars were shipped overseas, but now we were confronted with cargo ships loaded with vehicles. Those skippers were not going to slow down for us. We would see them as tiny specks in the distance and in minutes they would pass us, powering full speed ahead. They soon left us far behind to ride over the huge waves of their wake. The river, frothy and angry at being disturbed, wobbled *The Princess Matilda* roughly about. The first time this happened we heard plates smashing and glasses breaking in the galley. I rushed down below to check out the damage. By the time I had cleared up the remains of our breakfast things, we were approaching the huge Queen Elizabeth suspension bridge, the last bridge on the River Thames, joining Kent to Essex via the M25. Tim and I have crossed this bridge countless times and seen huge ships heading out to sea. The river from the bridge looks immense. From our tiny boat the river felt like an ocean.

Tim and I looked up to the bridge with its four lanes of traffic thundering over 400 feet above our heads. The weather was not looking too good. About half a mile behind us I could see rain clouds and a squall blowing. The tide had turned and the wind had picked up. We saw crests of white horses coming towards us. Red sky in the morning; the prediction may have been right. Tim got his notes out, supplied by the St Pancras Cruising Club. Basically, all they provided for our guidance was a list of buoys. I hoped Tim had not noticed the squall heading our way. He was so busy looking ahead I didn't want him to worry. But I kept looking back, watching the sheet of darkness chasing our tail. A cruise ship the size of the Tower of London was moored in Tilbury Docks. I peered through the binoculars to see if I could see through the portholes.

Tim was annoyed. 'Give me the binoculars, I have to find the next buoy!'

We both searched the horizon.

'What colour's the buoy Timmy?'

'Green.'

'Yes, there it is … I think?'

He kept calling out the names: Mucking, West Blyth and Mid Blyth. The buoys are all different. Some are shaped like a bell, some square; Mid Blyth is shaped like the Eiffel Tower. I was very pleased with myself when I spotted them, but I was forever looking at the rain clouds behind us.

Tim grabbed the binoculars off me again, pointing. 'Shane! Look, that's Southend Pier.' It was a long way away. All I could see was the sea and the oil refinery by Canvey Island. Huge tankers were taking on fuel and I didn't want to think what would happen if we got in their way. I looked at the road map and wondered how much further we had to go.

Tim had worked out his course into the Medway with no cutting of corners. He took the AA map off me and pointed to the Isle of Grain. 'When this dries out,' he said, 'the sandbank stretches for miles.'

The Isle of Grain looked far bigger in reality than it did on our road map. The wind was now gusting and we had a bit of an argument about something. We were overtired and tension was rising. We had not expected the estuary to be this wide. Enormous ships were heading towards us, so we kept out of the shipping lane, but Tim was afraid we would get stuck on a sandbank. I was getting cold and feeling irritable. What had begun as a romantic dawn adventure was turning into a nightmare. Books and video tapes had been knocked off the shelves. The inside of our boat looked like it had been turned over by burglars.

I had gone below to find a coat when Tim yelled at the top of his voice. 'Shane, come up here, we've lost the steering!'

I ignored him and put the kettle on and began to pick up books.

'For fuck's sake, come up here!'

I still didn't believe him. I really thought he was making it up until I saw his face. I have seen that face only two other times in my life. He was grey. My heart sank. Fighting the panic out of my voice I said, 'What's wrong?'

He spun the steering wheel around and nothing happened.

'We've lost the steering! The boat won't turn, the tide's going out and there're sandbanks out here!'

Any boat which has lost its steering is in a perilous position, at the mercy of the sea and the wind and other traffic on the waters. Huge ships take miles to stop, as the skipper of the *Titanic* discovered.

The Princess Matilda kept drifting with the tide. Tim and I were scared and felt increasingly helpless. We both tried to hide our fear. Tim went down into the engine room and came out with the emergency tiller. He fixed it to a bit of apparatus, hidden under a hatch on the back deck, which attached directly to the rudder. Still *The Princess Matilda* stubbornly would not go the way we wanted. I saw a boat and Tim waved his arms up and down to attract their attention. Later we found out this was actually the international sign for distress – very convenient. It was just as well it didn't mean, 'Go away, everything is fine.'

It was the Sheerness pilot boat that came to our rescue. The boat pulled alongside us and we threw them a rope.

'Hello Tim,' they said. 'Nice boat, how are you, mate?'

I am used to people addressing my husband as if they know him, but this was a first. It was if they were expecting to see him. They showed no surprise. The pilots towed us into Sheerness Harbour and tied us expertly to the high sea wall. It was getting dark, the wind was now howling and the harbour wall offered us protection. We were so relieved to be in that safe haven.

A couple of the pilots came onboard and took a look at the rudder. One of the guys thought he could fix it and asked if we had an extension lead so he could see what he was doing. Another pilot joined them and they all took a look, shook their heads and tutted.

'No mate, sorry, it's too big a job for us, but you'll be OK here for a couple of days while you get someone out to fix it.'

They left us standing in the wheelhouse, which was now strewn with tools.

Tim said, 'I'll put this lot away.'

I went below to finish making dinner. At least we had food and drink. I made us each a very large gin. We went to bed early with an extra blanket on the bed. The boat rocked about all night long, banging against the wall. Every time the pilot boat left to escort a ship into the estuary, we slammed against the wall twice as much. What a day. This wasn't what I had imagined at all. We had been sorely tested and now we were both truly exhausted. We eventually fell into a fitful sleep.

Chapter Five
The Lifeboat

'Bugger me,' Tim shouted. 'It's a tower block, a floating council estate!'

During the night a timber boat had tied up outside the harbour. It was a gigantic ship, towering above us. We had not been so close to something this big before. In the corner of the harbour was a tiny yacht that the lifeboat had rescued. The mast was broken and looked like it had taken a real battering. Tim told me the lifeboat had gone out, all the lights ablaze, while I had slept. He had had very little sleep. The tide was in when I awoke and *The Princess Matilda* was now at the top of the harbour wall. I didn't need to climb the ladder to take a look around our new mooring.

We had noticed several lifeboat crew members around the harbour. One of them, someone who had a badge that said he was a 'coxswain', came over and asked if he could help. We invited him on board and more crew joined him.

'I think the coxswain is the gaffer,' Tim whispered to me as I put the kettle on to make them a pot of tea. He went back up to the wheelhouse and I stayed in the galley flicking through the road atlas while waiting for the water to come to the boil. The ring binder cut straight through the Isle of Sheppey, but as far as I could see we were just off the A249. I took the tea tray up to the crowded wheelhouse and heard one of the crew say, 'She needs to be put into dry dock unless someone can work on the rudder underwater.'

Tim asked if they knew of any divers. Before he or I could finish our tea, a chap called Little Ray appeared in his RNLI dry suit and jumped into the harbour. His tea went cold while he did the job for us. We were so grateful.

Everyone seemed satisfied that we could now safely continue our journey. The coxswain asked if we had any sea-charts. We didn't, but we pretended we did. We already felt like a couple of fools so we had to keep a little bit of face. He also asked us if we would like an escort. Tim and I had looked at the sea as it hurtled passed the timber boat. The waves had white crests and were jagged grey and unforgiving. We gladly took up the coxswain's offer. He put Little Ray aboard and he and the other lifesavers (for this is what the RNLI are) followed us in their RIB. Ray said it stood for 'rigid inflatable boat'. I shall always remember Ray. He was only about 19 or 20 then, and he showed Tim the way. We would not have had a clue without him. Whichever way we looked there was the sea, docks and wharves. Ray stood next to Tim and pointed to the left. 'That's the River Swale,' he said. 'Just a few hundred metres down there is Queenborough. I think that's where you were hoping to get to last night. It's where most boats stop over before crossing the Channel to France.'

I was tempted to go and have another look in my road atlas but I am glad I resisted because he continued, 'We had a shout a couple of years ago, a young bloke who'd bought a boat in Gillingham. He lived in Brighton, so he filled her up with petrol and set off with just a road map. Someone told him as long as he kept land on his right-hand side he'd be fine. And that's what he did, he got all the way around the Isle of Sheppey and came back up the Swale. He ran out of petrol so we towed him back to where he'd begun!'

'What a dick!' I said guiltily and quickly disappeared below to hide our *AA Concise Road Atlas of Britain*.

The Medway is a busy, wide river, with powerboats, cargo ships, yachts and jet skis. My idea of a river is when you can swim to the other bank. Here it took us nearly an hour of travel before the riverbanks narrowed to that point.

Ray pointed upstream and said, 'That's the gasworks at Gillingham. You can't get lost now. The visitor moorings are below Rochester Castle, just beyond the bridge about 2 nautical miles upstream from here.' Then the lifeboat RIB picked him up and we waved them goodbye.

'What's a nautical mile?' I asked Tim.

'Get me a book of nautical terms for our wedding anniversary,' he replied.

It was a sunny, autumnal afternoon as we came underneath Rochester's railway and road bridges. We saw there were several powerboats moored against pontoons. At first glance there appeared to be no room for us, but as we drew closer we saw there was a space on the inside of the visitor's berth. Tim reversed 35 tons of *The Princess Matilda* against the tide, which made it easier to stop and tie up. The moored boaters looked at us with interest. We locked the boat up very quickly, taking a £1 token from a machine. The sign told us we needed a token to get back into the security gate at the top of the jetty. This was not the only sign. In bold letters another said *No Overnight Mooring.* We decided we would address this problem after lunch.

Rochester has one of the handsomest high streets we had ever seen. It was utterly Dickensian. We almost expected to be run over by a stagecoach delivering the man himself to the old Corn Exchange. Attached to the grand building is what Dickens called a 'moon-faced clock'. It was built in 1706, commissioned by the Admiral Sir Cloudesley Shovell. That first Sunday, Tim and I had no idea just how much time we would spend looking up at the timepiece that hangs over the high street or how often we would pay £1 for a token to get back on to the mooring.

We had no choice but to moor in Rochester that night. By the time we got back onboard, the boat was all alone and sitting on the mud. The tide had gone out and we could not have left the mooring even if we had wanted to. We watched water rats running amongst the reeds. There was nothing we could do but make the most of our situation. We were safe and had a secure temporary mooring, but time was running out and the days were getting shorter. Ray had told us the weather was about to change; winter was just around the corner. No way could we get *The Princess Matilda* to Ramsgate before then. Tim and I tried to hide our anxiety from each other, but he took the words out of my mouth.

'This is supposed to be fun. What if we can't find anywhere to moor her?'

I looked at him and sighed, 'Why are we doing this?'

*

Midnight
Why is this happening to us? It's not fair, who said life is fair? This is what I say to the kids when they complain. I used to look at those big billboard ads, with three people on them. One of them was blacked out. It said one in three people will get cancer, but actually these figures are wrong – I know they are. More like three out of three, first my dad, then Krissy and now you.

*

The next day we rang every single mooring on the Medway, thinking we had been really stupid for not making enquiries before setting out from Limehouse. The last person Tim spoke to suggested we phone up Chatham Maritime Marina next to the Historic Dockyard. Someone called Charlotte said they could squeeze us in. I called the Ramsgate harbour master and said we had changed our minds and would not need a winter mooring after all.

Tim and I both understood we had done something really stupid. We had underestimated the danger involved in going out to sea. We had no VHF radio, compass, life raft or flares. In other words, we were a couple of idiots. The Sheerness lifeboat volunteers didn't say anything, but we must have been their worst nightmare. We were very fortunate that the pilot boat arrived when it did, because we didn't have a signal on either of our mobiles to call out the coastguard. Not that we knew how to do that either.

'Well that's one less thing to worry about,' Tim said as we entered the lock to our new home. 'But I didn't have Chatham in mind when we got the boat built.'

'I love it already Tim, and I don't care if we never go to sea ever, ever again!' I replied.

Chapter Six
The Future and the Past

My wish nearly came true, and in the end we remained in Chatham for two winters. My negativity aside, we had not planned to stay so long but Tim got a film. His job always has to be a top priority as it pays for everything else. We spent three months in New York during the spring and summer of 2006 while he worked on a Disney film, *Enchanted*, with Amy Adams. On his day off we used to walk down to the Hudson River and look longingly at the houseboats moored on the quays. We had lots of visitors while we were in New York. Our close friends Brenda Blethyn and her husband Michael Mayhew came over and so did Pascale and Matilda. Matilda was now a toddler with an Australian accent.

'We'll soon turn you into a Londoner,' Sadie said to her when she came to visit. Sadie was acting chaperone to Tim's mum, Sylvia. Seeing so much of our family meant we weren't too homesick, but we did miss the boat.

I am convinced *The Princess Matilda* has a soul. She may be a hunk of welded metal but there is something majestic about her, and it's not just her name. It was not her fault we had had teething troubles with the steering when we came out into the estuary. I blamed the mattress. I worried constantly in case she was lonely or felt unloved. While we were in New York, Tim and I even made enquiries about having her craned out of the water and shipped over the Atlantic. It would have cost us a fortune. Fortunately Charlotte, who managed the marina, had her blokes keep an eye on the boat.

When we were finally able to spend time on *The Princess Matilda* again it was late September 2006 and we were really looking forward to our first autumn mooring walk. We had to wrap ourselves up against the howling wind as we walked up the steps of the marina lock overlooking Upnor Castle. The Elizabethan castle has a funny little fence around it that sticks out of the water at low tide. When the castle is lit up it looks like something from a Disney theme park. But when the lights of Upnor Castle are out, you must walk along the sea wall, which was built by prisoners in the nineteenth century, in complete darkness.

Along this bleak walkway we had many wonderful, bracing outings and would always peer over the wall to see the state of the tide. Sometimes our boat guests joined us. Come to think of it, there weren't too many that autumn. Only Brenda, Michael and our friends Miriam Jones and Jimmy Nail came to visit us in 'unglamorous' Chatham. But no matter how cold or wet it got, we would set out each evening, bracing ourselves against the wind. Down to the old crane and then 30 yards or so down to the end of the jetty. It felt like we were walking on water. When the wind was in the wrong direction, we heard the noise of the aggregate boats, unloading on one of the wharves. Tim and I loved those walks, but they were scary too.

'Somebody told me that a cabin boy had been brutally murdered on a ship anchored out there…'

'Don't look for ghosts, Tim!'

We would be fearful at high tide when the waves seemed to be slapping a mere yard or two under our feet. Low tide made us even more apprehensive in case the ruddy brown sludge might suck us in.

Prison hulks used to anchor near the jetty, filled with convicts bound for the penal colonies. Charles Dickens would have seen these rotting maritime carcasses. His father was a clerk in the Naval Pay Office in Chatham Dockyard. Perhaps, like us, he imagined primeval monsters emerging out of the mud at low tide. Or maybe he saw the bones of some poor convict who didn't make it ashore. Magwitch escaped from one of these hulks in *Great Expectations*; he makes it to the church-yard to terrify young Pip. We visited a number of churchyards trying to find the one where we imagined these adventures might have happened. We discovered Dickens based that grave-yard on many separate Medway churches. But there is one at Lower Halstow that we think fits the bill.

*

We had Brenda and Michael with us for New Year's Eve. I cooked dinner and we had a fire and candles lit. It was so warm, we had the doors to the wheelhouse open and went up the steps to look at the stars. The marina was quiet, except for our laughter and the howling wind. At about 11:40 we blew out the candles and threw on our coats to walk down to the scary jetty. Tim opened the outside door, which was ripped out of his hand by a mighty gust.

I shouted to them as they climbed out of the boat, 'You go on, I'll catch up!' and disappeared back inside the boat.

Under the fitted sofa in our saloon are three drawers. I knew we had a kite in one of them so I crawled under the table. I found the kite in the first drawer I opened, and hurried out of the boat, running to catch up with Tim and our guests. We never bothered locking *The Princess Matilda* in Chatham. The tide was in and water slopped beneath us as we walked down the jetty. We took it in turns flying the kite. The might of the wind lifted it high into the air until there was no more string to let out. Tim was flying it as I looked at my watch. It was almost midnight, and I waited for a couple of minutes before shouting over the wind.

'Happy New Year! Let the kite go Timmy, set it free!'

Brenda shouted, 'Yes let it go! Happy New Year!'

Tim turned to Michael yelling, 'What do you reckon Mike?'

Michael never yells, he is too cool, but he nodded. Tim let

go of the string and called out, 'Fly, fly free, let this signify good luck and love for the New Year.'

We all expected the kite to soar out over the river and up into the ether. The contrary wind took it back towards the crane. It dropped and fluttered in ever decreasing circles and plummeted sharply to the ground. All four of us ran giggling like school children at our failed poetic gesture to see who could retrieve it first.

*

Tim and I learnt so much while we were moored on the Medway. The river has a strong and challenging tide. Getting into the marina lock could be tricky, but we had plenty of practice. We also took a VHF radio course taught by Corporal Jase, a Royal Engineer.

'Sierra Papa Alpha Lima Lima, how do you do Mr and Mrs Spall?'

Jase was a mine of information, with polished boots and a spine like a ramrod. 'If you'd had radio when you'd lost your steering you could have called the coastguard on channel 16 and given your position. In your case you were in the vicinity of the SS *Richard Montgomery*, which sank during the war carrying thousands of tons of explosive! It's too dangerous to move.'

Tim asked if it had masts that stick out of the water.

'That's correct, she broke her back on a sandbank,' said Corporal Jase. 'Don't tell me you were thinking about throwing a rope around one of them Mr Spall.'

Tim laughed and said, 'It did enter my mind Jase!'

Tim and I gave the wreck a wide berth the next time we passed by. It still sits there ominously, the biggest unexploded bomb in Europe. If it went up it would take half of the Isle of Sheppey with it.

*

In March 2007 Tim was making *Sweeney Todd* at Bray Studios. He had a couple of weeks off so we thought it would be a good idea to take the boat up from the Medway to Windsor, which is close to Bray Studios. With our VHF radio and brand new sea-charts, we set out again, down the Medway and into the Thames Estuary. Tim had spent months studying the charts and reading various 'teach yourself' books on tides and navigation. For instance, Tim now knew that white horses, sometimes, are caused by the wind blowing in one direction and the tide moving in the other.

'It's called "wind across tide",' he said proudly. 'We'll make slow progress until the tide turns and then pick up considerable speed.'

He was quite right. At one point we were doing about 12 knots. By the time we got to Tilbury the wind had increased somewhat and so had the waves. The bow of *The Princess Matilda* was ploughing into them and they were breaking over the wheelhouse.

Tim was not too worried. 'My book says this happens because the river is becoming narrower and the wind is blowing from the east and we are travelling west.'

With Tim's skippering skills improving, we felt more confident. We found out later we had been in a Beaufort Scale Force Six.

The trip up the Thames that early spring was cold. As it turned out Tim didn't use *The Princess Matilda* while he was filming because Johnny Depp's daughter was taken seriously ill and the film was put on hold. Thank goodness she made a full recovery. Tim and I know all about illness, but to have a child so sick must be so dreadful. While Mr Depp's daughter was getting better, we decided to go further up the Thames to Henley and then made it back to Chatham on the Medway.

A few weeks later we waved goodbye to Chatham again, to

go to Ramsgate. Tim felt more confident now and said we would go around the outside of the Isle of Sheppey.

We got as far as Sheerness, where we had spent our first night courtesy of the pilots and lifeboat crew. We were just discussing this when I received a text from our daughter Sadie. 'DID YOU FEEL THE EARTHQUAKE?'

Tim then got a phone call from his best friend, Rennie.

'Did you feel the earthquake?'

We put the news on and heard: 'Homes in five streets in Folkestone had to be evacuated because of structural damage including cracked walls and fallen chimneys. The magnitude 4.3 tremor struck at 0819 BST and experts said its epicentre was a few miles off the coast in the English Channel.'

Well, we weren't going to go out in the Channel now that was for sure.

Brenda and Michael had a cosy holiday flat in Folkestone. Tim and I wondered if it had been damaged. They had let us use it a couple of times. Their flat was on the top floor of a Victorian house. Brenda used to make all the beds up for us and fill the fridge. The last time we had stayed there Tim had become very breathless climbing the stairs. A few days later Brenda had called me from Heathrow where she had learnt that Tim wasn't going to Cannes for the premiere of *Secrets and Lies*. She had been told he had flu.

*

'Shane I've just heard, poor Tim, we will miss him, it won't be the same without him!' 'He'll be all right Bren, serve him right won't it?' You and she had lived and breathed Secrets and Lies *for over a year. The two of you played brother and sister. You love Bren. The last thing you'd want is for her to worry about you, so I pretend it is something minor. 'We'll see you when you get back Bren. Have a smashing time, and make sure you have a drink for Tim.'*

Sky TV News cut back to a pre-recorded interview with Mike Leigh. 'What does it feel like to have your film opening the Cannes Film Festival?' I ask you if you want me to turn it off. 'No!' The doctor comes in, the one who told us about 'The Protocol'. You are very excited, there's the scene of Maurice with his arms around Cynthia on the TV. 'That's my film!' I don't think the doctor understands; he's Greek and hasn't a clue who you are and asks, 'How are you feeling?' You look back at the TV, the clip is finished and it has cut back to live coverage of Brenda and Mike and the rest of the cast walking on the red carpet. 'Well doctor, let's put it this way, I'd rather be there walking down the Croisette, than having this stuff dripped into me!' Dr Panos said, 'You are lucky to be here. You have 90 per cent leukaemic cells. Even a small internal haemorrhage could kill you.'

*

I phoned Brenda and she said the flat had suffered no damage from the earthquake, and it was on the market, would we like to buy it? They had bought a new place in Broadstairs.

'Oh, you will love it, it used to be a hotel. We've got an apartment on the second floor with views across the bay. On a clear day I swear I can see Calais. Make sure you let us know when you pass us by, so we can wave.'

'I don't think we are ever going to leave the Medway, Bren, we're starting to call it the river of entrapment!'

I hung up the phone and looked at my map-book. 'If only we could get to the Bristol Channel, Tim, we could stay in Wales for a bit, then get back on to the inland waterways via Bristol, go on the Kennet and Avon and then back on the Thames at Reading, what do you think?'

'I think we should have stuck with our narrowboats!' he replied.

Chapter Seven
Don't Give Up!

The next time we attempted to leave the Medway to go to Ramsgate we decided to go via the River Swale.

Little Ray from the Sheerness lifeboat had explained the river was a 13-mile channel that separates the mainland of Kent from the Isle of Sheppey. 'If you go that way,' he said, 'you should be OK as long as you keep land to starboard when you come out of the Swale.'

Tim studied his sea-charts, read the pilot book and we set out once again, waving goodbye to Corporal Jase. He had come to wish us *bon voyage*.

'Don't be tempted to take any shortcuts, Tim!' he shouted as we came out of the lock.

Four hours later Tim took a shortcut by the old ferry crossing. The ferry stopped running from the mainland to Sheppey years ago but our pilot book said it used to be possible to walk across on a causeway at low tide. It was an ebbing tide when we took our 'shortcut', and suddenly our boat stopped dead in its track with a horrid scratching, grating sound. *The Princess Matilda* had run aground. Tim put her into reverse gear, but she would not budge.

'I think we just found a bit of the causeway.'

Three hours later we were having our dinner in *Matilda*, the boat marooned on top of a hill, surrounded by a snow-white beach. If we had had a ladder we could have climbed down and explored: the Swale had become a ditch. As the tide eventually began to creep back in, we watched greedy wading birds pull worms out of the mudflats. The waves started sweeping up the ditch, slowly at first, then gaining momentum. If you have ever held a shell to your ear, you will know the noise the small wavelets made. Swoosh, swoosh, the sea turning over the sand then retreating. Swoosh, swoosh ... we were hypnotised, watching a scene that has been played out twice a day for millions of years. After two hours the waves were slapping on our bow, slip, slap, slop. Tantalisingly the waves fell back but each time they returned the slipslop became louder until our boat began to rock, the little waves nudging her off the sand.

Tim kept testing the depth with our barge pole until at last he said, 'I think we have enough water to move now!'

'Are you sure?'

'Yes I think so.'

Tim called a local boatyard who advised us to moor for the night on a barge upstream from where we had run aground. It was almost pitch-black now and we didn't want to navigate the Swale in the dark.

Our mooring for the night was a huge old rusty iron barge with open hatches and fishing nets designed to trip us up and send us tumbling into the dark, dripping bilge water in the hold. The man at the boatyard told Tim that local fishermen from the Faversham oyster fishery used it. The next morning we discovered bags of large shells hanging down into the Swale. We left a bottle of wine and a note with our phone number to say thank you to the oystermen. The bottle of wine might still be there for all we know. We went back to Chatham Marina with our tail between our legs.

It was a Saturday morning and the marina was busy. A large catamaran called *Top Cat* had been put on our mooring. Charlotte from the marina office called us on the radio. '*Princess Matilda, there's room for you on the end. I'll send someone down to give you a hand.*'

We saw Jase was waiting for us in his civvies. He took a line from me and I went to the stern to help Tim move the fenders around. Jase marched towards us and gave me a kiss on the cheek and shook Tim's hand. He said, 'I thought you'd gone for good this time.'

'Tim and I are going to give it one more go to get around to Ramsgate. And if we fail next time we'll hire a pilot to take us over the Channel and put her on the Midi Canal,' I said.

Tim interrupted me, as he attached the shore power to the boat. 'We're not going to do that, Shane. We're going to turn right and take her to Ramsgate, then we're going to turn right again and again. We're going to take *The Princess Matilda* all the way around the British Isles. One way or another, that's what we are going to do!'

'It will take us bloody years at this rate. I'll settle for Wales,' I complained.

We waved Jase goodbye and put on the telly.

'We'll go in the morning,' Tim said. 'We will do it, I promise you, Shane!'

*

The wind was blowing from every direction. Tim and I battled our way against the force of the Kentish tempest along the grunting pontoons towards our mooring. Both of us were bent double against the force of the wind. Daggers of sleet stung any exposed flesh. We were laden with victuals from the local Co-op, ready for our departure.

Tim yelled over the screech of the storm, 'We're not going anywhere in this!'

We approached the *The Princess Matilda*, which, like us, was fighting against the punishing weather. Huge gusts were pushing the boat out some distance from the pontoon and straining the ropes more each time. Experience had taught us

to cut her some slack, so Tim needed to haul on a taut resist-
ing stern rope to pull her in. But the tide and wind were
determined to undermine him, so I put down my shopping
and heaved on our centre-line.

'Get ready,' Tim bellowed, as *The Princess Matilda* obsti-
nately drew slowly closer. 'Now, quick!'

I leapt on the lowest part of our gunwale, hauling myself
up, the line still taut in my hand, while Tim threw on our shopping bags and jumped on before I got rope burn.

A while later, Tim was poking the fire as steam from our
drying clothes fogged up the windows. I checked the weather
forecast on my laptop.

I said, 'There's a high front coming over.'

Tim had his charts on the floor and was cross-referencing
his tidal flows. 'You said that yesterday.' He stood up and used
his sleeve to wipe away the condensation so he could peer out
of the saloon window. 'It looks like the rain is going to knock
the glass in.'

'I love that noise, it sounds like fine grit being thrown on
the roof.'

My husband went back to his charts, a pencil behind his
ear, and began measuring things with his protractor. 'Put the
VHF radio on darlin' please?'

I tuned it in and caught the end of the Met Office Broad-
cast for the next 24 hours: '*Gibraltar Point to North Foreland
… Sea state, calm or slight.*'

'That sounds OK,' Tim said, lifting up his charts. 'We'll go
tomorrow!'

*

I had a couple of eggs coming up to the boil with my timer at
the ready. Tim was in the engine room doing things with span-
ners and rags. The eggs began to roll so I flicked over the
hourglass sand timer and poured two cups of tea.

'Do you want it down there?' I said, peering over the open flap of the engine room.

He looked up at me, wiping his hands on the oily torn remnants of an old shirt. He took the cup from me, taking a sip and shook his head. 'We ain't going anywhere today darlin'! We've got a leak in the inlet pipe. I'll have to order a new one.'

The Princess Matilda has a pipe that sucks up water from the sea to cool the engine, then spits it out the other side. Tim turned off the engine room light and climbed up the ladder. He turned off the engine and shut the hatch with a resounding boom. The inlet pipe was fixed a couple of days later, but we still could not leave because Tim had to rush back to London to do a voice-over. This is a convenient way of paying for new inlet pipes and mooring fees. He sent me a text telling me what time his train was due back in Chatham, so I texted back saying I would meet him at the station. I had time to kill, so I thought I would walk through the grounds of what used to be one of the most important dockyards in the country. The navy left in 1984. It is now a museum and renamed The Historic Dockyard. Ships have been built and mended on this atmospheric and somewhat eerie site for centuries.

I was walking in the footsteps of Sir Francis Drake, Captain Cook and the infamous Captain Bligh. Whenever Bligh comes up in conversation, Tim does his impersonation of Charles Laughton in the 1930s version of *Mutiny on the Bounty*. He cannot resist. He sticks out and then drops his bottom lip. His eyes take on the look of a malevolent nautical martinet. Slightly modified for full daftness, he will deliver his line: 'Mr Christian, you are stealing my chips!' I don't know if *Bounty* was built in Chatham, but I know *HMS Victory* was, because Tim and I watched the fireworks over the dockyard on 21 October 2005, the bicentenary of the Battle of Trafalgar.

The oak timbers that became the keel of *HMS Victory* were brought to Chatham's Royal Dockyard in 1759, but work was not completed until 1765. The warship spent her early years on the River Medway where a 12-year-old Horatio Nelson began his naval career. The body of Lord Nelson, preserved in a barrel of brandy, was returned to Sheerness from Gibraltar, then travelled up the River Thames. His remains lay in state in the Painted Chamber in Greenwich Hospital before being taken to St Paul's for burial. I wondered if Tim and I would ever make it to Portsmouth on *The Princess Matilda* and see *HMS Victory* in all her restored glory. Somehow I doubted it. We had yet to get to Ramsgate.

Tim and I took a taxi back to the marina from the station. He had seen the river as he crossed over the Medway on the train and thought it looked perfect for us to leave. The cab dropped us off by the lock and we climbed the steps to look out on the river.

'Nelson served as a "Captain's Servant" to his uncle on a ship anchored out there,' I said to Tim as we gazed across to Upnor Castle.

Tim shaded his eyes against the glare of the sun and replied, 'One of the pilots who took us into Sheerness Gun Wharf, otherwise known as the Camber, told me Nelson took on ammunition and gunpowder for the Battle of Trafalgar just close to where we were moored that first night.'

'Bloody hell,' I said, 'you have been doing your homework. I am impressed.'

Like a couple of meerkats, we looked right then left.

'The river's like a mill pond, Tim.'

'No, a mirror,' he replied. 'See the reflection of the castle. What do you think?'

Not a ripple or a breath of air distorted the parallel image.

'We'll leave at slack water, Shane, and go to Sheerness then turn south and moor on a buoy in Queenborough.'

Charlotte in the marina office high above the lock saw us and waved. We had got to know her during the time we moored in

Chatham. She is surprisingly young for such a position; a really attractive woman who holds her own in the male-dominated world of marina operations. Charlotte is unperturbedly efficient. She shouted down to us from the viewpoint balcony. 'It's looking good out there, you won't come back this time.'

We laughed and Tim yelled, 'Don't bank on it Charlotte, don't give our mooring away too soon, we'll probably be back this afternoon. But just in case, give our regards to Corporal Jase.'

Tim and I walked back to the boat and both agreed we would miss Charlotte. She had been so helpful and had a good team working for her. They all came out of the office and waved us goodbye as we locked through. We had 'Good luck!' resonating in our ears from many directions.

'I really think this is it,' I said, as *The Princess Matilda* came out on to the river.

Tim smiled and put his arm around my shoulders. His hand crept down to my bum. I knew then everything would be fine.

'Let's not tempt fate, but by my calculations,' Tim said as we turned downstream, 'the tide should turn when we pass the power station, so we should be at Sheerness in no time.'

I grabbed his marauding hand and kissed his fingers.

'Are you nervous?' I asked.

He laughed and replied, 'No, I'm not nervous, I'm terrified!'

'Why?' I replied. 'You've done your research. We'll be fine.'

*

The Medway is exceedingly industrial in parts, but Tim and I love that; the monolithic concrete sprawl of a power station on one bank and miles of secret inlets and creeks on the other. Even the names are evocative: Lower Halstow, Slaughterhouse Point, Slayhills Marshes and Hoo St Werburgh, or as my scatological husband calls it Poo St Turdburgh. It's not a reflection on the place itself; he just has a habit of making everything sound like a bowel movement. As Tim predicted, the tide turned as we passed Kingsnorth Power Station on the Hoo Peninsula – no prizes for what he calls it. Our trip downstream went without incident. I think instinctively we knew there would be no going back. Sometimes you know there is no rehearsal.

The last time we had attempted to get to Ramsgate we had run aground, so we weren't going to make the same mistake. This time we were going to do the journey over two days and moor overnight in Queenborough, which is tucked just inside the Swale, which comes off the Medway. But first we were going to take one last look at Sheerness and the estuary. Sheerness is approximately 9 miles from Chatham. What had seemed so alien to us when we came off the Thames was now familiar. The huge, busy container terminals with ships coming in and out didn't look so bewildering or threatening. Tim wanted us to get our sea legs so we went out into the channel. We passed the rotund, dumpy Grain Tower Battery that was built in 1855 to repel invaders. The Dutch had raided the Medway in 1667, so a few harsh lessons had been learnt. But the Spanish, Dutch, French and German navies no longer constitute a threat to the men of Kent.

The now derelict battery is connected to the Isle of Grain by a causeway that can be crossed on foot at low water.

'It looks more sinister at high tide,' I said.

A four-storey observation deck was added during the Second World War. It is odd to see flights of concrete steps coming out of the sea. The estuary was flat and inviting and for about ten seconds we were tempted to cross over towards Essex and have a closer look at Southend Pier.

'No!' Tim said, resolution in his voice. 'I've planned our passage and the book says it's a bad idea to change your mind. Look what happened last time we did something on a whim.'

The Princess Matilda left a marine crop circle behind as we turned 180 degrees and headed back into the mouth of the

Medway, passing what we now knew was the Camber. The Sheerness lifeboat and pilot boats were hidden behind the high harbour wall. We slowly passed the entrance, just in case there was anyone about, but the little harbour was inactive. I sent Little Ray a text. 'WE ARE LEAVING FOR RAMSGATE TOMMOROW. MOORING ON A SWING BUOY IN QUEENBOROUGH! THANKS FOR ALL YOUR HELP RAY AND SAY HELLO TO ALL THE REST OF THE RNLI CREW.'

We were finally on our way!

Chapter Eight
Mad About the Buoy

Queenborough to Ramsgate: 33 nautical miles

A swing buoy is a sturdy float with a fixed ring on the top that is attached to a heavy chain anchored into the sea or riverbed. Well, that is what it says in our 'teach yourself' manual. I stood on the bow of *The Princess Matilda* with a six-foot-long plastic gadget we had bought from a chandlery. The instructions made it sound easy. 'Attach a line to the hook, which when hooked on to the buoy, slides off the boathook enabling you to haul the buoy up.' Like Calamity Jane with a lasso; I had practised attaching my line on all kinds of things on dry land and it had worked perfectly fine.

The instructions didn't say anything about other boats getting in the way. The buoy we were after was smack in the middle of several smart moored yachts sitting midstream. After our first attempt at snagging a buoy we noticed a few heads appearing out of various cockpits and portholes. One ancient mariner doddered speedily to his bow and grabbed two huge angry-looking orange fenders. They were almost as big as he was and with abject panic and accusation in his watery old eyes he tied them to the side of his classic yacht. The wind had picked up a wee bit and every time I missed, Tim had to turn *The Princess Matilda* around. Then he had to weave her in and out of the moored vessels to renegotiate our approach.

There was a strong tidal stream that was determined to take us in the opposite direction. I stood on the bow armed like Boadicea, leading her warriors into battle.

'Forward! Forward!' I cried, waving my plastic spear-like pole. Only I could see where the buoy was as we drew near. Then, less regally, I would screech, 'STOP!' and clamber down the side deck, trying to get my hook into the little ring on top of the buoy. It was like threading a needle, but way more perilous. It would have been easier pushing an angry python through a mouse-hole. I noticed the ancient mariner repositioning his fenders, which I now took as a personal insult. He did this several times.

Finally in triumph I yelled, 'I've got it!'

Tim rushed to my side to help me. But the pull of the tide was moving us further away by the second. Then my helpful gadget snapped and so did my temper.

'What a piece of fucking shit!'

We eventually achieved our objective at low tide. Meanwhile we had had an audience taking photographs. Voices travel over open water, especially raised voices liberally peppered with expletives. The chap with the orange fenders untied them. I hope he heard where I told him to shove 'em.

Early the next day we set off once again down the Swale. Our first milestone was passing the fishermen's barge. We saw no sign of the wine bottle and we gave a wide berth to the shallow water that had caught us out on the river last time. I say 'river' but according to our pilot book, the Swale is 'a submerged valley'.

I read this out to Tim, who laughed. 'It's not submerged at low tide! And I've been studying that pilot for ages, and we have to make sure we watch out for the buoys because the tide flows through both ends.'

I took out the *AA Concise Road Atlas*, and put the pilot book next to it. Tim had his charts out on the table. He had a pencil in his hand and pointed to an area.

'The tides will meet around here, if I've worked it out correctly, by Milton Creek. Keep your eyes peeled because the direction of the buoyage will change.'

I looked at the AA map book. 'Milton Creek goes up to Sittingbourne.'

'Yes,' Tim replied, 'and dries at low tide, put that down and use the pilot.'

I almost did what I was told, reading out the instructions from the pilot book, but furtively sneaking a look at the *Concise*.

Tim looked through the binoculars then gave them to me. 'That's Shellness over there.'

I could see a few cottages above the shell-shingled beach. Tim opened the other wheelhouse door.

'I'm a bit worried because we should be able to see Whitstable by now.'

I looked at the AA map. Shellness is on the Isle of Sheppey and Whitstable on the mainland. We had both been looking forward to seeing Whitstable but a hazy mist had fallen. Tim kept checking his charts and was clearly anxious.

'It's too late to turn back now. The tide would be against us. We've no choice but to continue to Ramsgate. Look out for a red and a green buoy.'

We both scanned the horizon. 'Over there!' I said eagerly.

'Where?' Tim asked.

I pointed. 'There. Can you see them?'

My long-sight is better than his, so he used the binoculars, then put on his reading glasses to look at his chart, where he had drawn our passage in pencil.

'I just hope I've got it right, or we're buggered. Have a look in the *Reeds*, Shane, see what it says about Whitstable Street.'

Reeds Nautical Almanac is the sailor's bible and weighs as much as our old family tome. We had bought the book when we bought the useless gadget to grab a swing buoy, and neither of them was cheap. Tim keeps the *Reeds* by the side of the bed and reads it before he falls asleep and as soon as he wakes. This was the first time I had opened it and I fumbled about turning pages randomly. Tim tutted and took it from me. He found the right page in an instant and pointed.

'Read me out the navigation notes.'

'Hang on!' I said irritably, scanning the page. 'OK it says, "From the east keep well seaward of Whitstable Street, a hard drying sandpit, which extends 1 mile north from the coast…"'

Tim interrupted, 'Right, OK, what's it say about approaching from the west?' He was busy doing things with protractors and rulers on the chart.

I continued, '"From the west avoid Columbine and Pollard Spits."'

With a sweep of his pencil he pointed to an area of green on the chart and then at the buoys on the horizon. 'Those are the buoys marking the edge of the sandbanks and marshes. Do you remember that pub in Seasalter?'

I shook my head.

'The Rose in Bloom. Sadie used to play in the garden.'

'The one with that plastic pixie treehouse and slide?' I asked.

He nodded, 'That's the one. It overlooks Whitstable Flats and that's where we'll end up if I've made a mistake.'

Neither of us spoke until we had cleared the buoys. Tim broke the silence.

'Once we pass Whitstable Street I can relax for a little while.'

We were disappointed not to be able to see the seaside resort. Whitstable is an appealing town. Tim and I often used to take the kids there for a day out, as it is so close to London. There is a stony beach and a restaurant right on the shore called the Royal Native Oyster Stores, but when our kids were small we could not afford to eat there. We made do with a boiled egg picnic. The little town still has a small fishing fleet, a fish market and the famous native oyster beds. Most of the old fishermen's sheds are now luxury apartments. The low-lying mist hid the old whitewashed fishermen's houses and the neighbouring seaside towns of Tankerton and Herne Bay from view. But then out of the hazy low-lying mist we saw what looked like a martini glass.

'That's the water tower that overlooks Herne Bay,' Tim said, a catch of excitement in his voice. 'Now if we can see Reculver...'

I interrupted, 'Reculver Towers? Over there, look, look.'

High up on the hillside we saw the well known Kentish landmark. It felt so good to see something familiar after being at sea so long. Usually it is the other way around. Our family has a competition and a prize for who spots the sea first when we are travelling together.

Reculver used to be on a headland centuries ago, when the dribble that is now the River Wantsum was a thriving shipping lane that separated the Isle of Thanet from the mainland of Kent. Ships carrying cargo from the east coast of England and continental Europe used the Wantsum Channel, but it became silted up during the Middle Ages. It is almost impossible to imagine that the stream that now goes under the A299 was once a busy sea channel.

The mist cleared completely as we approached Margate Bay. Charles Dickens used to get a packet boat from London to Margate for his summer holidays in Kent. This destination was also popular with the Spall family, who would drive down the A299 in a two-tone Ford Anglia estate. We could now see the small seaside hotels on the outskirts of Margate. Tim gave me the binoculars.

'That's the Beachcomber Hotel. And that's Westbrook beach.' His face lit up as he pointed out memorable places from his childhood. 'Look there's the cafe and beach huts. We'd rent the same one every year. Our mum used to bury bottles of Guinness in front of ours...'

I interrupted him. 'What on earth for?'

'It was her personal minibar; kept the bottles cold for her to drink the next day.'

I could picture Sylvia in her sexy pin-up one-piece, sipping chilled stout.

'Whenever she went for a swim,' Tim reminisced, 'me, Dad and Nick used to clap and shout, "she's going in!" She'd have a home perm, so she could come out of the sea like a movie star – with a mere shake of her head the perm would spring back into shape. Mum was always so proud of her white strap marks, wearing an off the shoulder frock when we had dinner. She was so glamorous. Dad was so proud of her.'

'I think it's time I had a Guinness,' I said.

'Don't be long,' Tim replied as I went below. Then he shouted, 'I want to show you the Royal Sea Bathing Hospital.'

I looked through the galley window as I opened a chilled can and saw the scruffy backside of the sanatorium. Tim and I have driven past this hospital many times. From the front it looks like a Georgian stately home. 'SEA BATHING' is embossed above the Grecian columns of the entrance hall. 'Founded in 1791', below. It was built 'for the relief of the poor whose diseases required sea bathing'. George III had made sea bathing fashionable in Weymouth. I took our drinks up to the wheelhouse.

Tim said, 'It doesn't look so grand from the back, hey?'

'Red hat, no knickers.'

Tim looked wistfully back towards the Beachcomber Hotel then back to the old hospital.

'I think it was used as a troop hospital during the war, but Mum said it's where victims of TB went for a cure. I remember seeing patients sitting in bath chairs, some still in their beds being wheeled into the sun.'

I looked with curiosity at the beach where Timothy had spent his childhood holidays. There wasn't much there.

'What did you and Nicky do all day, didn't you get bored?'

Tim shook his head. 'Oh we used to go exploring. Me and Nick used to walk down the promenade to Dreamland, ride the big dipper and dodgems, play on the slot machines. It was fantastic!'

The Princess Matilda was now about 300 yards off shore, but we could see the huge tatty sign: 'Welcome to Dreamland Pleasure Park'.

'Margate's seen better days,' Tim said. 'But Mum and Dad loved it. It's a shame they couldn't retire down here together. That was their dream. When Dad came out of hospital I treated him and Mum to a holiday. They could have gone anywhere but chose the Beachcomber.'

I put my arm around him. 'Poor Joe.'

Tim's dad died soon after we were married; he was only 55.

There were just a few people on Margate beach, most walking dogs, but shimmering in the hazy sun was the long arm of the harbour wall. The old fishermen's lock-ups are painted pink, orange and red. Tim and I have walked along this wall countless times. The harbour dries at low tide and the seaweed that is left behind bakes, ferments and stinks in the sun. Sylvia used to rent a flat overlooking the harbour wall and the Custom House. The old 'white' Custom House has an elegant clock tower topped in green bronze. There is a sign that says thousands of Dunkirk troops disembarked there. To save money the local council had painted the building white only where it was visible from the road. From the sea, it looked shabby and unloved.

'I think that's where they're going to build the Turner Centre,' Tim said, pointing to a car park behind the Georgian clock tower. He continued, 'Turner described Margate Bay as having the loveliest sky in England. I think he lived in a house nearby.'

'Just as well your mum moved then or she'd have lost her views.'

Tim had recently bought Sylvia a flat in a new retirement block just up the coast in Cliftonville. He called his mother as we passed Margate lifeboat station, to warn her we were on our way.

'Look out of the window, Mum, can you see us? Look through your binoculars!'

He put her on speakerphone.

'Is that you out there in that big blue tug thing?'

We assured her it was but we couldn't get any closer in because of the shallow water.

'Call me when you get to Ramsgate,' she shouted, as if her voice would carry over the sea, not the telephone.

'I will, Mum,' Tim said, and we both waved our arms furiously.

I dashed down below and came back up with a white table-cloth that I save for special occasions. Tim and I each took a corner. The offshore breeze lifted up the linen.

'Oh, what's that you're waving?' Sylvia demanded. 'A pair of Shane's drawers?'

When her block of flats was out of sight, I folded up the tablecloth.

Tim said, 'I can't believe we just waved to my mum from our own boat.'

*

Karen, the nurse, has just told us about 'Protective Isolation for the Protection of Immunocompromised Patients against Infection'. We must remove outdoor clothes and put on an apron and then disinfect our hands before we come into your room.

Sadie has been reading a booklet and pipes up cheerfully, 'Daddy, I know exactly how many platelets you had missing. 143!' She was pleased at her mental arithmetic skills. But I couldn't congratulate her, because we'd not heard this word before today.

Now we know platelets are what you need in your blood to help it coagulate. You had a transfusion of them this morning. The pump goes beep, beep and lights flash.

The information book Karen just gave me makes my heart race! YOU COULD HAVE CAUGHT PNEUMONIA ON THE MOORS! YOU COULD HAVE HAD A BRAIN HAEMORRHAGE! YOU COULD HAVE DIED!

Just a few days ago, we went to Sloane Square, me to Peter Jones to buy the red gloves, you to see Dr Gaynor. We were early for the appointment so we drove around Battersea Park where you used to work at the funfair. The familiarity and the stories of the park made me sad, just out of the blue I cried and you said, 'I'm happy, don't spoil it!' And now when I cry, I feel my heart will break. I had cried for Krissy and all the times we used to walk through the park. Now I cry for us, for you and me and the kids.

I bought a new sofa, and the gloves. You had a blood test.

Pascale drove the kids in. The telly is on. You and Rafe are watching the football. Sadie wants to watch a different channel.

This is normal.

'It's play-offs, it's Palace.'

'It's Palace and Charlton, Rafie.'

'It's the first minute, Dad.'

'Can't we watch Eastenders?' our youngest girl complains.

'I want to watch this, so don't moan please. What did you have for pudding Sadie?' Tim asks.

'Soup,' is her reply.

Pas is on her mobile, texting.

This is not normal.

You wee blue urine into a plastic bottle. The digital beep on the machine at the side of your hospital bed flickers, reassuring Karen that the drugs are dripping though at the right dose. One blue bag. One clear. I've been told the blue bag is the killer. I am afraid to ask what it will kill.

*

Our next landmark was the lighthouse on the North Fore-land. Tim showed me where it was on his chart.

'The lighthouse marks the southerly entrance to the Thames and the hazard of Margate Rocks.'

We could see the lighthouse in the distance, a huge white turret with a circular glass dome on the top. Fields of cabbages tumbled down the slope of the Kentish hillside like a skirt of spring greens. We knew we would be on the home straight once we passed by. Tim and I have driven by this lighthouse many times and now at last we were seeing it from the sea. Just around the headland was Ramsgate.

The sea meanwhile had changed completely. We could see white horses.

'Why's it got so rough Tim?' I asked, as the force of a wave threw me against him.

'I was expecting this,' he replied. 'You'd better hold on! It's going get choppy for a little while.'

I perched myself on the step holding on to the grab bar to steady myself.

Tim held on to the steering wheel and like some old sea dog he said, 'Two tides!'

'What the hell does that mean?'

The Princess Matilda was getting tossed about, up and down and from side to side.

Tim put on the windscreen wiper to get rid of the spray and said, 'It's because of the headland.'

SPLASH BANG. *The Princess Matilda* thudded over a wave. The skipper held on to the steering wheel with grim determination and continued, 'The east-going tide is converg-ing with the south-going tide!'

SPLASH BANG. And then the rocking stopped and I was able to stand up.

'That was exciting,' I said. 'It was like riding that roller-coaster in Dreamland.'

We looked out of the salt-caked window and saw the star-tlingly white chalk cliffs above Broadstairs. I stood behind Tim as he steered our boat, my chin on his shoulder and my arms around his waist.

'I can't believe we're passing Broadstairs. Who'd have thought it, who'd have guessed?'

He turned around and with one hand on the steering wheel, he stroked my face and said, 'I love that beach, and I love you!'

Then he burped.

Curvaceous crescents of brightly painted beach huts are built under the cliffs at Broadstairs, with the shops and hotels above. It is an attractive town but we had no time to linger. Tim wanted to make the most of the tide to take us to our destination.

'Look, look!' I said. 'That's Brenda and Michael's new flat over there.'

I made him slow down so I could take photos. I called them on their landline, but there was no answer, so I texted Brenda a photo of their flat and sent it without any message attached.

The Princess Matilda hugged the snow-white cliffs for a few more miles. The main road and seaside resort disappeared from sight, but then Ramsgate's sea cliffs came into view. Tim kept by the buoyed channel as we passed the San Clu Hotel, which is high up on the red-bricked fortified east cliff.

Ahead of us were the eastern harbour sea wall and the piled-up boulders of the breakwater. Tim called Ramsgate Port Control on our VHF radio. We were advised to hold off while a ferry came out. This was a first for us. We weren't going to argue and waited patiently for the Ostend ferry to leave the port. Tim and I waved to the passengers lining the decks of the *Pride of Aquitaine*. Her powerful engines roared and throbbed as it passed us by. She picked up speed once she was clear of the breakwater and left behind plumes of grey smoke that billowed out of the pillar-box red funnel. Tim steered into the ferry's substantial wake so we would ride over the foam of the waves rather than have it slap us on our side.

Tim called Port Control again for permission to enter the harbour. A disembodied female voice crackled over our radio.

'Princess Matilda, Princess Matilda. *You may now enter. Welcome to Ramsgate. Change to channel 80 for berthing instructions.*'

The berthing master directed us to the eastern pontoons. Tim and I were congratulating ourselves when we heard our call sign over the radio. A man's voice this time.

'Princess Matilda, Princess Matilda. *This is Ramsgate Marina, you are heading for a sandbank. I repeat you are heading for a sandbank. I advise you to reverse and turn hard to port! Over.*'

'Bollocks!' Tim said, sticking the boat into reverse gear at full throttle. He pressed the button on the radio to transmit. 'Ramsgate Marina this is *The Princess Matilda*, I read you. Thank you! Out.'

The four golden curved blades of our propeller squealed to brake our forward progress. We had our fingers crossed as we waited for the spume of seawater to kick up behind us to indicate *The Princess Matilda* had changed direction.

'Now I know how the captain of the *Titanic* felt!' Tim spat through gritted teeth. His knuckles were white on the reverse control lever. *The Princess Matilda* came to a halt and then began to move backwards, a froth of angry water kicking up seaweed and detritus and leading us away from the submerged bank.

As soon as we were back in the deeper water, Tim remarked miserably, 'Well I buggered that up. It says to watch out for the bank in the pilot book and the *Reeds*.'

'Oh for goodness sake,' I retorted angrily. 'They shouldn't have a bloody hill in the middle of a harbour. Aren't they supposed to dredge it?'

Tim, laughing now, 'reprieve' written all over his face, said, 'If we'd got stuck on that we'd have been there until the next tide!'

He started giggling, almost choking to get his words out.

'At least ... when we ran aground ... before ... there was no one around ...'

Tears were rolling down his face and he was holding his chest. He is often amused at potential disaster and near misses. This usually makes me annoyed and mad at him.

'Stop messing about! It's not funny, you are not a school boy!' is my usual reply.

But I could see the relief in his face. I joined in. We both giggled hysterically, each making the other giggle even more.

'Stop it!' I begged. 'My sides are hurting!'

We both calmed down and suddenly Tim became very serious. 'That was our first proper sea voyage!'

But I could not congratulate him, as we had to prepare to moor.

The eastern pontoons, we discovered, is where Ramsgate's fishing fleet moor. And where there are fishing vessels there are greedy, opportunistic seagulls. There were about 100 of them sitting on our allocated berth. They knew we had nothing to offer so ignored us as we drew alongside. It took a great deal of ingenuity to tie up our ropes. We sent our new neighbours scattering and squawking their annoyance at being disturbed. Tim and I were intent on keeping our ropes shit-free. But once we were secured, the pair of us jumped up and down, away from the bird poo, embracing and hugging and slapping each other on the back. We felt like Mr and Mrs Vasco Da Gama. I was so proud of Tim.

'You got us here my darling. You did it with your compass and charts! Jase will be so proud, I'm going to send him a text.'

'Yeah, tell him I was good on the radio as well.'

He stood there, beaming.

Chapter Nine
Who is Sylvia?

It had been a long day and we were both starving, so we locked up the boat and made our way to the Harbour Office. It was quite a long walk because we were right at the end of the lengthy fishermen's pontoons, which are stuck together like Meccano. Little bridges on rollers span the gaps. There is a gantry leading up to the dockside. It was a steep climb and there was a type of filled-in ladder that helped us get a foothold.

Ramsgate is the largest seaside town on Thanet and the harbour is in a central position. We walked hand in hand around the inner harbour by the Sailors' Church. The seafront is split in two by the east and west cliffs which are lined by huge redbrick buildings overlooking the harbour. The inner quay nearest to the east cliff has cafes and restaurants, while the inner wharf to the west has old workshops cut under a road that goes up to the top of the cliff. There is a flight of stairs called Jacob's Ladder next to the Sailors' Church and the old Smack Boys' Home. Both are built into the cliff.

'Smacks' were a type of trawler that fished the North Sea in the nineteenth century. The deck boys were taken from reformatories and orphanages and weren't looked after particularly well by their employers. The Smack Boys' Home opened in 1881 but is now the home of the Harbour Office and this is where Tim and I went first, in order to give our details. The lady inside the office told us a little about the history of the port.

'Where we are now is called Military Road, because it was one of the main embarkation harbours during the Napoleonic Wars. And we have a couple of Little Ships, which rescued the soldiers off Dunkirk, moored in the harbour.'

Tim and I already knew a little about the port, but were looking forward to finding out more about the Little Ships.

Ramsgate is a large, busy harbour, which, according to the lady in the office, dates from Roman times. King George IV landed here in 1820 and decreed the harbour should have the right to add Royal to its name. It is the only Royal Harbour in the UK, if not the world. It also has our favourite Pizza Express in Kent because it overlooks the quay. We have been there many times with Tim's mum and his brother Nicky. I had sent Nick a text while waiting for the ferry to leave the harbour. He was going to join us when he finished work.

Mandy, the pretty, petite manager of Pizza Express greeted us at the door. 'Hi! Where's your mum, Tim?'

'She's not with us – we just arrived here on our boat!' Tim replied.

'You're kidding me, you didn't really come by boat?'

Frankly, Tim and I were just as surprised as Mandy. She took our order and came back with two Peronis. Nicky joined us as our starters arrived.

'Congratulations bruv!' he said. 'Welcome to Ramsgate. How long are you going to stay?'

Tim stood and they embraced and affectionately tapped each other on the back.

'As long as they'll have us.'

Nicky asked us many questions about our journey. He had been in the merchant navy as a young man and was keen to look at Tim's charts. We all went back to *The Princess Matilda* after our late lunch.

Brenda called me on my mobile just as we approached the boat.

'I got your photograph of our flat. I can't believe I missed you go by. Where are you? Can I come and see you?'

'Of course you can Bren,' I replied. 'I hope you're wearing

your trainers, 'cos it's a bit tricky, so be careful. It's a death trap down here.'

I told her where we were moored. About 20 fishing boats were unloading as we returned to the boat, which meant Brenda would have to manoeuvre around boxes of fish, dripping nets, lobster pots, crab creels, flies and dive bombing seagulls. She would also have to concentrate on keeping upright. The long pontoons, slippery with fish scales and seagull shit, were undulating up and down.

'What's causing all this movement?' I asked Nicky shortly after he and Tim grabbed me to break my fall as I staggered alarmingly. I completely lost my balance and was tottering towards the drink. I had only had two beers and a Sambuca in Pizza Express.

Nicky laughed. 'You shouldn't have had the liqueur! It's high tide. The sea's got nowhere else to go so it's just bouncing off the harbour walls.'

The little roller bridges linking the pontoons together belong in a theme park. They groaned and moved a couple of feet back and forth. I had to time my leap so as not to loose a limb.

Soon Brenda arrived from Broadstairs and we anxiously watched her progress along the pontoons. She took the roller bridges in her stride, leaping like a gazelle and balancing with the dexterity of a ballerina. Being a local girl, Brenda had been to school with many of the fishermen unloading their catch. She stopped and wobbled up and down and passed the time of day with them. It took her a while to make her way to *The Princess Matilda*.

'I can't believe you are here!' she said as we welcomed her aboard.

The boat was rocking from side to side so we told her to be careful going down the steps into the saloon.

'Oh I think I have my sea legs now,' she said. 'It was like something from an army assault course. I'm so pleased to see you got here safe and sound. It's so different from Chatham.'

'How long are you going to stay in Ramsgate?' was Brenda's first question.

Nicky laughed and said, 'That's exactly what I asked them. Hello Bren, how are you darlin'?'

Nick gave Brenda a kiss.

'You look well Nicky. Tim and Shane are going to love it here aren't they? Wait until they see the sun setting over the inner harbour.'

Tim had his charts on the table, showing them the pencil lines he had drawn for our passage.

'Poor Tim,' I said to Brenda. 'I never take any notice.'

But she and Nicky were genuinely interested.

'We were in the Four Fathoms Channel by the Reculver Towers,' Tim explained, pointing to the chart. 'See that black Eiffel Tower symbol with the orange stripe, that's Spaniard. It's an East Cardinal Buoy warning you away from the shallow waters. I couldn't see it but I knew it was there. We had to get into Horse Channel between Hook Spit and East Last, which is a red buoy – very apt because we were about to enter the Gore Channel, then up past Longnose. Spaniard, Longnose! I love these names! I conjure them up in my imagination and they become people, characters. Look,' he said to Nicky who had his reading glasses perched on the end of his nose, 'that's the North Foreland. I sighted Elbow ...'

Brenda interrupted, 'Isn't Elbow a character out of *Measure for Measure*?'

Tim laughed, 'I think he is Bren, and gets his words mixed up as I recall.'

Now it was Nicky's turn to butt in. 'Have you heard Elbow, mate? A great band from Manchester.'

Tim poured Brenda a glass of wine and opened a beer for his brother, who asked, 'Are you going to see Mum tomorrow?'

Tim nodded while putting away his charts. 'We're going to meet her for lunch, but I can't see her walking down those pontoons can you?'

As I washed up the breakfast things the following morning, it became apparent that we could not let them drain. I could see the waves lapping through the narrow opening of the outer harbour. At low tide there was the sandbank, the one that was almost our undoing. It was covered in sea birds looking for whatever juicy morsels dwelt below the mud. The sandbank slowly disappeared from sight, and the seagulls flew away to seek a fresh feeding ground, be it a landfill or an incoming fishing boat. As the tide swept in, *The Princess Matilda* bounced about and the newly washed cups and breakfast plates clattered back into the sink before Tim could wipe them up. My favourite mug got broken. Tim went outside to wash the salt and seagull shit off the windows as I cleared up the mess and hung the surviving cup in the cupboard. I noticed a man heading our way.

When everything breakable, including a vase of yellow roses, was secured, I opened a newly washed window. Tim's legs were going up and down. His knees kept disappearing. I tapped him on the shin bone and pointed to the man. I heard him tell Tim that he was a fan of his work and his name was Steve and he worked at the harbour. Tim invited him in for a cup of tea. Steve was in his mid-thirties, an instantly likeable man, with a quick wit and sense of humour.

'Nice little ship you have here Mr and Mrs Spall, how long are we going to be honoured by your presence?'

Tim lost his balance and went sprawling over a stool.

Steve laughed. 'I think we can find you something a bit more comfortable!' He pulled out his mobile and made a call.

'Tony, when's *Proud Sea Horse* back?' He hung up and said, 'It'll be a bit tight but I think we'll get you in the inner harbour, but you'll have to wait until the bridge opens.' He looked at his watch. 'Let's say noon.'

He finished his tea and walked back up the bucking pontoon. You could tell he had done this many times. With the gait of a drunken sailor, he waved us goodbye.

Ramsgate has three harbours, the eastern part where we were moored is the least comfortable because it has little protection from the tidal surge. The western part has more shelter and is where all the leisure boats and visiting yachts go. A Custom's ship and the lifeboat were on that side too. Steve had said he was part of the lifeboat crew. The inner harbour has a tidal sea lock flap. The bridge and the lock opens twice a day either side of high tide.

Tim phoned Sylvia and said we would meet her at about 1:30 after we had moved the boat. He warned her, 'Don't wear heels, Mum, if you want to come onboard!'

*

I screamed anguish all the way over Waterloo Bridge. I wanted to be with you! Who could see me cry at 6:30 am?

You bend over a bit, stroking your chest. Your Hickman Line, which delivers the toxic drugs straight into your heart, is strapped to your torso. You won't let me call a nurse. 'It's only wind!'

Sylvia said she'd be at the hospital at about six this evening and at half past you start worrying. 'Where are they?' I've run out of excuses, and I can see you are panicking. I can't get her on the mobile. Brenda and Michael are outside the room putting on protective aprons and disinfecting their hands so I tell you to stop it and you become angry. It's horrible, and we can't concentrate on what they are saying. You keep saying 'Phone her again', and eventually I say, 'I'm going outside in case she's parking.' Still no sign of her, so I go back and say, 'I've just spoken to her, they had to go back home because Sadie was sick.' You know I'm lying but choose to believe me. They turned up ten minutes later, with Sylvia all of a flutter, because she'd got monstrously lost. Poor Sylvia, how dreadful for her. How do you tell a mother her son has cancer? How did I tell my kids? I phoned Pas, she was working. I used the public phone in the hospital. She couldn't hear me. She kept shouting tetchily, 'Speak up Mamma!' 'YOUR DAD HAS...'

Rafe had been so upset. I'd sat him and Sadie down. 'Dad won't be home for a while, he's got something wrong with his blood.' 'Will he be OK?' 'Yes of course! But he has to stay in hospital.' Rafe's face crumpled. 'How long, Mum, how long?' I have to be strong for my kids. I'm not ready to end their childhood. This is what I fear the most. I smiled and said, 'He will be home as soon as he's better and I'm going to get Nanny Sylvia and then Grandma to take care of you! You will like that. They will spoil you to death!'

*

Sylvia said she'd get a cab down to the harbour, as her car was being serviced. 'And anyway love, I've had a few drinks …'

She arrived in her taxi and Tim walked up the short, stable pontoon from our new sheltered mooring to help her. My mother-in-law likes to make an entrance, but Tim was determined she would get onboard in one piece.

'Just take your time, Mum, take my arm,' I heard him say.

I waved to her as she made her way tentatively down the jetty to our berth. She was wearing trainers and not her usual high heels. Sylvia might be in her mid-seventies, but she doesn't put her nose out of the door unless she is wearing a smart suit and full make-up. And she never has a hair out of place: she used to be a hairdresser. Sylvia was famous for giving the best bouffant in Battersea.

'Where'd you get the trainers from, Sylv?' I asked as Tim heaved her on to the boat. She is only five foot nothing.

'Hello dear,' she said, 'lovely to see you. I got them in Marks & Spencer's but I'm so disappointed they've shut down the Margate branch. I loved that Marks.'

It was a gorgeous day and after Tim had shown her around the boat, we sat out on the deck and had lunch on two small fold-up tables, which we joined together. All the doors to the wheelhouse were open and we basked in the warmth of the spring sun. The bricks of the Sailors' Church and Smack Boys' Home opposite us looked like they had sunburn.

As the late afternoon drew on, it became quite chilly, so I fetched a cashmere blanket and a thick cardigan for my mother-in-law. Sylvia feels the cold. Whenever she visits our house she complains, 'Oh it's freezing in here, feel the draft coming under that door!' We all strip off layers of clothes as she piles them on.

As I wrapped her up against the chill of the setting sun, five different shades of gold drifted above the cliff face. Brenda had been quite right: it was spectacular. Swathes of red blushed clouds hovered above the west cliffs. Little wonder Turner used to paint the skies above Thanet.

'Oh I wish I could paint that! What a sky,' my mother-in-law remarked. She is a talented self-taught painter herself. The buildings over the other side of the harbour were now illuminated. 'I've not seen it from this angle before. The Sailors' Church looks more like a cathedral lit up like that.'

The last of the daylight brought out small shy groups of roosting starlings. Soon they covered almost every yacht in the harbour, the wires blackened as they perched in neat rows. Above Pizza Express was a cartwheel of birds, and the starlings on the wire joined in with their sunset dance, swooping and tying themselves in ever more complex choreographed knots.

Sylvia wiped away a tear as I refilled her glass, and with a tremor in her voice said, 'Oh it's so lovely you are here on your boat. If only Joe had lived to see it.'

Tim touched her gently on her shoulder. 'Don't get upset, Mum. Dad would be happy knowing you're being looked after.'

Sylvia smiled. 'Oh, you know me, I'd cry to see a pudding crawl.'

Tim always laughs when she says this. 'Didn't you and Dad spend your honeymoon in Ramsgate?' he asked.

'We didn't call it a honeymoon in those days,' Sylvia responded. 'It was four months after we were married and Joe was on leave from the army. I fell for your elder brother Richard just up the road from here. Dumpton, you must've passed it on the boat. We stayed in a little B&B near to where Nicky lives now.'

'Didn't Dad's twin sister go with you as well, Mum?'

'Oh no dear,' Sylvia replied, 'two of his sisters came along.'

I almost choked on my gin and tonic. 'You went on your honeymoon with your sisters-in-law? You're kidding me! Didn't that put a damper on the proceedings Sylvie?'

'No, love. I remember I got horrible sunburn on my shins. I must have fell for Richard before then, because I couldn't bear the sheets near me, never mind my Joe.'

Sylvia took a tissue out of her handbag and asked us, 'You must have passed The Beachcomber on your way here?'

Tim nodded his head.

Sylvia continued, 'When I first moved down here, I used to sit on the beach and reminisce; it used to make me feel closer to Joe. I'd pretend he was a seagull, swooping free up in the air. I remembered all the happy times we spent on that beach. He used to love it when I went in for a swim with him.'

Tim put his arm around her. 'I know you loved him, Mum, and he feels that even if he is a seagull.'

Sylvia took out her compact to repair her make-up and called Tim a silly sod. She then took out a little notebook. For a number of years she has been in the habit of writing down questions to ask Tim whenever she speaks to him.

'Now then love, didn't you mention you were going to work abroad? You'll have to tell me when and what time you take off, so I can pray for your safe landing. And then you'd best call me a cab now, before I get too tiddly to walk up that jetty!'

We were pleased to have found such a wonderful and secure mooring in the inner harbour, because we would shortly have to leave the boat for a month while Tim worked. The job Sylvia was referring to was *A Room with a View* for ITV. Timothy was going to play Mr Emerson Senior, and Rafe Spall would play Mr Emerson Junior. This was the first time they would be acting together and we were to be put up in a beautiful, albeit slightly tatty, hotel in Florence, a street away from the shallow, swiftly running River Arno. There were no boats on the river, but lots of tourists on its bank. While Tim and Rafe went to work, I walked miles along the medieval back streets, enjoying the piazzas while they did all the hard work. I would meet them for lunch on their break then go back to the hotel for a siesta. My dad would have said I was living the life of Riley, which is quite true. I was. I do.

*

A motorbike courier called me a stupid bitch for changing lanes at the lights. I opened the window trying to say sorry it was my fault, but then his bastard shittiness pissed me off, so I screamed, 'I'm fucking sorry do you hear? I'm fucking sorry!' He pulled in front of me and I could see him looking at me in his mirror shrugging his shoulders at the people on the bus as if I was crazy. Of course I'm crazy. I have a son whose face crumpled. I don't think Sadie really understands, but Rafe does.

Mike Leigh had phoned from the airport. I was going to do

the same as I did with Brenda, but he had that annoyed Salford
tone in his voice, as if Tim had pulled out of the trip for a silly
reason. I was trying to work out how to tell my young kids when
he rang. Accusingly he asked me:

'Why isn't Tim coming?'
'He can't, he's in hospital.'
'Why? Why?'
'He's got leukaemia!'

*

Once Tim wrapped on *A Room with a View*, we flew home
then drove straight down to Ramsgate, stopping off in
Cliftonville to see Sylvia on the way. Sylvia is so proud of all her
sons, but her immaculate flat is homage to Tim. He smiles out
of blown-up stills in every corner of her apartment. Tim and I
love the view from the balcony. It looks out on an anchorage
for large vessels waiting to make a passage to the Thames. At
low tide we can see waves breaking over Margate Sands, which
hide deceptively just under the water.

'See, that's why we had to be so careful, Mum. If we'd got
stuck on that sandbank we'd have been in trouble, especially if
the weather had turned.'

Sylvia loves the view out of her window too.

'I worry about the ships, some of them stay for days and
days waiting for a break in the weather. Sometimes I see the
lifeboat go out and say a prayer.'

Sylvia remembers us all in her prayers. She has a hotline
with God.

Chapter Ten
Our Mutual Friends

The Isle of Thanet has a microclimate, and over those magical first few weeks Tim and I often used to swim in the sea at Ramsgate and Broadstairs. Pascale was over from Australia, so Tim and I had baby Matilda with us for a couple of weeks. I say 'baby', but she was now a toddler wearing clothes designed for a four year old: a big girl for her age. One afternoon we had quite a few people visiting us: Sadie, my sister Jen and a couple of actor friends, Chris Fulford and his wife, Camille Coduri. Chris and Tim had first worked together in the early 1980s. The last job they did was *Pierrepoint: The Last Hangman*. We told all of our shipmates to bring their swimming costumes, as we would go for a sunset swim.

Camille at the time was appearing in *Dr Who*, so Tim and I thought it was best if we ate on *The Princess Matilda*. After lunch we took them out for a little spin on the boat. Camille and Jen loved it, but Chris and Sadie looked really anxious.

'You'll be all right babe,' Camille said to Chris. 'Tim knows what he's doing. Do us a little dance, Timmy.'

Tim is always up for doing a turn and started to dance the hornpipe, his arms and legs going in all directions, his lips pursed together to make the sound of a kazoo. This had Camille in fits of giggles, her blonde hair falling over her heart-shaped face. It had the opposite effect on Chris and Sadie, whose faces were grey. Their look of terror increased.

I called Brenda on her mobile as we passed Broadstairs. 'Bren? Look out of your window you'll see us, we're just passing your flat. We're gonna go for a swim when we get back – come and join us!'

Camille and I climbed on the roof wearing our life jackets and waved and shouted. Down in the wheelhouse Sadie had Matilda (now called Tilda by all and sundry) on her lap.

'I'm going to be sick, Dad, take me back!' Sadie said.

Finally Tim relented. We took the boat back to Ramsgate and went to the beach instead.

We had the shoreline to ourselves. Tilda held hands with me and Jen as we paddled, jumping over the waves. Camille kept her thigh-high boots on and sat on the blanket next to Sadie. They sipped wine out of paper cups and shouted encouragement. Tim and Chris ran and dived into the sea. There were some big waves rolling in, and one swept my feet from under me. Jen managed to remain upright with Tilda, so I swam out to Tim and Chris. The sea was warm and felt like silk. When I reached them, Tim pulled me under the water; he always does that. If I want to stay above water, I have to jump on him and try to drown him instead. We both spluttered, laughing and screeching. Our squealing mingled with the shriek of the seagulls and we looked at the girls building sandcastles. Tilda's little legs ran down to the water's edge with the bucket to collect water.

I yelled out to her, 'Hi Til, come in and swim with Grandma and Granddad!'

Her slight shadow was lengthening on the sand. I thought I spotted Brenda on the promenade. Sometimes if you are lucky you experience perfect moments of happiness, and this was one of them.

*

Ten days of chemotherapy will be over tonight. When all is said and done you have not done too badly, far better than we thought, although these last few days you've stayed in bed and most of the time have been asleep. This morning you were up when I arrived, pouring a glass of water with your eyes closed, because they are hurting you. They were really watering. The doctor suspects an infection, and the antibiotic eye drops seem to be working. I read your horoscope to you: 'Planetary pressures throw up challenges in your career and home to strengthen or weaken your position. The test is daunting but if you can get through it then you will never look back and what you gain can never be taken away. Because there is an intense whiff of fate in what's happening to you now, certain things are out of control ... to know it means you can overcome it.'

Just at the moment, though, you have diarrhoea and your stomach is giving you trouble. You've hardly eaten anything since Thursday. Your temperature is still up and the nurse has sorted out some oxygen in case you become breathless. I suppose your red blood cells must be low. I've learnt that you slept so much before you came in because you had too many white blast cells, from the bone marrow. They reproduced and left no room for anything else. This is why your platelets were so low. There's a feature about you in The Telegraph *today. You did the interview ages ago and you can't read it now. But you do open one eye and look at the photo, which has you with a carrot dangling in front of your face. 'God I'm ugly!'*

You give a derisory laugh when I read out, 'Yet apart from a hairy interval three years ago, when a ten-month hiatus in work collided with a £70,000 tax bill, the Battersea born actor seems to have led a charmed life.' We're both worried about money, and how we will manage if you're not able to work. 'I can always get a job down the pub!' This always makes you laugh. I don't know why, I used to be a great barmaid. 'You've not worked behind a bar since 1978!' Terry our accountant reckons we'll have to pay £70,000 tax in December, and we still owe £37,000 from last year. We have over £4,000 a month of direct debits and standing orders. I change the subject.

'Me, Mom and the kids went to see Secrets and Lies *at a*

are in surgery having a new Hickman Line and I'm waiting. It's 9:30. You should be back soon to begin your second course.

*

Broadstairs is the quaintest and prettiest of harbours, with a golden beach with donkeys and deckchairs for hire. Dickens visited the town regularly from 1837. He used to stay at the Albion Hotel and later bought a house in the town. Fort House stands on the top of a cliff with views over the bay; he called it his 'airy nest'. He wrote parts of *David Copperfield* here, watching the tide roll in and out, a continuingly changing vista. The house and the views inspired him to write *Bleak House*, but Tim and I both agree the house looks more fort than bleak. Just below the house is a car park, and we have sat in our car when a gale has been blowing and the screaming sea crashes over the wall. Bleak but thrilling.

I invited two of my girlfriends, Miriam Jones and Madeline Newton, down to Ramsgate to spend a couple of days on *The Princess Matilda* while Tim was filming *Harry Potter and the Prisoner of Azkaban*. In the 1980s they were both married to actors in *Auf Wiedersehen Pet*. The first time I met Madeline, the *AWP* cast was filming on location in Germany. She had come over to visit her boyfriend, Kevin Whately. She was smoking a cigarette when she introduced herself. 'Hello, I'm Madeline.'

I knew who she was. She didn't have to tell me because in the late 70s she had been in a very popular television series called *When the Boat Comes In*. She and I were sitting on a crew bus, waiting for Tim and Kevin to finish a scene. They were filming across the road, surrounded by technicians. Kevin was standing patiently having his make-up touched up, while Tim had a soundman pulling wires through the back of his costume.

'You and me are the only girlfriend and wife out here then?' Mad said, indicating the activity outside with a slight flick of her cigarette.

'Frau and girlfriend,' I replied, as I finished rolling a cigarette. 'We're a couple of FAGs, got a light?'

I took the FAGs for a walk along the beach to Broadstairs.
Madeline said it was the furthest she had walked for years, as
she lit another cigarette. The walk took twice as long because
we chatted the whole way. Madeline is a Geordie with red hair
and white skin, which she kept under the shade of a massive
hat that seemed to trap her cigarette smoke, giving her a double
dose of nicotine. My dad was a smoker and had taken a huge
shine to her when they first met. He insisted on calling her
Dolly, the character she played in *When the Boat Comes In*.

I would admonish him, 'It's not her real name, Dad!'

Mad would laugh flirtatiously and take his hand, blowing
smoke out of her nose like Marlene Dietrich. 'Oh I don't mind.
Jim can call me whatever he likes.'

Miriam and Mad used to crew for me on our narrowboats
when Tim was working. Sometimes he is in limbo, otherwise
known as being on stand-by. This means he has a day off but
has to be prepared to get on the set at a moment's notice. It is
not always convenient, but it is part of our way of life. On one
occasion Tim had to leave us at the top of a challenging flight
of 21 locks above Warwick Castle. Sadie was with us too. It was
midsummer and pouring with the type of rain that hits you
twice, once coming down and then stinging you again on the
rebound. Three hours after Tim left, we had run out of dry
waterproofs. The rain dripped from our noses and dribbled
down our necks to squelch in our Wellington boots. And we
had only travelled a mile and still had another 10 locks to go.
My crew was getting the hang of entering a lock while I
shouted instructions from the towpath. As I recall, neither
Miriam nor Madeline spilt the slightest drop of watered-down
champagne out of their plastic cups.

I did, however, become rather concerned at one point, as I
prepared a lock ready for them. I saw Sadie, height four foot

six inches, walking along the gunwale dragging a 12-foot barge pole behind her. *The Colleen Bawn* had run aground. There was nothing I could do but wait. Miriam went up to help her push the barge pole at a 45 degree angle into the sloppy mud that had entrapped them.

Madeline stood by the tiller on the open back deck, dexterously smoking a long, cool, thin Consulate menthol cigarette. Occasionally she would shout encouragement. 'You can do it canny hinnies!'

She held an umbrella to stop her fag being extinguished, the cigarette gripped between her lips in grim determination. Her eyes squinted against the smoke as she put the boat into a screaming reverse gear. The boat inched backwards, Sadie and Miriam still pushing on the barge pole.

'We're off!' Miriam yelled.

But Sadie was still attached to the barge pole, which was now standing upright, her body leaning alarmingly at an 85 degree angle. Miriam lunged and grabbed her. The barge pole was left sticking out of the mud like the lady of the lake offering up Excalibur. Madeline meanwhile did a little twirl, taking in a length of rope. Through the horizontal sheet of steely grey tepid rain I saw Mad take another drag of her menthol-infused fag. With her free hand she gave a gentle tug as Sadie made her way back to the safety of the back deck. My youngest daughter had the end of Mad's rope tied around her waist.

Sadie was a great crew member until she reached puberty. Then she gave up wearing wellies and exchanged them for boots made of Italian leather.

Chapter Eleven
A Whiff of Sea Air

Sadie was not keen on wearing her posh boots when she visited us while we were moored in Ramsgate. Especially during the winter. The gale-force winds pounded the sea over the harbour walls, but we were well protected. That winter there was a little yacht called *Cailin* next to us, with two crew, Paula and Ron. Paula was a supply teacher who only worked during the winter months. She didn't walk anywhere, but skipped and jumped. I recognised her footwork.

'Are you a morris dancer?' I asked her.

'How did you know?' she replied.

Ron played the accordion, and we often heard him practising. Paula told us they were doing the same as us, navigating around the country clockwise. It felt a bit rich for us to be saying that we had only made it from London to Ramsgate, and even that had taken what seemed like years.

Christmas came and went. Pascale and her husband were over from Melbourne for a visit, and we took Tilda down to Ramsgate on Boxing Day. She had grown so much since the summer and made the boat her own, toys everywhere. I heard her calling to me every morning.

'Chum, Chum!'

My daughters call me 'Mum Chum', so she copied them. Tilda and I would both get dressed very quietly so as not to wake up Tim and then creep out of the boat. I would put her in her pushchair and wrap a blanket around her to keep her warm. Her eyes and nose ran in equal measure, and her little cheeks would go bright red. We would stop to chat with our neighbours, asking if we could get them anything from the shops. Tilda's favourite was the baker's shop. That is the great thing about being a grandparent: you can buy a sausage roll and a cake covered in hundreds and thousands for breakfast. She would blow her nose then blow on her sausage roll before nibbling, her breath white from the cold.

Brenda, who is patron of the Granville Theatre, high up on the east cliff, got us tickets to see *Jack and the Beanstalk*. Tilda loved it and after the show Brenda said, 'Come on Tilda, let's go and see the fairy godmother, she'd love to meet you!'

And she took us to meet the actors on the stage, where they all made a huge fuss of Tilda. Afterwards Brenda drove us back to the boat. Tim had passed on the pantomime and Brenda came onboard for a drink. Matilda was excited and told her granddad all about Jack and the fairy. Later Tim walked Brenda to the car while I put Matilda to bed. I could tell something was bothering him, so was anxious for him to come back. He locked up the doors once onboard and poked the fire.

'Catherine Wearing died,' he said.

His shoulders shook and I gave him a hug, holding him close to me. Catherine and Tim had a production company together and had a couple of projects on the go. She had produced *Our Mutual Friend* in 1997. They had both been nominated for a Bafta.

'Poor Catherine, she was so young. She went into a coma and didn't wake up.'

Catherine had a complex diabetic condition and died on New Year's Eve. She was only 41.

*

Secrets and Lies won the Palme d'Or, Brenda won Best Actress and Mike Leigh got Foreign Critics Award. I wish you had got Best Actor! You deserve it! You should be rewarded at this time, you poor sod. I open a small bottle of champagne, the kids are all here and very excited. You are so pleased for Brenda and Mike, and of course I wouldn't begrudge them anything, but it's not fair. Who said life was fair, who says? 'Well Brenda got it, fucking wonderful,' you just said. Lying there in bed with your eyes shut because they are so sore. You are covered in blankets because your temperature is up. I bet Brenda and Mike are thinking of us tonight. I make you a cucumber sandwich. I suspect you are becoming depressed. You say, 'You can't communicate when you can't open your eyes, you just turn inside yourself.' I wonder what we'll be doing this time next year.

When I arrive this morning your room is full of people, taking blood, temperature, emptying the waste bin, wanting the keys, polishing the floor. I wait, feeling useless. Your temperature shot up last night. You tell me, 'I was delirious, and I'm scared of it going up because it makes me feel so wretched.' Panos says this is because your blood count has been completely wiped out. We have to wait for it to get back to normal before you can come home. What kind of life can we have from now on? Moments, hours, days, weeks? A life that is dictated by a slight change in body temperature? Physically you have lost 12 pounds, and your hands have a yellow tint, the skin like parchment. Your hands were one of the first things I noticed about you. Nine stone nothing with little claw-like hands poking out of your blue leather jacket. A carrier bag full of the contents of the Holiday Inn minibar and a lonely heart, because your dad was dying. I'm glad we met. Even when you have really, really annoyed me, drastically annoyed me, I've never wanted to live with anyone else but you.

*

It was time for *The Princess Matilda* to come out of the water to have her backside painted. We had finally agreed that we would attempt to get to Wales that summer of 2008. It didn't look that far away on my road atlas. There are four slipways of differing sizes in Ramsgate harbour. They service all kinds of vessels. The governor of the slipway is a Geordie and Tim had had several conversations with him about lifting our boat. We were away the day she was pulled out of the water, but we went down to Ramsgate ten days later. It was strange seeing her on a big iron cradle several feet above the hard concrete. Workmen were climbing up and down a flimsy-looking ladder.

Tim, scatological as ever said, 'She looks like a 35-ton turtle, and talking of turtles I've got one too and its head's poking out. Let's get back to the hotel quickly!'

Tim and I were booked into a small boutique hotel high above the harbour. The views from our bedroom were wonderful. The lights were glittering on Deal Pier just across the bay. We could see the ferries queuing up to go into Dover just around the headland. The car and lorry transporters had all their lights ablaze as darkness threatened. As dusk drew in the sea became a steel grey, the same colour as the clouds. A disk of smudged yellow sun was visible low in the sky.

'I think there's snow up there,' I said, as I pulled a wrap around my shoulders.

It was a bitterly cold March day and there was a coal fire lit in our bedroom. Tim knelt on the hearth with several new sea-charts open before him. He had bought them in Stanford's, the map and travel bookshop in Covent Garden.

Tim had had his nose buried in his new charts ever since he got hold of them, cross-referencing tide tables and occasionally swearing. He looked up at me, the embers of the dying fire flickering across his face. I was cocooned under the boutique duvet where I was reading *Fear and Loathing in Las Vegas*.

'I wish you'd take an interest in this Shane,' he complained. 'Steve said we should go straight to Dover.'

Unfortunately the fire was dying down and I was loath to

leave my warm bed. 'I want to go up the River Stour to Sandwich first.'

Tim shook his head, a pencil wedged behind his ear. 'No, we can't risk it. Steve said the lifeboat has to go up there all the time to pull craft off the mud. We'll do a short hop and overnight in Dover. And if the weather's good we'll push on to Eastbourne, and Brighton.'

'Brighton!' I said, leaping out of bed, throwing the last of the coal on to the fire. 'Show me.'

Brighton is where we had our honeymoon.

*

The fire was out when we woke the next morning. We went down to breakfast wearing our coats. Just as well, as the radiators were all cold. Our teeth rattled as we ate.

'Let's sleep on the boat tonight,' I said, pulling on gloves to drink a tepid cup of tea.

'But what about the ladder, Shane?' Tim looked at me as if I were mad.

'Oh I'll be fine.'

It did seem a good idea until I stood at the bottom of the 18 rungs.

'Just don't look down,' Tim said. 'I'll be right behind you.'

I climbed and tried not think about the hard concrete beneath me or how many bones I would break if I fell. The ladder was placed halfway down the side deck of *The Princess Matilda*. My legs shook so much I could hardly move. It had snowed during the night, so the deck was slippery when I stepped off the top rung. I then had to turn around to take several bags of shopping and the rolled-up charts, encased in an elastic band, from Tim. I put everything on the deck and pushed it all towards a window with my foot to retrieve later. Keeping two gloved hands on the grab rail at all times, I shuffled 20 feet along the gunwale towards the stern. I bitterly regretted our decision to check out of the cold hotel.

'Oh for goodness sake Shane,' Tim said following behind. 'Hurry up before it snows again!'

My jaw was clenched too tightly to reply as I inched my way towards the wheelhouse. The side doors open outwards so I made my way to the back deck. There is a step and a safety rail all the way around this safe haven. I peered briefly over the stern, looking down to the iron rails that had carried the boat cradle out of the water. I had the key in the lock of the door when Tim stepped down into the wheelhouse. My computer bag was strapped over his shoulder but his feet slid from underneath him as he stepped, and my laptop and the step broke his fall.

'Oh my goodness, what have you done?' I said, dragging Tim to his feet. 'Are you OK?'

Tim grimaced in pain. 'I think I've cracked a rib!'

I got him inside and told him not to move as I recovered all the bags and charts through the window and got the fire alight and put the central heating on. When the saloon warmed up he lifted his shirt and showed me the beginnings of a mighty bruise. I poured him a glass of white wine – it didn't need chilling – and gave him a couple of painkillers. Tim never makes a fuss when he hurts himself.

'You'd better check I've not damaged your laptop.'

It had a huge dent in it but it still worked. The snow had begun to fall quite heavily. Snowflakes, backlit by the security lights, swirled and fell on the tiny beach next to our slipway. The incoming tide washed the snow away as soon as it landed. Tim gritted his teeth as he changed position, his charts spread before him on the table.

'I think we should have a night in don't you?'

Workmen using power tools woke us the next morning. I watched them from the wheelhouse as they walked along the side and roof as if the boat were only inches from the ground. David, the Geordie gaffer, said we should be ready to slip back into the water at high tide. We expected it to be like a lifeboat launch but it was a bit of an anticlimax, as we were gently winched down a few inches at a time. Tim had been told to turn on the engine when he felt we were clear of the cradle. A couple of the workmen stayed with us to untie all the safety straps. Steve was waiting for us once we were back in the water; he had said we could stay on the visitors' mooring by the lifeboat until we were ready to leave. I threw him a line and he pulled us alongside. He handed Tim a printout of the weather forecast. Tim glanced at it and passed it to me.

'That late snow blew in from Siberia,' Steve said. 'But the next few days are looking good. I'm going to miss you. Good luck! I hope you get to Wales!'

So did I, but Tim had only just told me it was over 400 nautical miles away.

Chapter Twelve
The African Queen

Ramsgate to Dover: 15 nautical miles

'If that's only a Force Three, Shane, I'll eat my own foot.'

Tim and I were standing at the end of the harbour wall watching a frothing, spume-flecked sea. It was high tide and rollers were breaking in.

'There're white horses breaking out there. In fact they're like cart horses. Look at them.'

'Don't exaggerate Tim.'

The Met Office had predicted a slight sea, but I had to agree with my husband. 'Slight' wasn't an adjective I would have used. On my Beaufort Scale, Kate Moss is slight and this sea was on the cusp of Marilyn Monroe.

'If we don't like it, we can come back, hey?'

Tim shook his head, 'It's not as easy as that.' He pointed out into the far distance. 'There're tidal issues and a 10-mile sandbank out there.'

'The Goodwin Sands?'

Tim nodded.

We had both spent the winter reading local books, and were aware that many vessels had been wrecked in that continuingly shifting area. The Great Storm of 1703 claimed over 2,000 lives.

'They used to play cricket on the sandbank at low tide,' Tim said, batting an imaginary ball. 'Even Shakespeare wrote about it. Do you care to hear?'

'You'll do it whether or not,' I responded.

He laughed and rolled his eyes to the heavens and flicked his tongue across his lips. With his right hand on his heart he spoke in a 1940s clipped staccato voice.

'Why, yet it lives there uncheck'd that Antonio hath a ship of rich lading wrecked on the narrow seas; the Goodwins, I think they call the place; a very dangerous flat and fatal, where the carcasses of many a tall ship lie buried, as they say, if my gossip Report be an honest woman of her word.'

'That was Al Jolson,' I said accusingly.

'Are you suggesting I'm an old ham and casting aspersions on my ability to impersonate one of our greatest Shakespearian actors?'

'If the cap fits … What's the quote from?'

'*The Merchant of Venice*.'

'I am always astounded how much you know.'

My husband laughed and threaded my arm through his. 'That's 'cos I've bin heducated by my profession innit? It was one of my early audition pieces where I shamefacedly copied Lord Larry Olivier.'

We walked around the little lighthouse at the end of the wall. Out on the bay was a colossal three-masted sailing barge with all of her sun-bleached red sails unfurled. Tim and I watched a ship that had probably sailed the seven seas, for seven generations.

'Do you think it's Venetian, carrying silk and ivory from the Arabian Seas?' I asked. 'I suppose the merchants would have taken their cargo to the Pool of London?'

Tim smiled and replied, 'This is the route they would have taken, maybe anchored off Margate Sands before going up the Thames Estuary.'

We stood quietly for a few minutes watching the crew letting down the sails. Tim broke the silence.

'What a beauty. She looks like she's heading in here, but

we'd better get back to the boat. I've still to double-check our course, just in case.'

On our way back to *The Princess Matilda*, we caught sight of Paula and Ron, our lovely morris dancing neighbours from the inner harbour. They had their yacht, *Cailin*, out of the water on wooden blocks. Both of them were busy getting their vessel ready to continue their journey around the coast. Paula's cheeks were rosy red from the whipping east wind. She was standing on tiptoes trying to get into an inaccessible place underneath the rudder. With her free hand she waved.

'We heard you might be leaving for Dover today?' she trilled, wiping her hand on her overalls.

'It looks a bit fresh out there,' Tim replied. 'But I had a chat with a local skipper who said it will be calmer once we clear the harbour, so we just might go for it.'

I laughed, 'It took us three attempts before we left Chatham, so if we go today we'll probably be back by teatime, but we're all shipshape, everything breakable's been shut in the cupboard. We're hoping to get to Wales…'

Tim interrupted. 'But we'll be spending most of the summer on the Solent.'

'So are we,' Paula said. 'But it looks like you'll have a head start. We've still an awful lot of antifouling and painting to do before we set out. We're fair-weather sailors so are going to wait a few more weeks. Good luck!'

She turned and skipped back to *Cailin*, her paintbrush at the ready.

By the time we got back to our boat the sailing barge was approaching the visitors' mooring. Tim went below to find the camera while I strolled down the pontoon to watch the vessel berth. As I drew near I heard someone calling to me in an exotic accent.

'Mizz! Mizz! Excuze me, Mizz!'

I looked up and saw a man holding a massive rope.

'Veel you be kind enouff to tuck zee line?' he shouted.

With a certain amount of trepidation I stepped forward. It was a huge, threatening, thick, black thing about the size of my wrist. The deck was full of passengers. They were looking down at me from the high foredeck. There was a look of expectation on many faces and most of them had a camera clicking away. I am the world's most useless catcher, but I caught this swinging beast at my first attempt. This does not happen very often. I received a spontaneous round of applause from those on the deck. I think they were Japanese. I bowed to my audience. I tied the line several times around the cleat and threw it back to the crew member. My rope chucking is even worse than my catching, but I did this first time too.

'*Dank je wel.*' the sailor cried, which I presumed meant thank you. Well, I hope it did. Tim joined me as the skipper put the ship in forward gear to bring around the helm. 'Amsterdam' was written on the bow.

Leaving Ramsgate was quite an anticlimax. There was no one about to wave us off. The Dutchmen and their human cargo had gone sightseeing. Tim and I just slipped our ropes and left. As we came out of the breakwater, *The Princess Matilda* seemed to grunt. She rolled a little, but Tim gave her more acceleration and aimed her head first into the waves. She smoothly cut through them. We were both thrilled to be back at sea, albeit our first outing was to be a short one. Dover was only 15 miles away but this was going to be an epic journey for us. The Strait is one of the world's busiest sea channels. It is used by hundreds of commercial ships criss-crossing the Channel in a choreographed waltz. The Port of Dover is Europe's largest ferry terminal. The French coast is only 20 odd miles away. A cross channel vessel arrives or departs the terminal on average every 15 minutes.

The sun came out as *The Princess Matilda* crossed Pegwell

towards Sandwich Bay. In the distance Tim and I could see the green, undulating, manicured turf of The Royal St George's Golf Club. We could just about make out the two-tone match-stick figures walking back up to the 19th hole.

Tim said, 'Do you promise to kill me if I take up golf?'

'Only if you promise to kill me if I take up line-dancing. Where's the camera?'

The man-made grassy greens of the golf club were a vivid backdrop to the rolling blonde sand dunes that skirted a now turquoise blue sea. Putting down the Lumix, I pointed.

'Those dunes have to be Kent's best-kept secret, hey Tim?'

'There's no one there, miles and miles of empty beach, a bird watcher's delight,' he replied.

*

Midnight
Mom and Sadie went to Frances Barber's party. Brenda joined them later on. Frances made a big fuss of my mom, put her in the place of honour with everyone coming to pay their respects like she was the queen. Lovely Alan Rickman sat next to her.

'Oh you won't have much luck with me,' she said. 'I'm past it,' or words to that effect. She loved him. Of course she hasn't a clue who he is. Brenda told me she was shouting above the music, 'And who's that over there, is she a Jew? I like Jews!' I presume she meant Suzanne Bertish, who gave her two letters to give to you and me. Mine is a lovely note. Everyone says the same thing: we love Tim, is there anything we can do? It's amazing the number of people who cried over the phone when I told them the news. It's almost a cathartic experience for me, passing my pain on a little I suppose. Except I've gained no proper relief. I miss you so much … It is a bereavement of sorts I'm suffering. I phoned Frances up on Friday because I was so miserable, a bit drunk. I'm not used to being on my own, I find it very hard.

*

I went below to make some cheese sandwiches and tea. When I got back up to the wheelhouse, Ramsgate was swiftly disappearing from view.

'It feels kind of lonely out here,' I said to Tim as I gazed longingly back towards Thanet.

'Lonely? Not from where I'm standing,' Tim said sharply. 'Look over there. That's the South Foreland Lighthouse.'

On the horizon beyond the lighthouse was a curved line of tiny evenly spaced vessels.

'They are the Dover–Calais ferries. It's hard to see which way they're heading. Are they coming or going? It's impossible to tell from this distance. I'm worried, we have to time our entrance into Dover in between arrivals and departures. It's a bit like that game the kids used to play on the GameBoy.'

'Super Mario?' I asked.

'That's the one. Where that big thing squashes everything,' Tim answered.

I gave him his tea.

'I could do with something stronger,' he said.

But before I could tell him off, we were both simultaneously distracted.

'Did you see that?' I asked.

'Bloody hell!' he answered. 'A blooming bumble bee! What on earth is a bee doing three miles out at sea on an April morning?'

'I reckon it's a good omen.'

Tim smiled and replied, 'Our bumble angel! We're going to need it. I gave the Goodwin Sands a wide berth, now all I have to do is dodge a few P&O ferries.'

Once we had crossed the wide bay I felt much happier. We were once again hugging the coast. Tim had recently bought us a life raft that was now stowed in a neat container on the back deck. It is designed to inflate as soon as it hits the water, appearing like magic out of the case. Well, that is what the man in the chandlery had said. I felt more secure now we had one because if we had to abandon ship we could always row to shore. I didn't share my thoughts with Tim; he would have been appalled. He would have quoted Corporal Jase. 'NEVER STEP DOWN ON TO A LIFE RAFT. ONLY STEP UP IN TO ONE.' Tim and I missed Jase.

I had been so absorbed with making tea and watching the bumble bee that I had failed to notice that the golden sand dunes of Sandwich Bay had been replaced with shingle. I looked at my road atlas. We had driven many times on the main road that goes inland to the town of Sandwich and reappears at Deal. There was a castle icon on the map. I searched for its physical presence through the binoculars and found it perched on top of a cliff. From the sea it looked squat with beige and shimmering white, brickwork. I pointed it out to Tim.

'According to the AA that's Deal Castle.'

'It's almost camouflaged from view,' he replied.

'Maybe that's what Henry VIII had in mind when he had it built?'

I squinted against the sun. The long, ugly pier off the seaside town is a more recent addition, the only new pier to be constructed after the Second World War. Tim showed me where it was marked on his sea-chart. You can't really miss a 1,000-foot mass of reinforced concrete jutting out like some obscene tongue into the sea.

As we passed Deal, *The Princess Matilda* had the company of a few fishing boats, bringing home their catch. They reminded us of suicidal whales marooning themselves on the beach. A few hours later, the entire Deal fishing fleet would be left stranded on the shore, waiting for the tide to take it off the shingle again the following day.

Both Tim and I had been monitoring the Dover ferries for the past hour. We were getting closer to the shipping channel.

As we drew nearer, the ferries grew larger. Tim is a dreadful worrier but I don't see the point of fretting about something until I have to. I picked up my road map. The next bay was called St Margaret's. Through the binoculars I could see three whitewashed flat-roofed art deco houses that made the white cliffs behind look grey and dowdy. I could sense Tim becoming increasingly fractious so I tried to distract his attention from the ferries.

'I wonder if those houses get flooded at high tide. That bit of a wall can't offer too much protection?'

Tim stopped counting the ferries and looked to the shore. 'That's White Cliffs,' he said.

'I can see that Tim.'

'No, not those white cliffs. That's what the houses are called. Noël Coward lived there. Do you remember that magical first weekend we had away after I came out of hospital?'

'Yes, of course. It's the only time you and I have ever been into a pub and both drank soda and lime,' I replied laughing. 'But that's because it was only 10:30am, and you were so knackered…'

Tim interrupted me, 'And the landlord told us we should walk down the cliffs…'

'Because Noël Coward used to live on the beach and Spencer Tracy and Katharine Hepburn used to stay with him and she used to swim in the sea. It took us three hours to walk back up the hill. It took you days to recover.'

'It was worth it though wasn't it?'

One of our favourite films is *The African Queen*. Tim does a marvellous Bogie. Come to think of it, he is pretty good at Kate and Coward too.

I no longer needed the road map to show me where we were. Another castle high up on the world-famous white cliffs of Dover had been in sight for quite a while. I swung my binoculars away from the castle towards a ferry that appeared to be heading straight at us. I thought about *The African Queen* trying to ram the German battleship. Water and binoculars play tricks with one's sense of distance. The ferry didn't look so close to the naked eye.

'How far?' I asked Tim.

'I'm not sure but I estimate they must be doing 30 knots,' Tim said with urgency in his voice.

He put *The Princess Matilda* into reverse gear and swung the steering wheel around like Popeye on speed.

'They must be able to see us,' I said.

My voice had gone up an octave and I noticed that Tim had become a character out of *The Battle of Britain*. I couldn't quite put my finger on it. Was he doing Kenneth More or Trevor Howard?

With a concise tone of authority in his voice he said, 'I'm going to turn 180 degrees to starboard and call Port Control. Look in the *Reeds*. What channel are they on?'

The *Reeds* was open on the Dover page, but I couldn't find my reading glasses. Fortunately I always keep a spare pair hidden away for such an emergency as this. My right hand felt inside my bra and withdrew the specs. The ferry showed no sign of slowing down. I tried to concentrate on the job in hand, scanning the page for the VHF number.

'Port Control, channel 74,' I said, swallowing panic with a hiccup.

'*Matilda*'s coming around,' Tim said calmly.

But I was not convinced as his arms were still grappling with the steering wheel. Oh God, I thought, I have seen this before. My eyes were drawn to the life raft but I shook my head. If the ferry couldn't see *The Princess Matilda*, what chance would we have on that? Tim was still wrestling with the wheel. Everything went into a slow-motion replay of what had happened when we first came out of the Thames Estuary. The rudder had not responded and *The Princess Matilda* had gone around in circles.

I dashed below to grab the things I knew I couldn't live without. I know on aeroplanes you are supposed to leave everything behind but I wasn't going to abandon ship without the Gordon's and my laptop memory stick. I slugged neat gin out of the half bottle before packing it into a waterproof grab bag. I rushed back up into the wheelhouse and a disembodied voice crackled over our VHF.

'*Princess Matilda, a ferry has just arrived and another will be leaving shortly, but if you hurry past the Southern Breakwater you will be fine.*'

Behind us we watched the stern of the ferry disappearing through the mouth of the harbour. Tim turned us around and a few minutes later *The Princess Matilda* followed it and we sped by the high sea wall.

'My God, that was a bottom twitcher,' I said to Tim as I loosened my life jacket so I could breathe. I had taken it in a notch as I swigged the gin.

'It wouldn't have hit us darling, I was just being over cautious. Let's get the old girl into port.'

'You're doing Kenneth More.'

'I am not, I'm doing me more scared,' Tim laughed, and took his Douglas Bader stance. All that was missing were the tin legs. Mine were like jelly.

Dover's inner harbour where we were headed is located between two piers. A large white cruise liner was moored against one of them. I had phoned ahead and booked an overnight mooring and we were directed to a berth. But Tim and I could not agree where the marina controller had told us to go.

'He said "C" Hammerhead.'

'No, Shane, he said "B" Hammerhead.'

'What is a bleeding Hammerhead anyway?'

As it turned out a chap was waiting for us on 'C'. As we were tying up, I asked the man what a Hammerhead was. He looked at me like I was truly daft. Our mooring was at the top of a jetty which had small limbs with boats moored either side of the central walkway. Because of the length of our boat we berthed on the longest pontoon at the top of the jetty. It looks like the head of a hammer. This only served to remind us just how inexperienced we really were. We felt foolish. It was a miracle we had made it here at all.

Chapter Thirteen
Chalk and Cheese

The sheet of the Dover rock face above us was the same colour and density as a sledgehammer. Discoloured by exhaust fumes, the iconic not-so-white cliffs blocked out phone and television reception in the harbour. I wanted to explore the tunnels that lead up the cliffs to the castle but they were still on winter opening hours.

'If the weather's good we'll leave before they are open; on the other hand if it's bad you will be sick of the tunnels,' Tim said as he opened his tide table.

I had read so much about the tunnels during the long Thanet winter. The first excavations were begun in the Middle Ages, and then expanded during the Napoleonic Wars. But Tim and I were more interested in 'Operation Dynamo'. The tunnels were the nerve centre during the evacuation of the allied forces from Dunkirk. Thousands of troops were rescued.

My dad used to say, 'We'd all be speaking German now if they'd been taken prisoner.' He should know; he spent his youth in the army.

Tim and I didn't get to see much of Dover except for a torrent of ferry traffic that we had to dodge to get to a shop. I say 'shop' but it was really a petrol station where we bought a loaf of bread for the following morning.

'I was born in London, you don't know how to cross a busy road!' Tim said as he grabbed my arm and pulled me into the path of a speeding coach.

Once we were safely on the pavement I shouted at him, 'For goodness sake! Are you trying to kill us?'

As we walked back to our mooring we saw a ferry waiting to get into the harbour.

'The last time you were on a ferry, you were with Krissy, weren't you?' Tim said taking my hand.

'I still miss her,' I replied.

*

Midnight
I feel so fucking useless.

I feel so lonely out there on my own. I find bedtime the worst. I find leaving the hospital the worst. You are all of me and I am a fish out of water now, not complete. 'I'm your best friend!' you said as I cried after Krissy died. I've begun running again, except our house is surrounded by graveyards. It doesn't help me much to see all those lonely neglected graves at the far end of the cemetery. You tell me to take it one day at a time. I do try, but every now and again I feel crushed by the enormity of the illness, this journey we are on. I could not witness another death. But you will not die, not for a long time...

Our bed is too big, too hard for me.

*

Dover to Eastbourne: 46 nautical miles

I looked at the road atlas as Tim did his engine checks. By car Eastbourne is approximately 50 miles away. The sea passage is about 46. This may not sound very much, but our boat only does a top speed of 7.5 knots, and nautical miles are slightly longer than road miles. In other words, we can average about six road miles an hour.

'It's going to be a long trip. How long will it take us?' I asked as I passed Tim some kitchen roll.

'About seven hours,' he replied.

He used the paper to wipe oil off the slimy dipstick, dropping the greasy litter into the proffered carrier bag.

'We should get there about 4:45.'

I put on my life jacket.

'I'm really looking forward to it, especially the power station.'

We passed Dungeness Nuclear Power Station at lunchtime. I was making cheese and pickled onion sandwiches from the garage's stale white sliced bread. From where I was standing in the galley the infamous power station looked like something from an episode of *The Quatermass Experiment*. The elegant old grey lighthouse is at odds with the silver spindly pointed pylons that carry electricity to the National Grid. I took the sandwiches up to the wheelhouse. Tim pointed towards the power station. The early spring sun had brought out families walking dogs and throwing frisbees on the shoreline.

'See those people further up?' Tim said, indicating figures perched on top of a high shingle bank. 'They look like they are sitting in an amphitheatre, waiting for the show below them to begin. I suppose the bank protects the power station from the ravages of the sea. It's a wild and bleak landscape in the winter. I drove down here with Mike Leigh when I was researching Phil in *All or Nothing*. Derek Jarman had an old fisherman's cottage on the beach…'

I interrupted, 'I love *All or Nothing* and thank God it's nice and calm for us today. Give me those Phil lines.'

His face changed before my eyes; he wasn't Tim Spall any more. Now he was a useless cab driver who thinks his wife doesn't love him any more. Exuding pathos and honest humanity, he is everyman. He delivers my favourite line from the film.

'*Sun comes up, sun goes down. Tide comes in, tide goes out.*'

'This is what our journey is all about,' I said, taking him by the hand.

He squeezed it with silent recognition and spoilt it by saying, 'Bugger off, I'm concentrating.'

The Princess Matilda rounded the headland, making passage towards Rye Bay. Meanwhile, the seashore was changing drastically. The shingle on the beach gave way to the Riviera-like coastline of East Sussex's Camber Sands. Every now and again we saw what appeared to be red and gold ribbons that gently danced in the breeze. But the ribbons changed colour and the water flickered in the sun like footage from an old fashioned movie. It was impossible to tell where the sky ended and the sea began. I thought the ribbons were the tails of kites flown from the shore.

'What are those flapping things?' I eventually asked Tim, with exasperation in my voice.

'They mark fishing pots,' he replied. 'If we get one of those tangled around the prop we'll be in trouble.'

I felt much easier now I knew what they were. 'I didn't think they would be allowed to fish around the corner from a nuclear reactor. Do you think the crabs glow in the dark?' I inquired. I peered through the windscreen of *The Princess Matilda* and thought I saw a bumble bee.

'What's that?' Tim said, snatching up the binoculars.

'I don't know,' I replied, as I realised the bee was an optical illusion.

'Whatever it is,' Tim said, 'it's heading our way.'

In moments a launch drew alongside us. As it drew closer the sun's rays turned the yellow warning sign to red. It was emblazoned 'M.O.D. FIRING RANGE SAFETY BOAT'. A head poked out of the cockpit.

'You must go out to sea. Firing practice is about to commence on the Lydd Ranges. For your own safety you need to go out at least four miles.'

'But I've got my passage marked on my sea-chart. And

there's a shipping lane out there,' Tim complained. 'How will I get back on course?'

The 'head' replied with a wave of his arm. 'Just head that way. Sou', sou'west!' He put his vessel into reverse and sped away.

'What does that mean?' Tim said as we watched the boat buzzing back to its hiding place.

'Which way is "that way" for fuck's sake? I worked it all out. This means I'll have to start all over again. What did he say? Sou', sou'west? We'll have to go out to sea and there're massive tankers out there and I don't know which way to go, or which course to plot. We're buggered!'

In these situations I always find it best to change the subject. 'Why is there a firing range by a nuclear power station?'

Tim shrugged his shoulders. He was looking at his chart. He scratched his head and turned *The Princess Matilda* out to sea. 'This will put two hours on our journey. It will probably be dark when we get to Eastbourne and there might not be enough water to get us through the lock. You steer, Shane, while I plot a new course. This will be the furthest we've been off land.'

'Thank God for that,' I exclaimed, 'because unless someone is slamming doors that's cannon fire!'

The sound of the dull thump of explosives stayed with us for quite a while. One and a half hours later Tim looked through the binoculars and whooped.

'I can see Beachy Head. We're back on course.'

I looked at my road map. 'Are you sure it's Beachy Head?'

'Yes, I've got it on my chart. Don't make me doubt myself, Shane,' Tim said, thrusting the binoculars into my hands. 'Put the map book down will you? Can you see it? It has to be Beachy Head.'

He snatched the binoculars out of my hands before I had time to focus.

'It's one of our major English landmarks, a great big chalk cliff, that's definitely it.'

'Well it looks white, but the chalk cliffs extend from Thanet to the Isle of Wight...'

A gust of wind blew through the wheelhouse and scattered Tim's sea-charts on to the deck. We both scooped them up but the chart he needed was at the bottom of the pile.

'Where are the protractors?' he said crossly.

We both searched, moving pilot books, half-eaten sandwiches and three-day-old newspapers. Eventually the protractors were found underneath my chair. *The Princess Matilda* came closer to land. I looked at my map and then through the binoculars.

'I can see a pier,' I said.

'That must be Eastbourne Pier,' Tim replied.

We drew ever nearer. Tim gave me the steering wheel while he did things with his protractor and the ruler, which had fallen into the waste bin. I could sense despondency emanating from him.

'What's up love?' I asked.

'That's Hastings Pier. We still have 12 more miles to go.'

We used to take the kids to Hastings. They always felt cheated with the gritty egg and tomato butties on the beach. A real treat would be a shared bag of chips and then a walk up and over the cliff. On one occasion we came across a local artist who was displaying her wares on the grass. Rafe walked straight over them. He was only a toddler with little bandy legs. The artist screeched at him. She reminded me of Betsey Trotwood in *David Copperfield*, shouting at the boy leading the donkey over the green in front of her Kentish cottage. Miss Trotwood pounced upon the lad, '*captured him, dragged him with his jacket over his head...*' I am sure the Hastings lady artist would have done this too but Rafe was wearing a sun bonnet and I gave her a look that stopped her in her tracks. I made Rafe apologise but I could see both points of view.

'But Mamma they were on the floor!'

On board *The Princess Matilda*, we experienced the last moments of warmth from the early spring sun. It was an iridescent globe of egg-yolk yellow, bleaching out everything on the horizon. I knew we had passed Bexhill-on-Sea three-quarters of an hour before. Tim looked at his watch.

'I reckon we still have about an hour before it gets dark. I wish I could see more against that glare. That's the trouble, we're sailing south-west, and going into the setting sun.'

It had become quite chilly. I found a jumper, bobble hat and gloves and clumsily turned over pages of the *Reeds*.

Tim said, 'We're crossing Pevensey Bay. I'm worried, there's a shoal out there. But once we spot Eastbourne's Martello Tower I'll know we're on track for the buoyed channel into the outer harbour.'

'We've never visited Pevensey have we?' I asked.

Tim squinted against the glare.

'When I was at RADA, me and my mate Michael Simkins said if we didn't make it as actors we'd open a fishmongers in Pevensey. I wonder what he's up to? I've not seen Simmo for ages. Do you remember we bumped into him on our honeymoon?'

'Yes of course. He's just written a book hasn't he?'

I looked through the binoculars. The sea was dead calm with shimmering specs of gold peppering the surface.

'I can't see anything, Tim.'

I gave him the binoculars. He put them on top of his chart.

'Take the helm, will you? And keep on that course, keep your eye on the compass reading, two degrees either side is fine, but no more.'

He picked up the protractors. I couldn't see what he was doing with them. I was concentrating too much on keeping the flickering needle on the compass in the right place. Tim doesn't take it kindly when I make detours. Fortunately he took the wheel back fairly quickly.

'Good girl,' he said in his John Mills voice. 'Perfect. According to my calculation we only have three more miles to run. I just wish we could see that damned tower.'

I put on my sunglasses to look through the binoculars and kept them there, scanning the horizon for what seemed like hours. 'I think I see something,' I said at last, passing the binoculars to Tim. 'Over there, about one o'clock from the windscreen wiper.'

'That's it! That's the Martello. If it had been Blackpool Tower we'd have spotted it ten miles away,' Tim exclaimed with excitement in his voice. 'I can see a red sail. It's a yacht. We'll follow it in.'

'Hurrah! I'd better make sure all our ropes are in the right place, and drop the fenders down.' I gave Tim a kiss.

'Be very careful. Keep one hand on the grab rail at all times. It's been a long day and we don't want to make any mistakes,' Tim said with concern in his voice.

What I have discovered about motor boating from our trips is this: you have hours doing nothing and then 20 minutes of frenzied activity. I think it was Corporal Jase who said it was the same in the army. Or he may have said, three hours of doing nothing then 24 hours of frantic action. I fastened all the doors back and checked Tim had his mooring lines to hand, then made my way down to the front of the boat. I had the camera in my pocket and the binoculars around my neck. The sun had disappeared and the sky reminded me of the shell of a battery-farmed egg. I had a grey handspun wrap around my shoulders. I shivered but didn't want to miss anything so I stayed where

I was instead of going below for a warm coat. From where I was standing the Martello Tower was a dumpy rotund structure, not so much a tower, I thought, as a squashed cigar. By the time we got through the breakwater into the outer harbour, the red-sailed yacht had locked through into the marina. We had to wait for the lock-keeper to reset it, so I had time to survey our new home. There was a lifeboat moored up ready for action, and a small sandy beach in front of a crescent of fairly new townhouses.

The green light came on, so Tim motored *The Princess Matilda* into the lock. It had been a while since we had been in one so I made sure we were tied up securely. The lock only went up a couple of inches, so I felt cheated. I like drama and enjoyed wrestling with ropes on the Thames. The gate opened and we entered a housing estate. It could have been anywhere, Manchester, Birmingham, Leeds or Limehouse. The same boring, generic architecture. 'Lifestyle' waterside housing. As for us, our new home was easy to find: the visitor's mooring was straight ahead. Tim and I got tied up to the berth fairly quickly. When I was done, I ran screeching with glee down the pontoon towards Tim, who was putting our electrics on shore power.

'We made it. Where's Eastbourne?'

Tim blew on his hands to warm them up. 'The marina's a couple of miles out of town.'

'But I'm starving!' I said. Then I sniffed. 'I can smell curry.'

Tim laughed and said, 'You can sniff out an Indian restaurant like a bloodhound following the trail of an escaped convict in a 1930s thriller.'

We locked up *The Princess Matilda* and checked into the marina office for the security code to get back on to our berth. Tim then followed my nose. Actually, this is a lie. The man in the office gave us a map.

*

Sovereign Harbour is a huge marina made up of several basins with lifting bridges to let through tall-masted yachts. It was a bit of a maze even with a map. I think it was luck more than anything that we eventually took the right path. We crossed a few bridges, and the last one led us to the Indian restaurant that overlooked our mooring. In fact *The Princess Matilda* was overlooked from all sides. Townhouses and apartments surround the marina. There is even an Asda supermarket.

'That'll be handy, we're running out of toilet paper,' I said to Tim as we tucked into the poppadoms. 'I can't believe we got here though, can you?'

'We brought our boat here by sea. How amazing is that?' Tim replied.

'Pretty special darling, and it's all down to you. You did it.'

'It does feel so satisfying,' Tim said, as he refilled my glass. 'I really thought we were lost at one point when that Firing Range Safety Boat told us to bugger off. I didn't like to worry you, but between Dungeness and here there are about 70 wrecks lying at the bottom of the sea.'

'How do you know that?'

'They're marked on the charts, I only just discovered what the symbol meant.'

'Well, you got us here safe and sound, that's the main thing and tomorrow we'll have a look at the Martello Tower and walk into town. I've sent a text to Miriam. She's going to catch a bus from Hove. I'll phone her later,' I said as I piled more lime pickle on to my side plate.

'I'm looking forward to seeing Miriam. But you'll need that toilet roll put in the freezer if you eat all that,' Tim chortled, in the mode of Eric Morecambe, his reading glasses rising over his eyebrows.

The next morning we walked a couple of miles along the shingled beach into Eastbourne. Unfortunately the Martello

Tower was inaccessible, although it looked taller on land than it did from the sea.

'So they were built to repel Napoleon,' I said to Tim.

'Apparently there aren't many left.'

'Just as well there aren't many Napoleons left either.'

We passed a few fishing boats that had been dragged up the pebble beach by a winch.

'The fishing industry must be in decline around here,' Tim said, walking around one of the many rusting winches. 'They look like they've not been used for years.'

'Well, there's a wet fish hut over there. Maybe Michael Simkins is filleting some skate.'

Tim laughed, 'Or pulling dead men's fingers out of a crab, or sticking live men's fingers up a dead eel.'

'Let's buy Miriam a crab.'

'No, she'll have to take it home on the bus. By the time we've eaten and had a walk down the pier it'll be festering. Everyone will think it's her that stinks.'

I was really looking forward to our lunch. Miriam is my best friend and had recently run away from London. I don't know what I would do without her. I used to think I lost my best friend when Krissy died, but it feels like Miriam has always been there for me. I remember the first time I saw her. I had met Jimmy Nail in Germany when he and Tim did the first series of *Auf Wiedersehen Pet*, but Miriam didn't go. We invited them both for Sunday lunch when we got back to London. My god, I thought, they are chalk and cheese, he is so BIG and she is so small.

*

I had lunch with Miriam in Heal's on Tottenham Court Road. It's just around the corner from UCLH. We shared half a bottle of champagne. I really love her. Miriam doesn't use a sympathy voice. I can't bear sympathy voices. She wrote what she had to say that first night when I was reeling.

Dear Shane,

When you rang to say Tim has leukaemia, I was completely devastated, so was Jimmy. Such a terrible thing, and so out of the blue. You must be in a state of shock as you try to come to terms with it. My own feelings were of disbelief and uselessness – I want to take it all off you both, but I can't...

Love Miriam

I know she means it. We share champagne and she knows...

The doctor has told you they might remove your Hickman Line because it's become so sore. Apparently they think your neutrophils, the cells that fight infection, are kicking back in. They are attacking the weakest spot, i.e. the line. You are afraid it will hurt, and you seem so discouraged. A new doctor says, 'It will only take a tug!' Poor Timmy. Easy for her to say. Nevertheless, she gives you some pethidine, but she suspects she gave it a little late or perhaps too soon. You still felt it. It wasn't as bad as you'd thought, and you get almost instant relief from the soreness around the line, which you've felt since you went down to X-ray on Friday. Your temperature has gone down too. It seems like the devil and the deep blue sea, because now you won't need so many antibiotics, but those you do need are to be put into a cannula in a vein on the back of your hand. When I was a junkie, that was always my vein of choice. But you don't have a choice do you?

Dr Rye says you may have a bone marrow biopsy to see how the marrow has reacted to the treatment. If it's not good, they will start the next chemo sooner rather than later. The rash on your abdomen is a lot better, but your legs are sore. This apparently is due to the neutrophils kicking in. This is a good sign, but you scratch like mad when I arrive this morning. I came a bit later than usual, I slept till 9:30. Mom and the kids have gone on the coach to Alton Towers. The amount of egg sandwiches she had made filled two bags. I didn't have the heart to tell her they wouldn't eat them, preferring shit from some over-priced self-service cafe. We'll see. At least they will have fun, the kids.

Rafe goes back to school tomorrow so I'll start coming in earlier again, get some kind of routine going. I need to begin work on my thesis but my heart isn't in it. Oh for normality. Why didn't I have an inkling our life was to change so abruptly on 8 May 1996?

Four more days and a month will have passed. A month, and I thought you'd be home by now, but it looks like you will have to stay in.

I'm not strong, everybody thinks/says I am, I survive from day to day, from hour to hour. Travelling through a world I'm no longer part of, on my way to and from the hospital. I try to vary the route. I went through the West End last night. Being a Saturday evening, people were thronging the streets. The girls were all dressed up, and the boys were hanging around the proverbial street corners. There was a sense of hysteria out there but amongst all the crowds was a silver-haired man. He looked like my dad. Old, with a face shrunk to the bones. His eyes were watching for the green man on the pelican crossing, oblivious to the mass of humanity around him. I wondered who would sit with him and hold his hand when he died. His mac was very shabby. Tears rolled down my face. Everyone was a baby once, and if you are lucky you are loved and cared for throughout your life. But I sensed this old man would die all alone.

*

After our lunch with Miriam, Tim and I caught a train up to London. Sometimes it seems we are forced back to the real world. We were looking forward to seeing Pascale, who had moved back to the UK. That was wonderful for us, but not so fantastic for her as her marriage had broken down. Of course, Pascale's return meant we would spend time with Tilda too and she was excited about visiting 'Princess Matilda Boat', as she refers to the barge. We took her back to Eastbourne with us when we returned a couple of weeks later. Tim dropped us off at the supermarket so we could get in some supplies, and we walked back to the boat. He had the hose out, with the jet spray attached. The wheelhouse was covered in seagull shit. Tilda and I stood well back as he attacked it with a scrubbing brush.

'Oh that's gwoss Gwanddad!' was her observation.

Chapter Fourteen
Princesses

Eastbourne to Brighton: 20 nautical miles

Tim and I had agreed that we would only go out to sea with Tilda on a perfectly calm sunny day, our grandchild being far too precious a cargo to risk. Our wish was granted. Our journey to Brighton was an uneventful passage: we weren't used as target practice and we didn't run aground. The gentle motion of *The Princess Matilda* rocked her namesake off to sleep on my lap. I was sitting on the back deck with a blanket wrapped around us. It was a sunny day, but the May Day sea breeze was chilly. I pointed towards a red and white candy-striped lighthouse, which was about half a mile to our starboard side. Tim looked at his chart.

'That really is Beachy Head. Look at the height of the cliffs,' he said.

'The chap in the marina office said most of the local RNLI shouts are to pick up dead bodies out of the sea. It must be so upsetting for them,' I said while tucking the blanket around Tilda's exposed arm. I shuddered. I once knew a man who killed himself and know a few more who have tried.

'I suppose you have to be really desperate to jump off,' Tim said. 'I think the Samaritans have installed a phone up there, so people who are thinking about throwing themselves off can speak to someone. We had a look once.'

'I remember, we drove along the South Downs and followed the sign…'

Tim interrupted. 'You refused to get out of the car.'

'It was windy. I didn't want to get blown away.'

'Oh, you were just too lazy.'

'I am not lazy!'

'Well, you're not lazy now we're doing this.'

'Sod off Timmy, I had three kids to look after and got a degree!'

*

Midnight

Every night, when I pass the Old Vic, I think of my thesis: Edith Lyttelton, and her connection with the theatre. Most evenings while I'm waiting for the lights to change, I think how lucky everyone else is, and how pissed on I am in the isolation of my smart, unwashed fast car. Tonight, through the windows of the theatre I see two floors of people enjoying interval drinks. I don't know what is showing. The weather was good yesterday so the pavement has taken the overflow of people wanting to make the most of the balmy night air. I'd like to be outside too. I feel like Joan of Arc in your room, bereft of the sunshine, which the blinds strain out. They are closed to stop prying eyes.

Two more bags of fresh frozen plasma arrived. You sleep off the drugs given to you this morning. You wake thirsty, and eat nothing but grapefruit. Yesterday you asked me to bring brown rice in. If anyone at the cast and crew showing of Secrets and Lies *(a month ago) had suggested my husband would soon be drinking just water and requesting brown rice, I'd have laughed in their face. How fucking ridiculous. We talk about the Hastings picnics we'll have with the kids when you are better.*

I was only out of the room for an hour, because Miriam had her car on a meter. And, anyway, I don't like being away from you too long. While she was getting a new ticket, I went upstairs and went into your room to find Panos leaning over your bum. What I presume to be bone marrow samples were all over the table.

It was a bit of a shock, I can tell you. I felt like puking so I left the room. I waited outside for about ten minutes before Panos came out. Miriam stayed with me till then. I went in the room and you were completely zonked. This really upset me because when I left before lunch you were back to your old self, complaining about the television. Now you are unconscious. I am angry with Panos. I swore at him. And I'm fucking angry with you too, for not phoning me. I could've been back in three minutes. I realise you just wanted to get it over and done with, but I also knew how much you'd been dreading it.

*

While we were squabbling Tilda woke up. Once she had stretched and rubbed the sleep out of her eyes Tim told her to look out for a black windmill. Tilda loves a task. She searched the shoreline for a few minutes before she spotted the windmill, which is a prominent landmark near to the rambling dual-spired Roedean girls' school on the South Downs. With a great deal of excitement she pointed.

'There it is Gwanddad.'

'And look over there, Til, can you see that big wall? That's where we are going to take Princess Matilda Boat.'

I sent a text to our friend Paul Sands as we approached the marina. Paul now lives near Brighton, and he was an old boyfriend of mine. I met him when he was playing fiddle in a group. My husband is not a jealous man. Paul was best man at our wedding and seeing him always reminds me of those days. Krissy, my best friend, was bridesmaid.

Krissy and I had met in Wales. She had just finished her A levels and was on holiday from London. I was living in what used to be known as a hippy commune, but actually it was a farm. It was owned by Robin Lawrence, who played drums in a band. I had a thing about musicians. The flute player was

Tim's mum Sylvia on her honeymoon, aged 19 on Ramsgate Beach.

Sylvia and Tim at a family party in 1981, just before we met.

My dad Jim Baker and I on a cruise in 1969.
My dad thought he was George Raft.

Me, in the foreground with the long skirt, at the Free Festival in Windsor Great Park after the police arrived.
(Photo Jeremy Browning)

Tim and I at a disco in the Midlands in 1981.

The first holiday Tim and I ever had together was on a narrowboat on the Llangollen canal, in June 1981. We ran aground a few times!

During a week's brief respite after Tim's first course of chemotherapy in June 1996, we took Rafe to Broadstairs.

Tim extremely ill after his second course of chemotherapy in August 1996.

The family on our fifteenth wedding anniversary – one I didn't think we would get to celebrate. Tim was still very weak after his second course of chemo. He's wearing a bandage around his thumb as he pulled the nail off shutting the curtains.

MY AUNTY JENNY HAS CLIMBED KILIMANJARO

Adventures on board the *Colleen Bawn*, our second narrowboat. Our great friend Michael Mayhew is on the bow on the Grand Union canal in 1999.

Tim, Alicia Silverstone, Sadie's friend Jill and Michael's wife Brenda Blethyn.

Reading the paper while I wait for Tim to work the lock!

Tim and Pascale in the saloon of the *Colleen Bawn*.

Tim on the helm and Nelly the bulldog in her lifejacket. She hated wearing it, but couldn't be trusted not to fall in.

Our first summer with *Matilda*,
here moored on the upper Thames.

The Princess Matilda moored
amongst the fishing fleet in
Ramsgate's outer harbour, spring 2007.

Inside *The Princess Matilda*. Making breakfast
on a chilly winter's morning, with the fire blazing…

… and the perfect end to a day at sea,
with the curtains shut and candles lit.

The Princess Matilda in Brighton
Marina. We felt like Vasco da Gama
when we arrived there in 2008.

Looking out of the window on a lovely sunny day.
(Photo Paul Crompton)

Michael Wilding Jnr, the son of the 1950s matinée film idol, and Elizabeth Taylor. The drummer kicked me out, so I hitch-hiked to London and cried for six months. Krissy was the only person I knew in the city and we lived together in a squat just off Portobello Road. It was she who took me to Windsor for the Free Festival in 1974. I had heard the drummer would be playing there but he didn't turn up. Krissy nursed my broken heart; she was the sensible one. She went to secretarial college and got a job in television and bought a house. I took drugs: speed, cocaine, mescaline, LSD and the odd mandrax. Then someone, when Krissy's back was turned, suggested I inject morphine. It seemed a good idea at the time.

Krissy drove Tim and me to Victoria Station after our wedding reception, which was held at her house. She gave us a chilled bottle of champagne and two glasses. A couple of hours later Tim and I woke up in Brighton. It was after midnight and there was just us and an empty bottle of Moët left on the train. Fortunately there was a taxi outside the station and the porter of The Royal Crescent Hotel let us in and showed us to our room. We had a brilliant time. Tim and I actually celebrate two anniversaries. The one I commemorate is 31 May because this is when he came into my life.

*

We have just watched 'Tim's Video', which Jimmy Nail organised. You loved it. Of course it is very moving and made me cry, especially the end when Rafe read his poem 'My Baldy Dad'. Trevor Nunn offered you a job at the National. You were truly humbled by the number of people who spoke on camera. Liza Tramontin, who won the Ronson Award the same year as you at RADA. Imelda Staunton, Chris Tiller, Wade and her sister, Mettin, Hugh Cruttwell, Suzanne Bertish, Robbie Coltrane, Gregor Fisher, Peter McDougall, Paul Sands, Martin Clunes, Dickie

Briers, Ken Branagh. Oh and loads more. I'm writing this on my laptop in the waiting room of the X-ray department, poor Tim, even less hair today. You are so vulnerable, I mean people always stare at sick people, you can almost hear them think, 'Oh poor sod, I wonder what's the matter with him? What a shame!' But you are a well-known actor so they look twice.

Midnight

To bed or not to bed, that is the question. Alone. My life is black and white. Any colour is in UCLH and I cannot dip my paint-brush in there. You need all your pigment. I'm jealous of the nurses because they do things for you. I say all the wrong things and feel useless and I can't cope. People think I'm strong but inside I'm jelly. I've no substance. You were my strength. I took it from you. And now you need to take it from me, but I walk from the car, which I've scraped on both sides, walk under the subway and try to dissipate my sadness so that I can be a little ray of sunshine for you. But I'm no actress. I've had a horrible day today, as if the rest lately have been any good! I've had no intimate moments with you. I know it's not your fault. I'm glad you liked Jimmy's film. I was afraid it had made you sad. I love you, I miss you, and I want you home. Fifteen years ago tonight you kissed me for the first time.

*

Brighton has to be the ugliest and most soulless marina in the world, I thought as *The Princess Matilda* entered the eastern breakwater. Tim sensed my thoughts.

'Give it a chance darlin'. It's the largest marina in Europe. There's room for over 1,000 boats in here. Somebody told me it was given the Concrete Society Award.'

'The Oscars of the cement industry? We learn something new every day,' I replied.

'I think they needed extra reinforced concrete. The sea can get really nasty, it must have taken some building. All we have to do is find our berth,' Tim said, scratching his head.

It took some finding.

While Tim and I moored, Tilda had been given instructions to stay inside the boat and not move out of her chair. She is such a good girl, she was sitting in exactly the same spot when I went down to bring her up into the wheelhouse.

'What do you think of our new home, Til?' I asked her.

'I like those!' she said, pointing upwards.

Above us were row upon row of yellow 'beach huts'. Stairs from the enormous pontoons lead up there. We were surrounded by every type of vessel: yachts, gin palaces, narrow-boats, Dutch barges. There were even some fishing boats hidden around the far corner. Unfortunately we could not see the sea. The colossal wall completely surrounds the marina. We walked up to the office to check in and were given a pin number to get into the security gate.

There are restaurants and bars on the boardwalk that leads to a multistorey car park near the marina. We met Paul Sands at the Pizza Express there.

'Well here you are in Brighton!' he said as he hugged us both. 'But the cup final's on this afternoon so can we hurry so we can get back to mine and watch the match?'

Tilda pulled a face.

'It's OK, Matilda, we have a couple of dogs for you to play with!'

*

Sadie joined us for a couple of days. She is happy on the boat as long as we remain moored in a marina. She and I took Tilda to the Royal Pavilion. I don't know who was more excited, Matilda or Sadie. There might be a 20-year age gap between them but they are both a couple of princesses. When I'm at a museum or gallery I have to read every single thing written near any artefact. My girls listened to the commentary on an audio device instead. Tilda would pay attention very carefully, concentration showing on her little face. In unison, she and my youngest daughter would both approach the same exhibit like a couple of remote controlled robots. My granddaughter removed the handset from her ear and looked around the gaudy Banqueting Room with the hanging chandeliers, palm tree columns and gilt wood furniture.

'The Prince Regent lived here when it was a farmhouse, Chum. Can we go and find him now?'

Sadie laughed. 'The prince doesn't live here, Til, he died.'

My written guide said it took 35 years to grow from the pastoral farmhouse to the oriental palace it is now.

Later on I walked Sadie and Matilda to the station to get a train back to London and told them how Tim and I had visited the Pavilion on our honeymoon.

'Many of the rooms were closed for renovation. I remember remarking to your dad that I though it odd that the Prince Regent would have chosen Brighton with its uncomfortable pebble beach rather than Camber Sands as his holiday home. "It used to be known as London by the sea," he said. "And they didn't actually walk on the beach. Horses dragged the bathing huts down to the shore."'

'He must have been a right princess that Prince Regent, no wonder he was so fat!' Sadie laughed as I waved them goodbye.

Brighton to Portsmouth: 42 nautical miles

'I've plotted two courses,' Tim said, as we left Brighton marina.

I was too busy looking at the scenery to pay much attention

to what he was saying. No matter how familiar you are with a town, it looks so different from the sea. Even the fairground rides on the end of the long, thin pier looked out of the ordinary. The famous Brighton shingle beach was packed with tourists fighting for room to lay down their towels and bottles of suntan lotion. *The Princess Matilda* was half a mile off shore and Tim and I had all the space in the world.

'One is 2 miles off the Bill, just south of Pullar Bank that extends off Selsey Bill rocks, but there's another way. I'm not sure which I'll take,' Tim continued.

'Sorry what did you say?'

'The North Foreland on Thanet to Selsey Bill in West Sussex is a division of the Met Office Inshore Weather Forecast. There's a reason for this. Both are tricky headlands. I've been worrying about this for a while.'

'Oh it'll be fine. Do you want a Coke?'

I came back to the wheelhouse with a couple of cans and put my feet up to enjoy the rays of the sun on the back deck.

A couple of hours sped by. I stood up and stretched and looked out of the wheelhouse window. I didn't like what I saw. Behind us the sea was blue, flat and friendly. Ahead it was ugly, scaly and black.

'We're not heading over there are we?' I asked with alarm in my voice.

Tim looked at his charts and the passage he had planned.

'Overfalls!' he replied.

'What's an overfall?' I asked, pretending I didn't care.

'Do you not listen to anything I say, Shane? I've told you again and again. Let me give you the idiot version.'

'I'm not an idiot!' I said crossly.

'Pass me that can of Coke please.'

'It's warm, you won't like it,' I said, passing him the can.

'I want you to imagine the can is a hill,' he said, placing it on its side on the table. 'OK, let's pretend I'm holding a hose, with the nozzle so the water flows in a straight line. Now what will happen when the jet of water hits the side of the hill?'

I thought for a few moments and replied, 'It would splash.'

'Exactly. We've been passing over deep water with a flat seabed. The tide and currents flow smoothly. But that black scaly line we can see is where the seabed rises and falls.'

'It's a bloody frothy line now,' I exclaimed.

'I can see that. I was expecting it. My *Learn to Navigate* says this is caused because the tide has to flow onwards and the only way it can go is up and over. It's going to be a bit choppy for a while.'

'Oh. Do I have time for a wee?'

'If you hurry!'

I went down the steps to the saloon. The guest bathroom was the closest. I opened the frosted window so I could look outside. The sky was clear, not a hint of cloud. The calm before the storm, I thought, as I washed my hands. I joined Tim in the wheelhouse.

'Are you sure we have to go over it?' I said as I looked longingly at the flat sea behind us.

'I'm afraid so, this is what's known as a confused sea,' Tim replied. 'This is where the elements show us who is boss!'

The surface of the ocean began to swirl and spurt into whirlpools as if it was being whisked by giant eggbeaters powered by the National Grid.

'Why are we doing this? I don't like it, that's a fucking ferocious wave…'

But before I could finish my protest, Tim yelled, 'Hang on Shane, hang on!'

I braced myself as *The Princess Matilda* rolled, bucked and quaked as her bow cut through the start of the overfalls. Tim pushed down on the accelerator to give her more power. We heard the engine race under our feet. I have a special place in the wheelhouse, just above the steps, where I can grab on to the hatch over the doors. God knows what Tim was doing. I was too busy trying to keep on my feet. We did not speak for several minutes. Corporal Jase once said that in times of danger his army mates would stop the banter and silence would reign as everyone concentrated on the job in hand. In my case this was keeping upright. I kept bending my legs to move with the boat as she righted herself from corkscrew waves that broke over the wheelhouse as we bounced through the maelstrom.

Then suddenly we were on a mirror. Tim and I both turned and looked behind us; we had come through a tempest. We both began to speak at the same time.

'Fuck me.'

'I need gin.'

All of Tim's charts had fallen on to the deck, so I picked them up while Tim looked through the binoculars.

'I can see the Spinnaker in Portsmouth I think,' he said. 'But those overfalls were worse than I excepted. That was a baptism of fire.'

'How far are we away now?' I asked as I flopped down on the step.

'About 16 miles, but I have to find the Nab Tower.'

I was too shaken to ask what the Nab Tower was. I reached for my road atlas, which I keep wedged by the waste bin. Tim knew what I was thinking.

'Yes, we could stop off in Chichester Harbour but I think we're too big and anyway Portsmouth and Southampton are ports that are protected by the Isle of Wight from the troughs of the Atlantic Ocean.'

'Troughs and overfalls. I want smooth!' I exclaimed with petulance in my voice.

'I have to keep my wits about me now, Shane, so will you keep a look out? We're entering a busy waterway.'

An hour later I sensed Tim becoming even more fractious and anxious. He kept snatching up the binoculars.

'What is it Tim?' I asked.

'There's a ship out there. It's about four miles away. I've been going full steam ahead to get out of the way and it's still heading straight for us.'

I took the binoculars off him and spent ten minutes focused on the ship.

'It must be anchored, it's actually not moving,' I said, giving the glasses back to him.

Tim looked down at his chart then looked through the binoculars once more. He began to laugh, his shoulders shaking with mirth. 'It's not a ship, it's the Nab Tower. It's a manmade fort that guards the eastern approach to the Solent. Those overfalls have discombobulated me.'

Portsmouth is a large natural haven that encloses a number of islands. The sheltered harbour is home to a dockyard port, ferry terminals and a small fishing fleet, and is a key naval base. As well as the navy vessels, *The Princess Matilda* also had to keep out of the way of commercial shipping, cross channel ferries, hovercraft, high-speed sea-catamarans and various other small boats that all operate in the area. We had never approached such a busy and sprawling port before. The tidal streams of the Solent are complex, but Tim had done his homework. There are numerous places to moor in Portsmouth. Tim chose Gosport. The city of Portsmouth, or Pompey as the locals call it, is on the eastern part of Portsea Island. Gosport, where we were heading, is directly opposite.

'We're following in the ship prints of the *Victory*, the *Mary Rose* and the *Ark Royal*. In fact we crossed directly over the place where the *Mary Rose* sank,' Tim said.

'I can't wait to see the preserved wreck of the *Mary Rose*. Can you believe we've got here? Do you remember how I used to say we'll never make it?'

Tim checked his charts.

'We've still a way to go. We're not home and dry yet. Listen to me! All of these nautical clichés are now starting to make sense.'

The Solent is a strait of water that separates the Isle of Wight from the mainland of England. Vessels from all over the world use this shipping route. Cruise liners from Quebec, oil tankers from Oman, container ships from China, sailing ships from Singapore and now a brave Dutch barge from Brentford. The Solent is also a Mecca for yachting. Cowes Week is an annual sailing event, but the only sailor we know is Denise Black, Paul's wife. She was rehearsing a play in Chichester. Denise had a lovely little sailing boat that she kept near Hayling Island. I sent her a text. 'WE WILL BE MOORING IN GOSPORT FOR A COUPLE OF WEEKS. BRING THE LOVELY DOREEN AND VISIT US.'

At the mouth of Gosport harbour is Southsea Castle, another one of Henry VIII's fortifications. Castles, warships and getting rid of surplus wives were his specialities. I went to the bow of *The Princess Matilda* to take photographs. Tim and I had seen the historic waterside of Old Portsmouth on the news when we were first married. The Navy was returning from the Falklands, and the waterside was thronged with thousands of cheering people. Anticipation was written across their faces as they waved to welcome their loved ones home from the war. I think their Tudor predecessors would have done much the same.

Tim called Gosport marina on the radio. It was easy to find but we had to do a great deal of ducking and diving, getting out of the way of all kinds of craft.

'It's like the M6,' I said to Tim as he put *The Princess Matilda* full steam ahead to avoid being hit broadside by something bigger than us.

Once we were safely tied up in the marina we took stock of our new home. It was such a contrast to Eastbourne and Brighton. For a start, we had a dramatic view looking out on to the Royal Naval Dockyard. Outside the yard was the Victorian warship *HMS Warrior*. She had her stately backside facing us and a pretty impressive sight it was too. Charles Dickens didn't share our opinion. On the contrary, he thought the hybrid steam and sailing ship to be 'A black vicious ugly customer as ever I saw, whale-like in size, and with as terrible a row of incisor teeth as ever closed on a French frigate.'

Whenever we tie up *The Princess Matilda* after a day's voyage, Tim and I are always starving and longing for a curry. We locked up quickly and reported to the marina office. The chap on reception said Gunwharf, across the harbour, was the best place to find somewhere to eat.

'There's a ferry due, if you hurry you should catch it.'

We were both quite breathless as we boarded and Tim apologised to the ticket collector as we had not had time to buy one.

'Oh it's you!' the man said. 'I can't believe it's you. It is you, isn't it?'

'It was when I got up this morning,' Tim replied.

'Oh come up to the bridge, meet the skipper, he's a huge fan,' the ticket collector said.

The crossing from Gosport across the harbour to Portsmouth only takes a few minutes, but it was time enough for all the crew to come and say hello to Tim. They all spoke at the same time.

'What are you doing in Gosport?'

'How long are you staying?'

'Have you got a boat?'

'Is it a blue Dutch barge?'

'Yes, that's the one,' I said, trying desperately to get a word in edgeways.

'You were very lucky, we almost rammed you, and just as well I slowed down,' the skipper called out against the din.

*

A few days later, Sadie brought Tilda down for a visit so we caught a ferry to the Isle of Wight. It was a far larger vessel than the Gosport commuter boat and we sat on the open deck and enjoyed the summer sunshine and the magnificent views. Our youngest daughter only feels seasick on our boat. Tim nipped down to the bar and brought up a couple of drinks. He wasn't driving. Sadie had been to the Isle of Wight when she was ten years old. Her dad had just spent four weeks in protective isolation in UCLH. Tim had been given a seven-day reprieve before his next course of chemotherapy and it coincided with a school outing of Sadie's. She had been so exited about both events. Tim and I decided she should go. It was while she was away that I took Tim and Rafe to Broadstairs.

*

Midnight

Some good came from your biopsy! You should be home in our bed by Thursday. Sadie goes on a school trip to the Isle of Wight. She's been looking forward to it so much – and her dad coming home too; you tell her of course she must go. I'm sitting here now on our bed, the door's open, and tomorrow night I won't be alone. We must both charge our batteries for next week ... get on with it again.

Dear Mum + Dad,

We arrived safely on the Isle of Wight we made sandcastles SARAH'S team won the competition they made a fish. We went to Osborne House and Carisbrooke castle (on the front). After we went on the beach and swam in the sea. We had ice cream, we went on the trampolines. Love SADIE

*

Sadie proudly showed us around Osborne House, telling Tilda about Queen Victoria. It really was a glorious afternoon and the views from Victoria's holiday home were extraordinary. I could see why she abandoned the Brighton Pavilion for the Isle of Wight.

'I bet there are people on the island who have never left,' Tim said. 'Now where shall we have our lunch?'

Sadie caught the train back to London when we got back to the mainland. Tilda stayed with us in Gosport for several days. She wore the *Hello Kitty* swimming costume I had bought her. After a Sunday carvery in a local hotel, Tim and I took her to the beach on Stokes Bay, close to the marina. We sat on a towel and watched Tilda's chubby little legs running hither and thither, collecting stones and shells. I received a text from Denise. 'THE LOVELY DOREEN IS MOORED NEXT TO YOU, ISN'T THIS WEATHER GLORIOUS? PAUL'S WITH ME! HELLO SAILOR!'

We lost no time returning to *The Princess Matilda*.

Paul is no sailor. He was writing a novel and I was convinced the trip out on *Lovely Doreen* with their two dogs was research. Denise said she didn't mind, she was just happy to have him onboard. It was Navy Week so there were air shows and displays going on over the harbour. We sat on the back deck with our fan blowing cool air over us. The elegant, petite *Lovely Doreen* is Denise's pride and joy and looked tiny moored next to the fat, solid *Princess Matilda*.

Tilda told them all about our visit to *HMS Victory*.

'Admiral Nelson got shot, but we couldn't go into his

bedroom because there was a rope across it and the sailors fired big cannons and slept in string sleeping bags. Can I play with your dogs now please?'

Denise took them for a walk and came back about half an hour later.

'I can't get over how clever she is, I forgot the pin number to get in the security gate…'

Tilda interrupted, 'I knew it, Chum!'

I poured Denise a glass of wine.

'So what are your plans for the rest of the summer? I'm really jealous,' she said.

Tim brought his charts up and they discussed our next journey.

'I'm thinking Cowes, Lymington then Poole. But we'll have to take Tilda back to her mum first as it will be too dangerous to take her along.'

Denise stared down at the chart.

'Ah, I see what you mean. The dreaded Needles. Good luck.'

Chapter Fifteen
The Odd Couple

Portsmouth to Poole: 35 nautical miles

A large, grey RIB that looked like it had red and white leather sofas was behind us. A middle-aged couple was sitting in it when we arrived. The two of them looked at our boat with expectation. Watching a vessel berth is a perk for those who are already safely moored. Sometimes things go wrong and people shout. Tim and I have witnessed some dreadful domestics, husbands spitting 'throw the rope darling' through clenched teeth. We hardly ever behave this way. I noticed one of our new neighbours was a blonde with a determined tilt to her chin, which she lifted, pausing at the job in hand. Actually it was a foot. She was painting her nails. Tim turned our vessel around so he could reverse on to our mooring. I did worry that the blonde's nail varnish would get blue exhaust fumes mingled with the fire-engine red that was already slashed over several of her toes. After Tim and I tied up, with hardly any cross words, we introduced ourselves. This is what you do when you arrive by sea to a new place.

'Hello, we're Tim and Shane Spall. Sorry about the diesel fumes.'

The blonde tightened the lid on the tiny bottle of nail polish. She pushed stray strands of bobbed hair off her face and smiled.

'We like your boat. I'm Anne and this is Vincent. Where have you come from?' 'Yarmouth, today,' Tim replied. 'Before that Lymington, Cowes and Portsmouth.'

'Oh where do you moor in Portsmouth?' the blonde asked.

'We had a couple of weeks in Gosport...'

The man, Vincent, interrupted me. 'So it's not your home mooring then? Where do you berth *The Princess Matilda*?'

Tim laughed. 'We don't have a home mooring yet, we're taking her to Wales.'

'You should make it this summer then,' Vincent replied.

'You could do it easily in your boat, but I think it will take us a good while longer,' Tim said, 'and if we're lucky we just might make it to Torquay this season, we've had some bad weather this year.'

The blonde, Anne, looked beyond us to our boat and raised one perfectly plucked, arched eyebrow.

'Where did you start from?'

'Limehouse,' Tim replied.

'No Tim. Brentford.'

'Oh really?' Anne said. 'How long has it taken you to get to Poole?'

Tim and I looked at each other, we were both tempted to fib, but honesty is always the best answer.

'Three years,' I said proudly, daring either of them to laugh.

I took Tim's arm as we began to walk away.

'Maybe see you later,' Vincent said.

Anne raised a manicured hand and gave us a regal wave. 'We're here a few days.'

'How long would it take them to get to London on their boat?' I asked Tim as we walked up the pontoon.

'With that outboard? The Thames Estuary is about 200 nautical miles from here, they would have to refuel, but they could do it in a day,' Tim replied.

We strolled towards the marina office to check in and get the pin number. The marina is a two-minute walk from the town centre. It was too early for dinner, so we wandered around and explored. Poole is not a large town. The waterfront was crowded with tourists, coming to look at the boats on the Town Quay. The yachts were rafted up four abreast. Tim and I shuddered. It is a cheaper option to moor on the Town Quay, but you pay the price, as we had discovered the previous day in Yarmouth.

At first we had been directed to moor against Yarmouth's East Quay. It was right next to the ferry terminal and the noise from the throbbing engines was dreadful. *The Princess Matilda* vibrated and so did I. I am noise phobic, so just in case my husband was not aware of this fact, I had a Tilda-esque tantrum. Tim phoned the harbour office and they suggested we move to the Town Quay.

'Well that sounds romantic,' I'd said as Tim had put our boat into forward gear.

'Where is it?'

He looked in the *Reeds*, then looked at the crowded harbour wall, which was about 100 yards long. The Town Quay was the wall.

'At least we won't feel so much vibration now,' Tim said, as we attempted to fit into the last remaining space.

It had taken some doing. When eventually we were moored against the wall, with numerous fenders and cunningly tied planks of wood to stop us being scraped against the bricks, Tim flopped into his fold-up canvas chair. I opened two bottles and brought some glasses and an ice bucket up to the back deck. It was a glorious afternoon. Tim savoured his first chilled goblet of wine.

'You deserve that,' I said as I sipped champagne.

'Cor that didn't touch the side. This is the life. Here we are on the Isle of Wight,' he said, as I topped up his glass.

'We are incredibly lucky...'

Tim jumped up out of the director's chair, almost knocking over his Chablis. He caught it with the dexterity of a juggler.

'Where's he going?' he said, pointing at something behind my head.

I turned around. A vessel was approaching us. Not just approaching but stopping.

'Hang on!' Tim yelled. 'You can't do that!'

A rope had been thrown around our handrail.

'You're moored on the Town Quay, you'd better get used to it. We'll only be here a couple of hours,' the skipper said, as the crew made fast against us.

They then all climbed across *The Princess Matilda*, without a 'by your leave'. I was more than annoyed. I was steaming with rage.

'Why didn't they ask if they could moor against us? This is our home. They are so rude, and look at their filthy footsteps on our deck. How dare they!'

'You must calm down darlin', let's just relax and enjoy the afternoon. I expect they've just nipped to the pub,' Tim said, in a placatory manner that I suspected was a device to assuage his own annoyance.

'I'm going to get some more ice and go to the toilet, not necessarily in that order.' I grabbed the ice bucket and went below.

I was only inside the boat for a few minutes. When I came back up the steps to the back deck there were three lanes of traffic on the tarmac of the Town Quay. Nearby were cars and coaches, white vans, petrol tankers, cars towing caravans, lorries, motorbikes and mopeds waiting to drive on to the ferry. They all had their engines running.

'There's less pollution in bleeding Oxford Circus,' I complained.

Tim grabbed my hand as I twisted my champagne bottle around in the newly replenished bucket.

'Look there,' he said.

He had his face burrowed in his shirt against the fumes, but his eyes directed me to a spot close by. There were two old ladies sitting sidesaddle on mobility scooters, greedily licking the drips from ice cream cones. Their open legs were in our eyeline.

'Will you promise,' I said as I refilled my glass, 'to kill me, if I ever wear Crimplene and sit with my legs akimbo?'

Tim laughed and said, 'It reminds me of a pair of old leather handbags with the zips ripped out!'

After the ferry had departed, we climbed up the short ladder on to the quay and asked a cabbie to take us to a good pub. We were hungry.

'I reckon we have about an hour of light,' Tim said as he paid the bill after our dinner. 'Let's walk back.'

We strolled along the riverbank, hoping we were going downstream towards the harbour.

'What's the river called, Tim?' I asked.

He didn't reply as his mobile rang. It was a balmy evening. We ambled along hand in hand in the twilight, which made the riverbank seem both tantalising and mysterious.

'I can see orange blobs,' I said. 'And bats.'

But Tim ignored me as he chatted to his manager in Los Angeles. When he finished, I asked him again, 'What's the name of the river?'

'Cor, did you see that?' was his reply. 'A bat! You love bats darlin' and you know what the river's called. Think about it. Where are we moored?'

I bent down and picked some buttercups. 'Yarmouth.'

Tim bent down and picked up a stick and started poking me with it.

'Stop it, Timmy!' I said, snatching it out of his hand.

We passed some brambles in the hedgerow that ran alongside the tidal river. I squeezed a berry but it was too dark to see the colour so I bit into it and spat it out.

'The blackberries will be ripe in a few days. My mother used to say it was the devil putting his footprint on the summer…'

Tim interrupted me. 'So what's the name of the river, Shane? Yar-mouth is the clue.'

I noticed he had another stick in his hand, so I threw a blackberry. This one was ripe and caught him on his cheek so I ran.

He chased me shouting, 'When I catch you I'm going to stick this stick right up your bum!'

We expected to see various crafts moored alongside *The Princess Matilda* when we got home. But we decided we would not mind.

'I can't see any masts can you?' I said with my fingers crossed as we approached the quay.

Tim went down the ladder that had lengthened slightly as the tide ebbed. I was pleased to get onboard before it became any longer. Tim unlocked the door to the wheelhouse and discovered a RIB the size of a cross channel ferry tied up against us. Once again we decided we did not care. Tim and I can do Zen. But after a couple of hours my Zen was on a short fuse. It was getting quite late and I was feeling tired.

'There's no point going to bed yet, Shane. You know how grumpy you are if you're woken up.'

I was doing some hand washing in the kitchen sink when I heard laughter and loud voices. Blackberry juice is a bugger to remove. Washing for me is a form of meditation. Some women embroider; I attack stains. I pulled up my sleeves and looked at my watch. It was past midnight. The boat rocked as about 12 people came around the gunwale. Through the open galley window I saw hairy, sunburnt legs of various sizes.

'Hello, are you all right?' I solicitously enquired.

The boarding party ignored me. I wrung out my laundry with renewed vigour. At the end of the queue were three kids. They followed the others and jumped off our boat on to the RIB. A woman wearing cream linen trousers brought up the rear.

'Life jackets darlings,' she instructed as she boarded her vessel.

'The discourteous buggers,' I grumbled under my breath.

'What kind of boat is that, Mummy?' one of the children chirped.

'Well, it's not a Yarmouth Harbour type boat darling,' was the reply.

The skipper fired up their huge outboard at that moment, which was a shame. They didn't hear Tim and I shout in perfect unison.

'Fuck off you bastards!'

*

There is a statue of Baden-Powell on the Town Quay in Poole. He is wearing his Scout hat and shorts.

'He had his first camp on Brownsea Island,' Tim said as we strolled along. 'We passed it as we came into Poole Harbour.'

'Were you ever a Scout?' I enquired.

'Na, army cadet,' Tim replied. 'Let's go and find a pub.'

After a drink I left him to have another pint and went back to *The Princess Matilda*. I had left some clean laundry in the washing machine. The RIB was still there. Anne was wearing a sarong over a dripping bathing costume. Her teeth were chattering.

'You've been for a swim!'

'Yes. It was marvellous!'

'Where are you staying tonight?'

She had a towel and a toilet bag in her hand.

'On the RIB. I'd better go to the facility block and get a shower, warm myself up,' Anne replied.

I watched her striding away. She was a tall, handsome-looking woman. I wanted to catch up with her and ask her if she had been a Girl Guide or a Valkyrie.

It was a chilly afternoon and my feet in my flip-flops were

freezing so I went below and put on Tim's fur-lined Uggs. My husband has quite a gay collection of shoes onboard, including a pair of pink Crocs that I bought him in Brighton. He returned as I was pegging out the washing. I had strung a line across the back deck. Tim stopped by the RIB and chatted for a few moments with Vincent.

'What's he doing?' I said, following Tim inside the boat.

'He's putting a cover over.'

I went back up to the wheelhouse to have another look. Anne was dressed now and was towel drying her hair.

'Do you want to use my line for your wet things?' I asked.

'That's very kind of you,' she replied.

I took them from her and pegged them out. I then saw a recognisable face coming along the pontoon. I waved.

'Paula, hello! How are you?'

I introduced her to Anne. 'Paula was our neighbour in Ramsgate harbour.'

'I'll leave you to it,' Anne said, and disappeared under the cover of the RIB.

Paula appeared to be in an agitated state. 'Ron and I saw *The Princess Matilda* coming into the marina earlier on. It's so wonderful to see a familiar face. How was your passage into Poole Harbour?'

'It was like a millpond. How about you?'

'Not so good! We've had some horrible weather.'

'Yes I know,' I replied. 'We got stuck in Brighton for a fortnight, then Lymington for 10 days.'

'Well, you were sensible for staying where you were. We left Yarmouth and came into Poole and decided to anchor near Brownsea Island in Blood Alley Lake. That's not an encouraging name is it?'

Before I could reply, Paula continued. 'We thought we'd found a good spot so we dropped the anchor and put the kettle on. As we sipped our tea all seemed well till *Cailin* began to settle on the bottom. We'd misjudged the tide and instead of flooding it was ebbing. We spent an uncomfortable night sitting in the cockpit wondering what would happen when the water came back. *Cailin* came up OK, but didn't float free. We were beneaped! The next day the wind picked up and the people on the ferry rollicking by in the Channel just a few yards away seemed surprised to see us there. Two tough looking RIBs arrived just before high water and dragged us off.'

'Oh my word Paula, is the boat OK?'

She shuffled her feet. It had begun to rain. 'It's going to cost us to get *Cailin* fixed, she was badly damaged. I'd better get back before I get drenched.'

I watched her walking wearily up the pontoon, her shoulders hunched and her head bent. I fasted up all the doors and went inside and told Tim about *Cailin*.

'Bloody hell,' Tim said. 'They were lucky.'

I kept nipping back up to the wheelhouse.

'Why do you keep doing that Shane?'

'I'm worried about Paula and Ron. Do you think they need anything?'

Then I saw the rain-lashed RIB behind us. I pretended to check out my sheltered washing and went below.

'I can't believe they're sleeping under a tarpaulin, it's tipping it down. If that was me, I'd be booked into the Executive Suite in the Thistle Hotel up there on the quay. Do you think I should offer them a hot-water bottle?' I asked Tim.

'They're probably asleep.'

'But there's a gale blowing.'

I searched in the drawer for our hot-water bottles but wasn't sure about the etiquette of knocking on a wet RIB so decided Tim was right and went to bed.

*

Midnight

You were home for seven days and seven nights and now it seems you were never here at all. We discovered a photographer outside the house as we were getting out of the car. He had a lens a mile long. I was so furious and ran across the road swearing at him. 'I didn't take anything!' he said. 'You can have the film.' I am stupid. I should have taken it there and then, but I was trembling too much. Pascale told me to go inside while she took down his details so she could phone Keith Schilling, Jimmy Nail's solicitor. He's taken out an injunction so the photos – if there are any – can't be published. A nice state of affairs. I spent the rest of the day on the phone, while you sat at the bottom of the garden. My sister Jen arrived while I was on the phone. It was all very traumatic.

I sorted a homeopath out to see you, to help with your taste buds. You say food tastes of metal. She arrived at three. I left with Jenny to collect the kids from school. Ruth, the homeopath, was still there when we got back. Michael Mayhew dropped off the remedy she prepared later on. Then Miranda Richardson came around. You seemed to be fine, but as soon as they all left you became irritable. I found it so very upsetting so I went for a bath. You came to bed. Next door's dogs started to bark. Those dogs drive me crazy. I rushed downstairs and went next door. The horrid woman responded to my knocking. 'It is not my dogs!' she lied. 'They are your dogs, you've left them outside for the past month, and I've had enough of sweating in my bed with the windows shut!' She slammed the door in my face. I was furious. And you were angry that I'd done that. It was a horrible night.

Sylvia and your little brother, Maff, came around. You did the usual Sunday stuff, except you didn't go to the pub. You bought me loads of flowers. It was a wonderful day, but as Sylvia left you noticed her car's back tyre was flat. Maff and I chased her, which was a real bore because we didn't catch up with her for miles, and we were on a dual carriageway when we did. Maff changed the tyre but I had to drive five miles the wrong way to come back. Sylvia phoned me later that night in tears to thank me for looking after you. To thank me for loving you. I drove you back to the hospital…

*

The next morning I woke up to a kaleidoscope of reflected, rippling sunrays that flickered and glittered through a tiny gap in our curtains. I left the two drapes on the pontoon side of our cabin shut. There is only one curtain on the other side because we have a wardrobe there. It was a beautiful day so I opened that curtain and the porthole too. I was secure in the knowledge we were not overlooked. Tim was up making the tea so I went back to bed to read some Thomas Hardy. Dorset is Hardy country. A few minutes later I felt the boat move as if someone had jumped onboard. I could hear clumping and thumping on the forward deck just behind my head. I sat bolt upright. Then through the porthole I saw a yacht coming really close to us. I was naked and some man with a stringy grey beard was staring at me. It took me a few seconds to work out what was happening.

'Tim!' I shouted as I used a pillow to preserve some modesty. 'There's someone on our bow and there's a Peeping Tom on a yacht!' I leapt out of bed just in time to see some man leaping on to the yacht. I was enraged. The porthole is too small to poke out my head. So I just yelled, 'You sneaky twats! Why didn't you just ask?' I threw on some clothes and rushed up to the wheelhouse.

Tim beat me to it. 'The cheeky dishonourable bastards!' he said angrily as we watched the yacht speeding away.

Quickly I climbed on to the roof, armed with a bag of recycling, but Tim said I would get arrested if I threw any bottles. I turned around and saw our new neighbours, Anne and Vincent, were sitting in their RIB. She looked perfectly refreshed and her blonde hair was immaculately groomed. On the pontoon next to them was a primus stove with a kettle coming to the boil. They could have been at Glyndebourne or Henley Regatta. We all waved and I realised I looked like a harpy. I was wearing Tim's curry-stained shirt that had been left on the stool ready to pre-soak. It was the first thing that had come to hand. I knew I had panda eyes because I had not removed last night's make-up. I tried to tame my pyramid of unbrushed hair.

I had a wash and changed my clothes. Then I set traps for anyone else who dared board *The Princess Matilda* without permission. Tim looked at my handy work. The bow was an assault course.

'You could get done for manslaughter,' he laughed.

'It will be worth it. I hope any predators get tangled up in the ropes and coal bucket, and I hope the hose trips them up so they fall head first into the water.'

Tim held out his arms and I jumped off the boat on to the pontoon.

'I'm going to the shop. I need some knicker elastic; I've another trap in mind.'

'Of course you do,' he said as he put me down.

I grabbed a carrier bag with the hot-water bottles from the wheelhouse and walked along the pontoon past the RIB. Anne and Vincent were sharing a croissant. I didn't feel it was the right time to give them something made of rubber.

'I'm going to Tesco. Do you want anything? Milk, a news-paper?' I asked them.

'A newspaper, yes please' Anne replied, wiping her hands on a napkin. 'What do you fancy Vincent?'

'The *Telegraph* would be nice, thank you, Shane.'

On my return I gave them the newspaper wrapped around the hot-water bottles.

'You reminded me of Betsey Trotwood chasing away the donkeys just now,' Anne said as she paid me for the paper.

'And hot-water bottles! How thoughtful of you, thank you so much.'

We got to know each other really well over the following few days.

Poole Quay Boat Haven is a pleasant but busy marina that is protected by a low breakwater. Tim used to put our chairs on the roof of our boat. We had pole position to see the comings and goings around the harbour. I was still on the look-out for our boarding party from our first morning. Sometimes we would have to stifle our laughter watching boats moor.

'It's mean to laugh at others' misfortune,' Tim would berate me, but sometimes he couldn't help himself either.

You have to be prepared to make a tit of yourself as soon as you board a boat. Tim and I have done our fair share of pontoon bashing and death-defying leaps to secure a mooring. Experience has taught us to do things extremely slowly and to take our time, but we still bicker. It is part of the fun, especially when it is pissing with rain and Tim is sheltered in the wheelhouse and I am standing on the gunwale trying to lasso a mooring cleat. I know for a fact that the one I will choose will be the wrong one. And so it is the world over.

Poole is the headquarters of the RNLI. It is where the crews come to train. It is also the home of Sunseeker Yachts. These vessels aren't our cup of tea, but each to their own. There was a 100-footer moored in the marina. It created a great deal of interest. A couple of trip boats operate from the Town Quay and we could hear the commentary.

'*The large vessel on your left-hand side is a Sunseeker Yacht. It's the ultimate plaything of footballers and millionaires. That one belongs to a Nigerian oilman, which is handy. At full throttle it burns £100 of fuel an hour. If you look very carefully you may also spot a classic yacht. The Princess Elizabeth and the Duke of Edinburgh used this after they were married. It has just been restored to its former glory, so if your numbers come up on the lottery, it's for sale. Not quite as grand, ladies and gentleman, is the blue narrowboat that is owned by Barry, from TV's* Auf Weidersehen Pet.'

'Come on, Barry,' I said. 'Let's go and do some shopping.'

Tim is not the best person to go into a shop with so I left him sitting outside Yates's wine bar in the High Street. He was talking to his older brother, Richard, when I came back. Tim's sister-in-law, Frances, had been dreadfully ill for a while. Tim hung up the phone. 'Poor Fran, it doesn't sound too good...'

Richard and his wife Frances used to use our narrowboats once or twice a year. We had promised them they could spend time on *The Princess Matilda* when Frances was feeling better, but we all knew this would never happen. Tim and I walked back to the boat in silence. We bumped into Paula and Ron by the security gate. They gave us an update. *Cailin* was on the mend and they were leaving on the tide.

'I don't think we'll get much further this year,' Paula said. 'The nights are drawing in.'

We both agreed it was unlikely we would get to Wales.

'Well it's not a race is it?' Tim said after we waved them goodbye.

Then we saw Vincent, who invited us for a sunset cocktail. It was freezing. I wish I had got in there first with the invitation. Tim and I unpacked our shopping and took a bottle of champagne to the RIB. We climbed on board and chatted. There were masses of seagulls on the breakwater, all squawking.

'Don't they disturb your sleep?' I asked.

Vincent replied, 'Only when a fishing boat comes in and they screech, but then the wash of the boats knocks us all over the shop. It's a bit like sleeping on a giant waterbed.'

I looked at Anne, who had just given me a refill.

'Erm, what do you do if you need a wee in the middle of the night?'

Vincent laughed and said, 'I'm all right!'

'And so am I!' said Anne. 'I have one of those gadgets where you can pee standing up. We are really looking forward to the hot-water bottles tonight, it's turned chilly again.'

'Tell Shane and Tim what happened to you last night,' Vincent said.

'Oh it was nothing, I fell in that was all,' Anne explained. 'Our friends all think we're completely barmy, but we love it…'

Vincent interrupted her, 'We are barmy Anne. We have a huge house in Winchester and we sleep on the floor of the RIB underneath a tarpaulin!'

Tim and I laughed.

'Have you seen *Ark Royal*? Someone said it was in Portsmouth a couple of weeks ago,' Anne enquired, changing the subject.

'It arrived the day we left…' I replied.

Tim interrupted. 'See it! It was 50 yards away from us. It was as big as Harrods, a majestic awe-inspiring war machine. All the crew was standing to attention on the decks. And right on the tip of the curved runway, where the fighter planes take off, was a sailor with a machine gun. We made eye contact, me through the binoculars and him through his telescopic sight. I put them down pretty sharpish.'

'That must have been quite a spectacle,' Vincent exclaimed.

I looked at my watch.

'We have to go back to London tomorrow,' I said. 'So we probably won't see you again after that.'

'I've got a job to do,' Tim clarified. 'It should pay for the next service on our engine. I'm doing the voice-over for a documentary. Every time I go in the studio the director asks what we've been doing on the boat. He says we should let him film…'

'That will be the day, Tim,' I interrupted, handing my empty glass to Anne. 'We're bringing our granddaughter back with us.'

When we returned to Poole with Tilda, the chap in the office gave us an envelope addressed to *Tim and Shane, The Princess Matilda*. Inside was the following message: 'We decided to stop in Cowes on our way to the Itchen River in Southampton to celebrate an OK crossing. We did it in an hour! If ever you land in Winchester and fancy a glass, give us a call. Anne & Vincent Oddie.

PS Are you going to take a look at the Bournemouth Airshow? We're thinking of taking the RIB.'

Chapter Sixteen
Barnacle Bill

'Do you want to see some big airplanes in the morning, Til?' I asked her as I got her ready for bed.

She yawned and replied, 'Can I have an ice cream?'

'In the morning, darling, and I think it's time I bought you some new pyjamas for Princess Matilda Boat, you are almost grown out of these.'

'Well I am almost four, Chum, my mummy says I grow in my sleep.'

The following day Tim and I anchored just off the beach for the air show. Bournemouth is fairly close to Poole. Tim, Tilda and I sat on the roof of *The Princess Matilda* with a picnic. Our granddaughter was more interested in the progress of several little tenders flying red Wall's Ice Cream flags than the Red Arrows. There must have been 40 vessels of all different sizes anchored off the shore. The ice cream boats did a roaring trade, but we saw no sign of the Oddies. One of the trip boats from Poole was lying about 60 yards away from us, but the skipper then pulled alongside us. Tilda didn't mind; she licked her ice cream and waved.

The next morning we caught a bus to the beach at Sandbanks. Tim was wearing his pink Brighton Crocs. Tilda was happy wearing her *Hello Kitty* bathing costume. I untied a knot on the straps of *Hello Kitty*; she had grown so much over the summer. With greasy hands I covered her in factor 50 and passed the tube to Tim. Sandbanks is a glorious beach. Later we took Tilda to the fair in Bournemouth. It was quiet after the bank holiday and Tilda and I rode on the carousel, my granddaughter in front of me. She adored it. Tim helped us off.

'I love this country,' he said as he bought Tilda a frothy cerise cloud of candyfloss.

He took his change and jangled it in his pocket. Tilda's head bounced into the foam of pink but she held out her hand at the same time. Gwandpa withdrew a pile of two pence pieces. We approached the slot machines and their tantalising cascades of coins that never fall. We watched as Tilda fed the pretend avalanche.

'Did you see who was riding the carousel behind you?' Tim asked me.

'No, I was too afraid to turn my head, that ride was too fast for my liking.'

'On the horse behind you was a Hasidic Jew holding on to his son. The little grinning boy was wearing a skullcap, the dad, an Edwardian frockcoat and a big furry donut hat. Riding on the galloping horse behind them was a Muslim in a jellabiya hanging on to his smiling daughter who was wearing a nun-like headscarf. And then there was you wearing a look of panic and Tilda a look of joy. We live in the best country in the world.'

*

Midnight
I cannot sleep. I walk from room to room in our silent house. Well, silent except for the barking dogs. Everyone is asleep. So many memories. I try to think of all the happy ones but I find myself in the morning room with a bottle of gin. I sit in a chair in the spot where my dad passed away. He came out of a coma the night before he died. For two days he had lain moribund. The nurses thought it only a matter of time. We had people coming around for dinner. I put a few off, so it was just people we knew really well, people who Dad liked. I kept nipping into the morning room, where we'd put his bed, and I'd chat to him as I had always done.

'We're having a party for you tonight, Dad, and our Jenny's flying down from Scotland specially to see you, so you'd better wake up...' My mother just sat there next to the bed without saying a word. I went back to the kitchen. The doorbell rang. It was the district nurse. I led her down the hall.

'He's still the same,' I said as I opened the door to the morning room and there he was, sitting up in bed with a smile on his face. Everyone who came for dinner sat and talked to him and there was so much laughter. The last words he said to me were, 'I love you darling...' I miss him so much sometimes it hurts, and you've only been back in the hospital one day and it feels like eternity.

*

The Sunseeker had been moved while we were away from our boat. Now it was moored directly in front of the marina office. It looked as if *HMS Ark Royal* had hit it. One side of the hull was badly damaged. A man out of the office joined us as we stood looking at the smashed fibreglass.

'They were trying to take her over the harbour to have her serviced, and the wind took her and she got smashed on the Town Quay. One of the professional crew was injured as he tried to fend off!' he explained.

'So it's not just us amateurs who make mistakes,' I replied.

Tim and I spent almost a month in Poole. We didn't plan to, but sometimes this is how things pan out. The beginning of September was a difficult time. Tim's sister-in-law, Frances, died. She was only 56. The Spalls are a close-knit family. Everything comes back to the same thing: family. Sylvia was extremely upset at the funeral. Richard is her first-born. It is hard to see any of your children so bereft. Poor Richard had to bear the sound of his own children weeping. Our hearts went out to them all.

Poole to Weymouth: 30 nautical miles

We left Poole on a silk-like sea.

'We have to go out 7 miles to miss the shallow overfalls. But the visibility is amazing,' Tim said. He gave me the binoculars.

'See that, those are the Needles behind us. I've had enough of needles in my time.'

There was a perfectly formed horizon as we headed on a passage towards Weymouth. *The Princess Matilda* was on an unspoiled azure sea that merged into a cloudless, hazy cerulean sky. I was wearing cashmere trousers when we set off, but changed into my swimming costume. Tim had put a deckchair on the roof for me where I sat enjoying the rays from the low-lying autumnal sun. I love Tim being the captain; he does all of the planning, the charts, tides and navigation. Now and again I sipped fizzy wine and ate crisps. I joined Tim in the wheelhouse as we entered Weymouth Bay. A crescent of Georgian terraces framed the packed beach. Tim called the harbour master to say we had reserved a mooring, and he directed us to the Town Quay.

'But I don't want to go on the Town Quay, Tim.'

'You sound like Tilda, you'll be stamping your foot next. We have no choice.'

One hour later, I was in the galley. Barely audibly, I hissed through gritted teeth.

'I hate Weymouth. Why do they have to moor next to us?'

'For goodness sake, Shane, stop it,' Tim whispered.

'No tell them to go away. Tell them I have epilepsy and need space.'

'But you've not had a seizure for years…'

'Well I might have one tonight. I can appreciate there's a lack of mooring on these Town Quays, but what's wrong with "Excuse me?" or "Please may I?" instead of just chucking a rope to raft against us. I know exactly what will happen. They'll go to the pub and you'll fall asleep before closing time.'

'Oh right, it's my fault is it?' Tim said, his voice rising before he remembered we could be overheard. 'I got us here and all you've done since we moored is moan. You sat on the roof sunbathing, quaffing champagne and I didn't even have the chance to take a leak.'

'You should've taken a leaf out of Vincent's book then and pissed over the side.'

In a huff, I stamped up into the wheelhouse to cool off, banging the doors behind me.

Barnacle Bill on the parasitic yacht was reclining on his deck wearing a blue blazer and a peaked Breton cap. He was also wearing white shorts and long socks. Unsurprisingly he had his legs wide open. Before I could avert my eyes I saw what looked like the foetus of an elephant with a very short trunk. Somewhere out of sight was a radio that was barking out the shipping forecast. I was in no mood for small talk about Dogger, Fisher or German Bight, so I shot him a murderous look. Kicking open the doors I thumped back down the steps into our saloon.

'Listen, let's not argue,' Tim said as he quickly shut the curtains.

I am sure I saw Barnacle Bill's trophy wife taking a shower.

'I'm not the one arguing!' I yelled. I didn't care who heard me now.

'Come on darlin' let's go and have a look around the town,' Tim said to placate me. 'There's a marina somewhere. Maybe they can fit us in there tomorrow, but tonight we have to put up with it.'

'I'm going for a shower. I may be some time,' I growled.

With a flick of my wrist I slammed our bedroom door shut behind me. I drew the curtains across all the portholes, feeling a little calmer now I had some privacy. The door to our en-suite was slightly ajar, so I pulled down the blind in there too. I threw my sarong on the floor and peeled down my bathing costume and sat on the loo. Through the small window above my head I watched high, skinny filaments of mare's tails whisping across the sky. Our bathroom is a room with a view. But it was not just clouds that caught my eye. Barnacle Bill Junior was in a bosun's chair hanging 20 feet up the mast of the yacht. He waved at me. I swore and stumbled and kicked the bathroom door shut behind me. Unsuccessfully I tried to hike up my swimwear, which was tangled around my thighs. I tripped and fell on to our king-sized double.

'Tim!' I yelled.

Tim came to my rescue. I was spreadeagled, wrestling with Lycra. We both looked upwards to the skylight above us. It was low tide and the high quay was thronged with tourists making the most of the Indian summer. They all had a bird's-eye view of our bed.

'I need gin,' I said, as Tim struggled to fill in the hole above with a blackout frame that sits snuggly in the ceiling in our cabin.

As we walked up the pontoon later on, we saw crowds of people gathered on the quayside, dangling their legs over the edge. I am sure I had seen most of them before. We heard hollering cries of excitement as crabs the colour and size of walnuts were dropped into small buckets. People were sitting outside the many waterside pubs.

'I think we're going to have a noisy night of it darlin',' Tim said. 'But you've got your earplugs.'

We heard some kind of alarm as we walked up the steep, brown stone steps by the road bridge.

'It looks like it's going to open,' I said, pointing at the bridge. Barriers were dropped and the traffic built up.

'I'm glad I'm not sitting on that bus in the full sun.' The bus driver turned off the engine.

The bridge split in two and yawned. We watched an armada of boats spewing through the gap from the inner harbour. Everyone was waving. It felt like a carnival, but we left the crowds and bridge behind us. The inner harbour was full of boats. A security fence ran alongside most of the way.

'It's not very attractive is it?' I observed. 'It's in the middle of a ring road, the gasworks and Debenhams.'

Tim's phone rang.

'It's my agent,' he said, taking the call. 'Hi Pip … yes … OK, what next week?'

Tim looked at me and took my arm.

'You're going to have to get used to Weymouth, Shane! Let's hope they can fit us in here for the winter. I have to go to Ireland next week. I told you about that script. The first Hammer House of Horror for 32 years. Then when I get back there's something being filmed on location here in Dorset. Think about it, it'll be so handy. I'll be able to stay on the boat instead of in a hotel!'

Chapter Seventeen

From Here to Eternity

Tim held the door open for me to come out of the marina reception.

'Barry's a nice chap,' I said after we had both said goodbye to him.

'He's more than a nice chap,' Tim replied. 'He's a star. And we have a new home for *The Princess Matilda* this winter. We just have to wait until tomorrow while they make room for us.'

'Is Barry the marina manager?'

'I'm not sure, but it will be a secure mooring that's for sure. We're very lucky they can fit us in.'

We walked to the pedestrian bridge at the head of the marina. The River Wey is channelled through a sluice in the wall.

'Let's have a walk upstream Tim.'

'We've got all winter to do that. Let's find our new local.'

Weymouth is a compact town, or so it seemed to us, for whichever way we walked we came to the beach or the Town Quay. On the esplanade is a colourful statue raised by 'The *grateful* inhabitants To GEORGE THE THIRD On His entering the 50th Year Of His REIGN.'

'Is he the one that went mad?' I asked Tim as we walked around the plinth. 'What's going on with his bits? I love the anti-seagull spikes as his crown.'

'I'll tell you what was going on with his bits, he's not wearing Calvin Klein and he had porphyria.'

'It's a beautiful statue.'

'Yes, it is,' Tim agreed, 'but he does have a bit of a deranged grin on his face.'

Close by is a replica bathing machine with an information board. We both studied it, but Tim read it out loud.

'So he came down to Weymouth to bathe, on his doctor's recommendation, because of his ill health. He would walk down the steps into the sea and a band played "God Save the King". Now that would have been the money shot, him pissing in the sea leaving a purple trail.'

'Trust you,' I said. 'Now as I recall, he was King of Great Britain and King of Ireland when he came to the throne, but after the union in 1801, he became King of the United Kingdom of Great Britain and Ireland. I wrote an essay about him when I was at college.'

'I'm looking forward to working in Ireland, they're finding us a cottage,' Tim said as we crossed the road to the beach. It was even busier than Brighton.

The quay was quieter when we returned and the yacht had disappeared. But a few feet behind us was a sea-cat ferry that could have swallowed us whole. We could see glittering lights across the bay through the gap in the parallel hulls. Tim and I were getting ready for bed when we heard something heavy being thrown on our roof.

'God, I hope that's not the ferry leaving,' I said, as Tim opened the bathroom window to see what was going on.

After a few minutes he shut the window and got into bed with me.

'Sorry love,' he said. 'We'll have to put up with it. Barnacle Bill's back, he said they just had a marvellous cruise to Lulworth Cove.'

'Did he mention anything about dolphins?' I asked innocently.

'As a matter of fact he did. He said you had heard a rumour...'

'Not me,' I said, yawning and reaching for a book. *The*

Picture of Dorian Gray came to hand. I took it to Ireland with me.

*

On our return from Ireland Tim began work on *From Time to Time*, a Julian Fellowes film with Maggie Smith. It was so handy having the boat 20 minutes away from the location, but the winter weather set in early in Weymouth. We had ice form on the skylight above the bed. I lit the first fire of the season.

'You'll be throwing off the bed clothes all night,' Tim complained.

We drove to Portland Bill to have a look at the ocean on his first day off. There is a causeway alongside Chesil Beach that joins the island to the mainland.

'It should be called plastic bag beach. I want to get out and clean it all up,' I complained.

The Isle of Portland made us feel quite sad. A whole road by the port was lined with closed pubs.

'Look at those,' Tim said. 'They would have been beautiful looking buildings once. Maybe the area's going to be redeveloped for the Olympics.'

'Barry said they are having all the sailing events here, but I hope they clear all the litter up off the beaches first.'

We found an open pub right on the beach, The Cove House Inn. The barmaid proudly told us that on their doorstep was a 16-mile beach of pebbles. Tim looked at the photographs on the wall. It was impossible to see out of the windows as they were too steamed up.

'Great,' he said, 'every single one of them is a picture of a wreck that's been swept up on the beach. I don't know if I'm in the right frame of mind to look at Portland Lighthouse now.'

I bullied him into it.

The red and white candy-striped lighthouse up there on the

point is very pretty. But its function is practical rather than aesthetic.

'Just visualise,' Tim said, 'that out there is a flat ledge of rock that sticks out half a mile into the sea. That's Portland Ledge. That's why the lighthouse is here. In places the sea is over 90 feet deep but on top of the ledge it's only 30. Like a babbling brook, the water speeds up in the shallows. So when the tide crosses Portland Ledge, just out there, that's where it runs quickest. Plus at certain times the flood tide travels from west to east and gathers speed over the ledge. Then it meets the slower water over the deeper parts, creating a standing wall of water. That's the Portland Race. The one that did for all the wrecks in the pub.'

'What the potman?'

Tim laughed.

'No my love.'

'But it's as flat as a pancake out there, Tim,' I said.

'It is at the moment but if we stayed long enough, we'd see the Race. My imagination is working overtime. We won't be going around Portland Bill until we have to.'

'Can we not just crane the boat out and put her on a lorry to Wales and cut out the scary bits please?' I pleaded.

Tim worked the next day so he missed seeing Miriam Jones.

'I'm seeing as much of the country as you,' she said.

I showed her around Weymouth and we had lunch in a little restaurant by the chip shop. She was going to stay the night but had to get back as her cat was sick. I walked her back to the station. Everywhere is walkable in Weymouth. When I got back to the boat it was bone-chillingly cold but we only had enough coal to keep the fire going during the night. I popped on the fan heater but noticed the electric control panel having a nervous breakdown. Red flashing lights are not good. I realised we had lost our shore power. I threw on my fleece and braved the cold. Fortunately there was someone on the boat next to us.

'Can I help you? My name's John,' he said. I explained the problem and he did things with a screwdriver.

'You've blown a fuse, my dear, so I'll put your lead into my power point until Barry can sort it out for you. Now, if there's anything else you need, my son and his family have a boat next door but one.'

We lost the shore power again two days later. Unfortunately neither Barry nor Granddad John were around. I had arranged to meet Tim in the Balti House after he finished work. We had been unanimous in deciding the Balti House was the best Indian in Weymouth. Not only is the food consistently excellent, but a meal there gave us an opportunity to walk past the house where Thomas Hardy lived. In his novels he called Weymouth 'Budmouth Regis'. Whenever we passed by the house with the blue plaque we touched it, just in case we could absorb his genius. Tim was already in the Balti when I arrived.

'It's perishing out there.'

The staff showed us to 'our table' by the fish tank. Tim sometimes became annoyed with me because my eyes follow the fish.

'Shane. You aren't listening to me.'

'Sorry, one of the fish sucks up pebbles and spits them out again. I find that so intriguing.'

'Bugger the fish, will you just concentrate on me for a minute please? I was saying I've got an early call in the morning. Did you get some more coal in?'

'It's in the boot of the car,' I replied. 'I'll bank up the fire tonight because we can't put on the central heating. The shore power's off again.'

Tim tutted as he squeezed lemon on to his tandoori.

'We'll have to preserve the batteries. I'll run the engine

when we get back to heat the water for a shower. I wonder why the power keeps failing?'

'Barry said it's because it's been raining non-stop and the water gets in the plug,' I replied. 'But I think it's because we're at the end of a very long pontoon and the electricity gives up the ghost by the time it gets to us.'

On the way back to *The Princess Matilda*, we stopped off in the Spar and bought some candles. Tim took the coal out of the boot and put it in a trolley. He pushed it through the security gate.

'Have you noticed the water has changed colour, Tim?'

'Funnily enough, I did this morning. It's gone from a steel grey to khaki. There must be a lot of mud coming downstream on the River Wey.'

He made a grab for me with his free hand.

'Wey hey!'

I giggled and struggled to escape his fingers.

'Oh, I forgot to tell you,' he said, 'the cast and crew have been invited to Julian's house tomorrow. One of the drivers is going to pick us up.'

*

Julian Fellowes opened the door. I handed him a bottle of champagne.

'Oh, we'll put it there and stare at it,' he said, putting it on a shelf.

Emma Kitchener-Fellowes, his wife, was resplendent in black and pink and gave us a guided tour of their beautiful Elizabethan manor house.

'This is our viewing room where we watch the rushes. Don't you love those tiny little lights? I threw Smarties and wherever they landed I drilled a hole and then a man came around and fitted in the lights. Timothy, ask me how many times Julian and I have watched *Pierrepoint*?'

Before he could answer, she opened the palms of her hands, with all but one thumb on show.

'Nine times, we watched it over and over.'

I drank canned Guinness and stared longingly at the champagne. I don't drink wine.

'Can I get you both another one of those?' Emma said.

There were pictures, vases and photographs of Lord Kitchener everywhere, the iconic finger pointing at us from all directions: *Your Country Needs You*.

I whispered to Tim, 'Our granddads answered his call in 1914. Was he Emma's grandfather?'

Tim shrugged his shoulders.

'I'm going to write to Michael Wilding, he'll know. He and Brooke spent Christmas in Scotland with them a few years ago. Michael's sister-in-law went to drama school with Julian I think. Did I tell you Michael and Brooke are coming to Paris in the spring? I hope they come to stay with us when they get to London.'

Tim and I had last seen the Wildings in Santa Fe, where they live. Tim had been doing a western in New Mexico. Michael is my oldest friend; I love him dearly.

'How long have you known Michael?' Tim asked as we sank into a sofa by a roaring fire.

'Wales, 1974. I can't work it out. I can't wait to see him.'

'Does he still play the flute?' Tim asked, shaking my empty can of Guinness. 'Shall I get you another?'

'No thanks, Pet.'

Julian came over and joined us.

'You do your final scene next week, Timothy,' he said. 'I shall miss you old boy.'

*

After a while it felt like we had always lived in Weymouth. We strolled around the old harbour and enjoyed a beer in a couple of pubs before having lunch. This it what we do; eating is our hobby.

'Let's eat in that restaurant by the old pier, Shane. What's it called again?'

'Hamilton's.'

The restaurant was a ten-minute walk along the promenade. The wind spat sand into our faces. It really was freezing cold. Tim and I held hands.

'It's hard to believe this beach was thronged with sunbathers a couple of months ago,' Tim observed.

'I love an empty beach, even though I have to squint to stop the sand blowing in my eyes.'

It was wonderful to escape from the wind into the restaurant. We were greeted like old friends.

'Ah, Mr and Mrs Spall, welcome back,' said the proprietor. 'May I suggest the Shambles Plaice for you sir. It was caught this morning, and your usual madam?'

'Yes please,' I replied. 'Egg mayonnaise and chips thank you.'

When we finished our meal Tim said, 'That's the best bit of fish I've ever eaten.'

*

Midnight

You have eaten nothing for over a week. The last few days have been hellish. You have been very ill. It is only as I write that I realise just how ill you have been. Last Sunday you began to have temperatures of 104°F which caused you to rigor. Your body goes into spasm and you shake. The whole bed shakes. I see fear in your eyes as they search the room to find mine. The nurses rush in to cover you in blankets. 'I'm freezing cold!' Someone puts a dose of pethidine into your new Hickman Line. Immediately your teeth stop rattling and the rigor dies down. I feel dread in my bones. You were doing so well.

I'm reading reams of Edwardian diaries for my thesis.

I wonder for who they were written. I wonder who I am writing for now. Were they private thoughts or thoughts to be read by someone else at a later date? If the latter, then the diary should illustrate just how much one has suffered. I ask myself, 'Am I guilty of this?' If it is the former, if I'm writing just for myself, then I must write freely. But I know not which. I think I am very vulnerable. I think I am exceedingly strong. Whatever meets in the middle of these extremes is me. I am lonely but I am not ill. You are. But I must be careful your illness doesn't make me sick too.

My sister Jack phoned at 11:45 and told me Mom's house in Spain had burned down, so I called my brother. I know it's late but I don't care, I don't have enough left over for anyone else. I say nothing to Mom, who is asleep in her room, because you are in nightmare land and I want it to be over now. This journey is taking everything I've got. I'm not sure how much I've got left.

*

'So what do you think about that director's email? He's really interested in making a documentary about our journey,' Tim said as we walked back to *The Princess Matilda* from Hamilton's.

'Dunno. What's he like?'

'Paul Crompton? He's a nice bloke. I think you'd like him, but do you want a film crew on the boat?'

'No, not really, but then again, it would be something to show the grandkids. Besides, I think we're doing something quite unique. For goodness sake love, you got us here with just your charts and a compass.'

'Let's think about it. We're not going anywhere until the spring.'

'Let's get my birthday and Christmas out the way first shall we? I might invite Anne and Vincent Oddie to my party, what do you think?'

Anne and I had become pen friends. At my birthday party, she mentioned they were planning to bring the RIB to

Weymouth for New Year's Eve. I talked her out of it, but we arranged to have lunch on the 31st.

'I bet you are glad you drove down,' I said as we walked to the pub after we left the restaurant. 'There were kids skating on the pontoons yesterday.'

Vincent laughed and said, 'I'm glad you talked her out of it Shane.'

'But Vincent, it would have been wonderful!' Anne complained.

Tim got a round of drinks in. The barman gave him his change, then asked, 'So are you dressing up tonight?'

Tim thought this was rather odd.

We waved goodbye to the Oddies and went back to *The Princess Matilda*. Tim and I have spent New Year on our various boats for over a decade. Sometimes we struggle to stay awake to hear the bells, but this year we were determined to go for a midnight walk on the beach. We could hear shouting so we reluctantly left the boat at about 11:15.

'The pedestrian bridge is thronged,' Tim said as we made our way up the long pontoons to the security gate.

'Everybody's in fancy dress!'

Usually Tim and I head away from crowds, but on this occasion we went with it. We were so intrigued. The atmosphere was electric as revelers crowded the narrow streets.

'It's like a scene from a Hardy novel, Tim.'

There were girls with bare feet and fairy wings and youths dressed as Superman. They were all blowing toy trumpets.

'Notting Hill Carnival, without the steel drums,' Tim said.

'Or Rio, without the maracas. Or the sunshine come to think of it,' I replied.

We stood outside a bar watching cabs dropping off angels, firemen, ballet dancers, cowgirls and cats. A *Hello Kitty* posse all queued up patiently to get past the bouncers standing outside the pubs. Across the road a cyberman and Captain Jack Sparrow watched Michael Jackson moonwalking while Madonna, in a gold conical bra, took photographs. When we got closer we saw it was a man. We noticed his muscles weren't as defined as the queen of pop.

'It's freezing cold, Timmy, look at us all wrapped up in layers of clothes. We are underdressed.'

We walked through the crowds towards the beach, 'Happy New Year!' resounding in our cold ears. By the statue of King George, a Scottish piper was playing Auld Lang Syne. The handsome Jubilee Clock across the road struck midnight. Fireworks erupted from every direction. I had our kite in my pocket – flying it on New Year's Eve is now an annual event – so Tim and I hurried on to the sand. We thought we had it to ourselves but were joined by two others, a superhero and a girl with tiny wings and a great deal of bare flesh.

'She'd look more at home in Rio, wearing that,' Tim said.

'What's Batman up to? Where's he going?' I replied.

Tim and I were trying to get the kite to fly, but I kept my eye on the girl as she frolicked like a water nymph in the sea.

'I don't know what she's taken but I'd like some.'

Tim didn't hear me. I could see by his face he was annoyed with the kite.

'The wind chill must be minus five,' I said through chattering teeth.

I wrapped my scarf around my mouth. Tim untangled the kite string and looked around. He looked at me and mouthed 'What happened to her boyfriend?' Then we saw Batman running through the surf. The next moment he had lifted the girl off her feet and scooped her into his arms.

'How romantic,' I said to Tim. 'It could be Burt Lancaster and Deborah Kerr…'

Tim interrupted me. 'Hardly. I think our superhero has more than a roll in the surf on his mind.'

The nymph was now on her knees. She was ripping down his tights.

'I think we should leave them to it, darlin',' Tim said, reeling in the kite. 'I bet Burt didn't get a blow job in *From Here to Eternity*.'

Chapter Eighteen
And the Band Played 'Waltzing Matilda'

After much deliberation, Tim and I invited Paul Crompton to come down to visit us with his 'little camera' to see how we got along. We took him out for a trip around Portland Harbour. Tim gave him some background.

'Apparently it's one of the biggest man-made harbours in the world.'

'It's huge!' Paul said. 'Will it be OK if I climb on the roof and do some filming?'

'Just be careful,' Tim replied. 'And for God's sake keep your life jacket on.'

When we were alone Tim asked, 'What do you think?'

'I like him, he's so enthusiastic, but I want to duck every time he points the camera at me.'

'Just be yourself, my love,' Tim said, putting his arm around my shoulders. He then poked his finger in my ear. This always annoys me.

Later on we drove Paul back to the station. He got out of the car and took his camera out of the boot. 'I should have a five-minute taster ready for you next week. I've had a brilliant day. I can't keep the smile off my face.'

'We're making no promises, but we plan to leave Weymouth very soon. It will be one of my biggest challenges, the Portland Race...'

I interrupted. 'Tim's had the whole winter to worry about the infamous Race.'

The weather improved over the next couple of weeks. We often walked along the beach to Hamilton's restaurant.

'There's still a keen wind. I'm pleased I brought my wrap, Tim.'

We stopped at the Anzac War Memorial. I read out the inscription. 'In memory of Anzac Volunteer Troops who after action in Gallipoli in 1915 passed through hospitals and training camps in Dorset.'

Tim began to sing. '*And the band played Waltzing Matilda, as the ship pulled away from the quay, and amidst all the cheers, flag-waving and tears, we sailed off for Gallipoli.*'

I joined in. We often play it on iTunes on my Mac. '*But the band played Waltzing Matilda, when we stopped to bury our slain. We buried ours, and the Turks buried theirs, then we started all over again.*'

'Shane MacGowan sings that so beautifully. I find these memorials so sad. They were so far away from home,' I said.

Across the road from the memorial are hotels that were used as hospitals during the Great War. Now they are full of pensioners, who arrive by the coach load. The men and women are all dressed up to the nines as they disembark the coaches. They huddle together, trying to find respite from the blustery weather, and smoke cigarettes.

*

Midnight
I'm glad I gave up cigarettes; it's bad enough I swig the gin. The bedroom would have nicotine stains by now. My mom was very brave about her house burning down, but I can't afford to take on anyone else's pain. I couldn't even bear to put my arm around her, because it would have opened a torrent of despair, hers and mine. I have felt this way before. Somewhere within me I have a rod of iron. I think back to the day that Pascale was born. It was such a

dreadful labour. I was a 22-year-old little hippy literally with flowers in my hair ... and the Welsh nurses didn't approve of me one bit. Thank God my mother was there. She came into the room where I'd been left on my own with a buzzer to press if I needed anything.

'Where are the midwives?' she asked.

'I don't know! I've been shaved and given an enema and that was it...' I mumbled through contractions.

'We'll see about that!' my mother said and strode out of the room.

She found them drinking tea and smoking fags and gave them a bollocking. I don't think this improved my situation, as one of them came in with a huge spike to break my waters.

'We can do it my way or your way,' she said as she grabbed hold of an ankle.

Pascale was born 12 hours later with my mother giving me encouragement when I said I couldn't do it any more. And then I held her in my arms, this tiny miracle and I felt such joy and then at the same time a stab of pain in my heart that was worse than any labour pains. The man that I loved wasn't there to share my joy. He'd left me nine days before. BUT I was so strong, Timmy. I watched all the women on my ward getting the 'baby blues' but not me. They all looked at me with such pity, me and my hippy baby in second-hand baby clothes, but I did not shed one single tear because I knew I wouldn't be able to stop. I didn't even cry when the social worker asked me if I would like to have my baby adopted. I looked at her and said, 'Why don't you fuck off?!'

*

Tim and I found shelter from the wind as we drew close to the old pier. There were several people sitting outside the restaurant. We ordered and I noticed a straggling hiking procession going by on the other side of the road. They were teenagers, with backpacks and camping gear. The stragglers were half an hour behind the rest. I looked back down towards the beach.

'Look at that Tim,' I said. 'There are two kids in bathing costumes. That little girl is determined to go into the water.'

Her sister was a little more sensible and played in the sand.

'It's only March.'

I received a text from Anne who apologised for not responding to my emails. I read part of it out to Tim.

'WE ARE IN ANTIGUA, BUT SHALL SEE YOU ABOUT 7 APRIL. VINCENT IS DETERMINED TO GO AROUND PORTLAND BILL WITH YOU!'

'Well that's good news,' Tim said. 'But the more I read about the Portland Race, the less I like it. But at least we have a satnav now. All I have to do is learn how to use it.'

*

Paul Crompton sent us a copy of the five-minute tape he made. We showed it to Anne and Vincent on their return from Antigua. They were camping on their RIB in Weymouth. Their 15-year-old son, Nick, was with them. Quite how they all slept was a mystery to me.

'Tim and I kept changing our minds about having someone film us,' I said as I pressed play.

'I think you should do it!' Anne said after she watched the tape.

Vincent and Nick agreed.

'We'll see,' Tim said. 'My agents have to approve the contract, it's complicated.'

'Well, I'm looking forward to seeing you go around the Bill,' Vincent said.

We spent the next hour checking various websites for weather updates.

'What do you think Tim?' Anne asked. 'Will it be the 7am tide tomorrow?'

'I'm not sure. Everyone I speak to gives me different

advice about the best time to get around. I don't want to put you all out, it can't be comfortable for you all kipping on the RIB, but thanks so much for helping me with the passage on the satnav.'

'It was our pleasure,' Nick said. 'And the RIB is hellish!'

'No it's not Nick! We're all fine,' Anne insisted. 'Especially now we have the blow heater. Let's go for a walk on the beach.'

The atmosphere of the town had changed considerably. On the beach, frames for the burger bars were being constructed and covered in matching white, blue and red plastic. For months Tim and I had passed the sign that says, 'All Aboard the Seafront Landtrain. The next train will be Easter.'

'It seemed so far away when we first came here,' I said to Anne as we passed the noticeboard.

'Easter is only next week, you will miss the train. Shame, Shane.'

Anne took my arm.

'Come on,' I said, 'let's show you the house with the cannonball from the civil war and our favourite plaque.'

We cut through the side street to the Town Quay and stood before the plaque. Anne read it out. 'The Black Death entered England in 1348 through this port. It killed 30 to 50 per cent of the country's total population.'

'Nice plaque,' Nick said, 'but there is quite a difference between 30 and 50 per cent, that's quite a wide margin. I can't wait to see the cannonball.'

'Shane stopped a fight underneath the cannonball,' Tim said as we went entered the side door of the harbour-side pub, The Sailors Return.

'There was a scuffle going on between three blokes and she got in between them and shouted "Leave him alone!" And they did. That was a huge relief or else I'd have had to become involved.'

It was folk night in the pub, which swiftly filled up with

fiddles and accordions. We stayed longer than planned. Anne clapped and jigged. Vincent had to drag her out.

'We have an early start in the morning, Anne,' he sweetly admonished her.

As it turned out, our early start was cancelled: the weather forecast changed overnight. The weather does this at times. We had to wave goodbye to the Oddies, who had to make a break and get back to Southampton before gales blew in. Tim went back to his charts and I went back to Thomas Hardy. I was reading *Return of the Native*. Three days later Tim and I waved goodbye to Barry and left the marina to moor on the Town Quay. The harbour master gave us a large sign to hang on the side of *The Princess Matilda* that said NO MOORING. We were grateful for that. For the next three days we rose with the expectation that today would be the day, but the weather did not let us go. Finally we awoke to bright sunshine. Tim and I undid our ropes from the visitor's mooring and left.

We returned half an hour later.

The sea outside the bay was huge and unkind. Tim and I sat in the wheelhouse and watched the blood-orange sunset over the gasworks and wondered how much longer we would have to wait.

'We're never going to get to Wales at this rate. Never!'

Chapter Nineteen
Domestics

Weymouth to Dartmouth: 60 nautical miles

Our aborted trip had knocked Tim's confidence, so I knew it was imperative to get him back in the saddle, figuratively speaking, as soon as possible. We both listened to the Met Office forecast over the VHF radio. It was the same as all the websites I had been checking obsessively the whole morning.

'This is it Tim. It's a slight sea. We won't get a better window, the high pressure is just what you wanted.'

'Oh Shane, you don't understand, if I've made a mistake with my calculations we could end up being bashed to buggery by the Race. And that bloke in the pub last night really wound me up. He said his mate got caught by the Race and almost sank...'

'Tim, you know exactly what time we should round the Bill. You've checked and treble-checked the times, so we'd better not hang around. We should leave now, or else we'll have to wait until tomorrow.'

'You are quite right,' he said. 'Let's go. We have to hit the Bill at exactly four hours after high tide. We'll go on the east side for about for two or three miles. The tide should be going with us.'

I helped him into his life jacket as he started up the engine and once again we left the quay. A man on a neighbouring boat shouted to us, 'DON'T COME BACK THIS TIME! GOOD LUCK!'

Weymouth Bay was pleasingly calm, but we knew it would be another story as we came around Portland Harbour. Over the radio we heard a 'Mayday' being called on channel 16. The lifeboat that had been moored just ahead of us on Weymouth Town Quay overtook us a few minutes later. Silently we watched the wake of the boat disappear into the far distance. It was an ominous start; somewhere at sea a vessel was in danger. It did occur to me that the lifeboat would now not be available if we got in to trouble.

The Princess Matilda passed the place where we had turned around a few days before.

'You made the right decision Tim.'

'No, I bottled it.'

'On the contrary, you were sensible.'

We could see the lighthouse on Portland Bill in the distance. Tim had decided to take the inside route, which meant we would be seeing it from fairly close quarters.

'It will take us an hour to get there,' Tim said. 'Go and put the kettle on love.'

Tim wasn't the only one of us worrying about what we were about to do. Everyone we had spoken to had told us a horror story about rounding this infamous headland.

'Oh we almost got smashed to pieces. You'll stand no chance in your boat…'

'The lifeboat brought them back; the mast was broken and the skipper had concussion…'

And in the pub just by the lifeboat station was a board with the details of the latest shout. They had plucked a crew from a sinking vessel just off the Bill.

I decided to phone Sadie while I was waiting for the kettle to come to the boil.

'Hi Sade, we might lose our phone signal, so will you phone the coast guard if you don't hear from us by 6:30?'

'Mum, you are kidding right?'

'No darling.'

There is nothing quite like spreading a bit of worry around.

When I came back up to the wheelhouse the lighthouse had grown and was increasing further in size as we drew closer.

'You can go as close to the cliffs as you like.' Someone in the harbour master's office had told us.

This is what we did.

Our radio crackled into life, 'Princess Matilda, Princess Matilda, *we're the fishing netter on your portside. You've got fair weather, we've had no more than a two-metre swell.*'

'Netter, good morning, we're planning on getting around the Bill as quickly as possible. We hope you get a good catch today, over,' Tim replied.

'*We're not doing too badly, but we won't be hanging about. In about 50 minutes we'll have the Portland Race with waves higher than Big Ben out here, so we'll be heading back to harbour. Good luck Matilda. Out.*'

I opened the door and Tim and I waved to them. There were a few jet skis out there too riding the larger waves. They bounced up and down several feet as we went by. Further out were a couple of other boats trawling for Shambles Plaice.

'They know what they're doing, they'll be pulling up their nets soon,' Tim said as we picked up speed to cross Lyme Bay towards Torquay.

The Princess Matilda rode over the swell, her nose rising and meeting the crest of the long, smooth waves.

'It's like that time when we went back up the Thames,' I said to Tim, 'do you remember?'

'When we went past Tilbury? It's not half as bad as that.'

He looked carefully at his charts and the satnav.

'We did it!' Tim said with excitement in his voice. 'We've just come around Portland Bill!'

'Was that it? What about the Race!' I said with incredulity in my voice.

'We got our timing right.'

To tell the truth I was oddly disappointed with the lack of drama, after all we had heard and read.

'We can relax now. We're taking a straight line across the bay towards Torquay, our first stop,' Tim said.

'Oh right, I'll read my book then, I feel oddly cheated!'

I took out my book. We were too far away from the land to see much. Tim was happy standing at the wheel. He kept looking at his satnav. A couple of calm hours passed.

'We're about 12 miles out at sea, but something's not quite right,' Tim said urgently. 'Take the wheel will you, Shane, where are the protractors?'

'I took my eye off the ball,' he said with annoyance in his voice. 'I lost concentration. We've actually been going backwards for the last hour. We must have picked up some bizarre southerly spring tide. It's going to take a while to get back on track.'

'Oh well,' I said, 'thank goodness there's nothing else about. I won't tell if you don't.'

Tim laughed, 'We do seem to have the ocean to ourselves. We've not seen another boat for hours.'

'Don't speak too soon,' I said, peering through the binoculars. 'What do they say about buses? I can see ten huge ships out on the horizon. I've counted them twice.'

'Bloody 'ell!' Tim said. 'I hope they have us on their radar.'

We kept a very close eye on them for the next hour or so. But when it became apparent they were anchored we relaxed.

'I vaguely remember reading something about them,' I said to Tim. 'I'll see if I still have the paper.'

I sorted through our recycling that was in a bag on the deck. Quickly I found the article I was looking for. It was dated 9 April 2009.

'I do enjoy a two-day-old local paper,' I said to Tim as I turned over the pages. They were inside out and back to front.

'Ah! There it is. There's even a photo.'

I showed it to Tim and read it out to him as he fiddled with his satnav.

'The number of giant tankers anchoring off the South Devon coast has been raised with maritime officials. Ten tankers currently anchored in Lyme Bay are set to remain stationed here until the price of oil picks up.'

'I'm looking forward to going in-between them,' Tim said, wrapping his arm around my shoulder.

I sent a text to Anne and Paul Crompton. 'WE CAME AROUND THE BILL AND ARE PLAYING CAT AND MOUSE WITH BP. ONE MORE HOUR AND WE'LL BE IN TORQUAY.'

The white villas of Torquay sit like false teeth above the marina. Tim called the harbour master, who directed us to our berth. There was the usual selection of yachts and Sunseekers in the marina. Most had people on the decks enjoying their Easter break. Some waved, others ignored us. I waved regardless. Tim and I were incredibly happy.

'Torquay, can you believe it?' Tim said.

'Look how clear the water is. I can see right to the bottom.'

Our revelry was curtailed because, shortly after we moored up, Tim received a phone call from Mike Leigh. I was busy adjusting the fenders. I could tell it was bad news.

'Simon died!' Tim said. 'It's so sad, poor Simon.'

Simon Channing-Williams was Mike's partner in Thin Man Films. He was the moneyman, the one who found the backers for Mike's projects. Everyone who knew him held him in the highest esteem, not just for the fact that he could raise money for a script that did not exist, but because he was a real gentleman.

We sat there on our boat with tears running down our faces. Simon, lovely, deliciously funny, flirtatious, charming and naughty Simon was gone. The man loved his food, a good cigar and his champagne, and we loved him. I remembered the letter Tim had received from Simon a couple of days after he was diagnosed with AML:

> *Mike shared with me the appalling news of your illness. I was shocked and deeply upset. We missed you greatly at the Cannes premiere; you would have been in your element. The reception of Secrets and Lies was extraordinary. Everyone is talking about your astonishing performance. We raised our glasses to you last night and we shall go on sending get well vibes until you're better.*

'Dear, darling Simon. I thought we'd get to see him when we get to Cornwall. He has a house near Penzance,' Tim said. 'I told Mike what we've just done, come around the Bill and how terrified I was. He said Simon would've been proud.'

'You're a long time dead, Timmy, that's why we have to make the most of our lives. We were given a second chance. Come on let's find a pub and raise a glass now to Simon.'

My phone rang as we entered a harbour-side bistro. We didn't like the look of any of the pubs. It was Sadie berating me for not letting her know we had arrived safely. I put her on speakerphone.

'I've been worrying myself sick all afternoon. Why can't you and Dad take up golf and do normal things, like everyone else?'

'Sorry darling, we forgot,' I guiltily replied.

'I'll forgive you this time! What's Torquay like, Mum?'

'I'm glad we didn't spend the winter here. It's a leery place, there are gangs of girls dressed to thrill.'

'They will all be undressed after six bottles of Bacardi Breezer,' Sadie replied.

'Are you speaking from experience?' Tim laughed.

'Me drink alcopops? You are joking, Dad!'

Another gaggle of girls went by the window.

'I thought Torquay was a blue rinse kind of town,' Tim said as I hung up the phone.

'Life goes on, darling.'

After a quick dinner we decided to escape the pub-crawling crowd, pausing briefly to look at a memorial close to the marina.

The commemorative stone is dedicated to the US 4th Infantry Division who embarked to Normandy as part of Operation Overlord on 5 June 1944.

'How brave they were,' I said. 'I wonder where my dad left from? I wish I could ask him. Come on let's go back to *The Princess Matilda* and shut out the world.'

Another group of girls passed us, laughing and shouting to each other.

'I quite like the marauding Torquay girls,' I continued once they had crossed the road. 'I bet their grandmas gave the Yanks a good time before they boarded the boats to Juno beach.'

'It's been one hell of a day. Let's get back on our sanctuary,' Tim said, leading the way.

When we got back onboard, Tim studied *The Shell Channel Pilot* and I read a local newspaper we had picked up off a park bench.

'Hey listen to this,' I said. 'The Shackleton expedition stopped off at Torquay for a meal in the Torbay Hotel before they went to Antarctica. I don't think they would now. I checked it out through the windows while you booked us into the marina office. The hotel's so grand outside, I had high hopes of white linen tablecloths and crystal wine glasses, but saw pink two-ply paper serviettes and a bowl of those horrid plastic things that spew mustard and brown sauce all over you as you tear them with your teeth.'

Tim laughed. 'I don't think the perfect seaside hotel exists any more, but if it does we'll find it. You want a place that serves egg mayonnaise made with salad cream and waitresses called Dolly, silver-serving tinned new potatoes.'

'New potatoes, cheese salad and beetroot, yum,' I replied.

Tim turned the page of the pilot book.

'We need diesel, so we'll go over the bay to Brixham tomorrow. The guy in the office said there's a fuel barge over there. It'll only take us 20 minutes,' he said.

The next day, a couple of coastguards helped us tie up to the Brixham fuel barge. One was from Birmingham and the other a Welshman, and they told us to watch out for the Brummie Navy.

'What does that mean?' I asked.

The Midlander laughed and replied, 'They droive down the M5 on a Fry-day noight, and teck their bowts out of the marina, must of 'em oinly goo from Brixham ter Weymouth and beck!'

'Well as a Midlander,' I replied, 'I'd rather share a Town Quay with the Brummie Navy than the rude ribbers and yachters from the Solent!'

He thought this highly amusing and suggested a pub we might like.

After we moored, Tim and I walked up some rambling steps and found The Maritime Inn. It was just across the road from the headquarters of the coastguard. The governor of the double-bow-windowed hostelry was from Liverpool.

'My name's Pat,' she said. 'Welcome to Brixham. What can I get you?'

'Do you think anyone was born here?' Tim said, as he brought back our drinks.

I had found a seat by one of the two roaring fires. Even though the sun streamed through the lead-latticed windows, it was chilly. The oak-beamed ceiling was festooned with chamber pots.

'Someone's been taking the piss,' Tim observed.

Then we heard a squawk. In the corner was a parrot on a perch.

'He's really friendly,' Pat assured us. 'But don't get too close.'

We left the pub reluctantly after we finished our drinks. Well, Tim did. He can sit in a bar all day long, but I was keen to have a look around the picturesque town. The houses that rise up the hill around the harbour are painted in differing shades of pink, blue and red.

'It's gotta be one of the prettiest towns we've ever seen,' Tim said as we made our way down another twisting flight of steps. We came out on to a car park on the harbour front. The only remaining vehicle was a midnight blue van facing the water. There was one hell of a domestic going on inside it. A beige blouson-wearing big-backed bottled blonde was screaming at the driver. The small man appeared to be cowering away from her. Tim took my arm.

'Come on, leave them to it,' he whispered, as I paused to intervene. 'I don't want to get into a ruck with her, Shane. Let's have a look around the other side of the harbour.'

*

I phoned the sweet night nurse after midnight. She said she was going to check you every 15 minutes. You were sleeping. She said you were a little bit better when I phoned at 6:20 this morning. I had a cup of tea, made some phone calls, left lots of notes for the kids and my mom, and left. I got to the hospital at seven. I wish the traffic was as easy every morning. I had no problem today.

You are asleep, and I think you look a little better than yesterday. When you wake I call a nurse and between the two of us we manage to get you sitting up. You give me a lopsided smile, but it's more of a grimace as we try to find some position that causes you less pain. The nurse leaves and I take a grapefruit out of my bag. I cut it in half and scoop out two segments and feed you. The juice dribbles down your chin. I wipe your mouth, but your hand grabs mine and pushes it away. You didn't eat at all yesterday. You ask me to put on the television.

The director Stephen Frears is on Sky News. The last time we had seen Stephen was at The Comedy Awards when you were nominated for Outside Edge. *It was at LWT on the South Bank of the Thames. Everyone was fed huge amounts of booze during the commercial breaks, but no food. I kept putting my hand over my glass – warm white wine does nothing for me – but you didn't seem to mind. Come to think of it, you didn't mind not winning the award either. The show was interminable but after the last acceptance speech was finished we were all herded into the hospitality suite. I used to think these functions were fun, but now find it annoying when I'm introduced to a person I have met at least 20 times. Mostly they briefly glance at me when you say, 'Have you met my wife before?' And nine times out of ten, without a flicker of recognition, they give me a perfunctory 'hello', turn their back and carry on talking to you.*

'Tim, I want to go home now.' You were deep in conversation with Frears. As always, you re-introduced me. I saw the look. 'I want to go home now, Tim.' But you ignored me. I walked away and left you to it and went to the Ladies. I was so pissed off and sat in the cubicle listening to everyone else having a good time. It took me about 20 minutes to find you again. You were still talking to the director. You were smoking a cigarette. I took it from you and said, 'Look, Tim, I don't smoke!' I took a drag, and then dropped it in your drink. I turned my back and left. I'd not had a cigarette for ten years. You ran after me and I was so annoyed because you were drunk. We had the most horrible argument by the river. When we have big rows they are dreadful. I yelled at you, 'Just leave me alone. Fuck off! Go away!' I saw two people and shouted, 'This man is bothering me!' I strode away and you were left with two strangers who thought you had been attacking me. I felt bad so I waited for you to catch up and then we went home.

*

It was 7pm when walked down the jetty towards *The Princess Matilda*. There was a 50-foot rigged trawler getting ready to leave. Tim and I stood in the twilight for a few minutes watching the crew. There was a great deal of hauling going on as the two sails were raised. We could see much activity on the rope ladders. As we came closer we realised the crew were all children.

'I would've loved to have done that when I was a kid,' Tim said quietly.

'I received a text from Paul today,' I said as I unlocked the door to the wheelhouse. 'He wants to come down next week and meet us, to talk about the TV project. What a shame he's not with us tonight.'

'Tell him we'll see him in Dartmouth, we'll be there tomorrow,' Tim replied, his eyes looking longingly at the trawler as the canvases were raised.

'Pull … Pull … Pull …' a hypnotic voice called as the children stood in lines heaving in unison on the hoisting ropes. The only other noise was that of the rising tide gently slapping on the bow. The red-sailed ship slipped silently away into a crimson-encrusted sunset.

The following morning, I walked into Brixham to get in some supplies while the skipper did his engine checks. By the marina there is a fairly new development that is out of character with the rest of the harbour. It reminded me of Eastbourne marina. Walking into the town, I expected to find a high street to match the characterful cottages up on the cliffs. I was disappointed. It could have been any street in any pedestrianised town centre. There were the usual shops: Co-op, Tesco Express, Subway, Specsavers and building societies. I took our shopping back to the boat feeling rather guilty. The Co-op was handy. Why search out butchers, bakers and candlestick makers when you can get it all under one roof? I resolved to try harder next time.

Back in the wheelhouse I stared at the newish houses at the top of the marina. Tim's head poked out of the engine room as I dropped the heavy bags on to the deck.

'A sign up there says the new houses were built on the site of J W & A Upham, a famous local boatbuilder that was founded in 1817. It built mainly fishing vessels...'

Tim interrupted me. 'Pass me a rag, love.'

I handed him some kitchen roll out of one of my shopping bags.

'Ta,' he said as he grabbed the bar to haul himself on to the deck. He threw the litter into the bin. 'Brixham still has a large fishing fleet though.'

'You didn't let me finish! A new dry dock was built in 1939. Come on, let me show you.'

Tim followed me up the jetty.

'There,' I said, pointing. 'The slipway before the breakwater is known as "the hard" and was built for the D-Day landings. Thousands of men left for Normandy from here, as they did from Weymouth, Portland and Torquay.'

Tim and I listened to the Met Office forecast when we got back to the boat. We both agreed that the predicted sou'easterly wind and the 'slight and occasionally moderate sea' sounded just the ticket.

'It's only a few miles around to Dartmouth,' Tim said. 'We'll be there in a couple of hours, in time for lunch. Have a look in *The Good Food Guide* and see what's on offer darlin'.'

I greedily scanned the index. 'We're spoilt for choice,' I declared.

The man in the Brixham marina office had advised Tim to give notice of our passage to the coastguard over the VHF radio. It wasn't something we had thought about doing before. He called them on channel 16 and they told him to change to another channel. Channel 16 is kept open for emergencies. We felt like proper sailors now.

Chapter Twenty
Castles in the Air

The sea was silk smooth as we came out into Brixham Bay. One hour later, we were both cursing the day we had bought a boat. We had become smug and complacent and had thought we were Sir Francis Chichester, because we had come around the North Foreland, Selsey Bill and the Portland Race.

The sea lifted the nose and arse of *The Princess Matilda* ten feet into the air. There she hovered for what seemed like forever before landing with a thud that vibrated throughout the boat. I could hear plates falling out of the cupboard. I remembered I had not shut the doors properly when I had unpacked the shopping. The next wave sent what I suspected were glasses crashing to the galley floor. Then I heard the kettle clatter across the saloon.

'You had better go and see what's happening inside,' Tim said.

'No fear, I can't stand up never mind go down the steps,' I said as another roller hit us. This time the boat slid sideways down the surf. If you have a surfboard this is a good thing; it's not so much fun on a boat. I leapt out of my canvas director's chair just as it skidded across the floor. I clutched on to Tim and watched as our bow disappeared under the next wave. Unfortunately I wasn't holding on to him firmly enough and I was thrown on to the deck of the wheelhouse. I lunged for the grab bar that Tim uses when he climbs out of the engine room. Tim was still hanging on to the steering wheel, his knees were braced and his knuckles were white.

'Now we know what the fuck a moderate sea means!' he said, yanking the wheel around. 'Brace yourself, this is going to be nasty. I have to change course!' Tim yelled.

CRASH went the contents of my store cupboard. *The Princess Matilda* weighs over 35 tons but we were being tossed around like a rag doll. If I could have unwrapped two fingers from the grab bar, I would have crossed them. Instead I sent up a silent prayer. I looked behind us and watched the sky disappear. A wall of grey water rose up. Moses and Cecil B DeMille came to mind. I expected the wave to engulf us as it did the Egyptians chasing the Israelites across the Red Sea. The breaking wave hit us broadside and the boat corkscrewed as Tim turned *The Princess Matilda* around. It took all of my strength to hang on to the bar and all of his to turn the wheel. We both knew it would get worse before it got better.

'Oh God,' I prayed. 'Please don't let our engine die.' And I am an atheist.

For a moment I found myself remembering how we had queued for hours to experience something similar at Universal Studios in Florida with the kids. But none of us were in danger of being swept overboard on the Jaws Ride. The back doors of *The Princess Matilda* were open. I tried not to think about what would happen if the steering failed or our propeller became fouled with a lobster pot. I knew Tim was thinking this too.

'It should get easier as soon as we get the waves off our broadside,' he said with determination in his voice.

Neither of us spoke for a few minutes. The mountainous waves battered us for what seemed like hours. In adversity, time slows down. Gradually the motion of our boat changed as the sea lifted up our bow, slid beneath us and spewed out behind us. This made it slightly easier to move so I was able to peer through the open door to the inside of the boat. I half expected to see seawater crashing through broken windowpanes.

'I'm going down below to make sure we're not taking in water anywhere,' I said, timing my departure from the wheelhouse to coincide with a lull between waves.

I staggered below like a punch-drunk boxer. The battered kettle was at the bottom of the steps. I picked it up and held it like a baby. Our saloon looked like it had fallen victim to an illegal rave. Books, DVDs, tins of spaghetti, broken cups, plates and glassware, and a split bag of dried mixed beans littered the floor. I now understood what 'after the horse has bolted' meant. The broom had fallen across my cupboard doors, I picked it up and fastened it back in the cupboard and shut the doors firmly. The fridge door was also swinging open so I made a grab for the gin before another wave hit us, then slammed it shut. I fell against the sink, where I threw the bottle, hoping it would not break. After I regained my balance I kicked the broken crockery out of the way. I knew I only had moments. I squared my feet against the bottom of the cooker and pressed my back against the cupboard. Wedged in firmly I waited patiently for the next wave to pass. During the next lull, I checked our cabin. All of my books were on the floor. I lay on the bed as I felt the next wave lifting up our bow. I had clean laundry hanging above me. The spray washed over the skylight above my head. I half expected it to drench my washing, which was behaving like a pendulum in a grandfather clock. At the next let-up I staggered to my feet and into our bathroom. Quickly I checked we didn't have seawater coming through the plugholes. We had not shut the seacocks to prevent this happening. I held on to the hand basin and towel rail as I felt and heard another wave breaking. Through the frosted glass I could see white froth. I managed to run downhill to the wheelhouse before the next wave came.

'Everything's fine. It's a mess, but we're OK down below,' I said breathlessly as I took my seat on the step with the grab bar. I took a swig of gin. The bottle had not been abandoned. 'How's it going up here?' I asked Tim as I leant over and passed him the bottle.

He threw back his head and took a glug before passing back the Gordon's.

Spluttering, he said, 'It is easier now we're riding the waves. At least we can time them. But what we've gained in comfort, we're losing in equal measure. In a nutshell, we're going in the opposite direction to the one we need to go. The Mew Stone is behind us and I have to turn around again and keep clear of the West Rocks and Castle Ledge. That's the entrance to the River Dart. The turning will be the worst, but once we're around I'll be able to zig-zag to get in there. Are you ready?'

'Of course,' I said, taking another nip out of the bottle.

'Hold on tight, darlin', we have a nasty ride ahead, but we should be in the shelter of the estuary very soon, I promise,' Tim said with a look in his eyes that told me, 'I'm so sorry, this is all my fault.'

'I love you!' I said as I put the gin in the bin next to my perch.

Neither of us spoke for the next 30 minutes. This was how long it took Tim to safely navigate *The Princess Matilda* into Dartmouth. It was a rollercoaster of a ride.

*

Midnight is the worst time for me. I try so hard to keep away all negative thoughts, to keep my imagination and underlying frenzy under control. I have to think about the positives. What are they? Come on, think. No, don't think. Write, don't think.

Your blood pressure dropped. Your poor body is swollen with fluid. A new doctor – pretty, young, unliked, I suspect, by everyone had the nurses do strange things with weird bits of wood so they could 'estimate' how much extra fluid you are carrying. It was positively medieval, and then the pretty unliked announced, 'You may have to go into Intensive Care.' Just like that. We've never seen her before; she looks like a bossy head-girl. 'When's Panos back?' I ask her. 'He's in Greece, his mother's ill,' one of the Irish nurses says. They all look a bit shifty. 'Where's the other doctor, Rye? I want to see Rye!' I demanded. 'She won't be in until the morning,' unliked says. 'Now, I have other patients to see to!' and leaves. Bridget, one of your favourite nurses, arrives to look after you. She strokes my arm and tucks you up. 'Well, Mr Spall, the doctor says we should give you some diuretics, so let's see how we get on with those.' Her calm Irish brogue reassures us. She leaves and comes back with the medication and an armful of plastic piss bottles, which she arranges like ten pins at the bowling alley. This makes us laugh … except your laugh is a pathetic bleat and mine is edged with hysteria.

*

Our arrival into the mouth of the River Dart was a triumphal one. Several boats were heading towards us. For a moment we both felt like Captain Cook being met by the Hawaiian islanders who rowed out to greet him in their canoes. I waved, expecting them to be some kind of welcoming party, but they ignored us and headed out to sea.

'They are obviously used to it,' I said.

Tim and I both looked behind us, but the sea looked benign.

'That passage has taught us two valuable lessons,' Tim said as he massaged his hands. 'Firstly, a moderate sea is a misnomer, and secondly, *The Princess Matilda* can take a bashing. I've lost all feeling in my fingers.'

'I'm not surprised. You must have blisters on your hands the way you clung on to that straining steering wheel. I want to go to the bow and take some photographs, but I don't trust myself to walk along the gunwale. I'm still trembling.'

'I'd better let Brixham Coastguard know we've arrived. I thought they sounded a bit strange when I said we were leaving,' Tim said, testing his fingers so he could tune the VHF radio to channel 16.

'But the sea was like a millpond, how did it change so quickly?' I asked, slightly distracted. While Tim had been massaging his hands, I had been rubbing my bum.

'The more we do, the less we know. The sea's a dangerous place, Shane.'

'Have I got a bruise on my arse?' I said, pulling down my tracksuit bottoms.

'That will be a beauty,' Tim said ignoring the radio.

'Take a photo of it. I like to keep a pictorial record of my boat injuries.'

'You'd better pull your pants up, there's a fishing boat about to overtake us.'

When the fishing boat had passed, I took the wheel and Tim called the coastguard. He then picked up the camera.

'How beautiful is this river?' he said with a catch in his voice.

On either side of the mouth of the Dart are fairytale castles. And then dual craggy precipices greeted us on both banks. Some of the rock was smudged with emeralds that I soon realised were evergreen trees and shrubs clinging on to the silver cliff faces. The cliffs gave way to a forest of embarrassed, naked ancient oak trees still awaiting their spring greenery. Huge mansions hid away in gaps in the woods. As we sailed upstream, chocolate-box cottages tumble randomly down the hillsides. They were painted in gaudy blues, pinks, yellows and lilacs and reminded me of one of Tilda's edible sweetie bracelets. Above the rooftops was lush high pasture with sheep grazing on the hillside.

'Is that another castle?' I asked Tim as we made our way upstream.

'I think so, and there's the ferry that crosses from Dartmouth to Kingswear, I'd better slow down to let it by.'

By Dover and Portsmouth standards, this was a small ferry. We waved to the passengers, a few of whom had climbed out of their cars for the short trip across the river.

'There's another ferry further up,' Tim said as he pushed down the throttle to give us more speed now the vessel had crossed our path.

I looked through my binoculars; we now had a pair each. 'I can see cars waiting by a slipway and a weird blue-looking thing…'

'That's the chain ferry,' Tim said. 'We've got a berth in a marina close by.'

We let this ferry cross before we turned about and moored as directed on a hammerhead. Across the river as we tied up were puffs of white smoke and a whistle. A jet-black steam train pulling cream and black coaches appeared to be travelling a few feet above the water line.

'Trains and boats, all we need now are some planes,' I said to Tim as he connected us to the shore power.

'I'm going to hose off the salt,' he replied. 'You start on the mess inside and I'll come and help as soon as I'm done out here.'

'Do you know what, Tim?' I said, giving him a kiss. 'I don't mind about the rough journey, it was worth it. I love this place, it's completely magical.'

He slapped me on my unbruised arse cheek but I disappeared back inside before he put the hose on. I surveyed the damage. It was pretty bad. I nudged a few DVDs to one side and spotted a CD amongst the jumble littering the floor. We had bought it in a charity shop the year before. It was the only CD we had on the boat – I had long ago copied everything else on to iTunes on my Mac. I turned on the TV and put on the CD to play out through the telly. It was a compilation of music hall songs. From under the sink I grabbed a black bin liner and found the dustpan and brush, then began to clear up the chaos surrounding me. Crystal glasses my mother had given me and part of an old dinner service from my youth lay shattered. Strangely, I didn't feel sad. I felt happy. They were just things. I can still remember my mother without looking at a glass. Tim and I were safe and sound and so was *The Princess Matilda*. I turned up the music and through the window I saw Tim with his hose, washing away the salt before it rusted the boat. He waved and I began to dance as I swept. I felt like Snow White, whistling while she worked. This was a celebration. Tim came down the steps and turned up the sound.

'There's no one else here,' he shouted as we jigged and danced.

We sang along to the lyrics remembered from our childhood. *Run Rabbit Run* may not sound electrifying, but we were thrilled by the harmonies of Flanagan and Allen. We acted it all out like Charlie's Angels.

'*BANG BANG BANG BANG GOES THE FARMER'S GUN, SO RUN RABBIT RUN RABBIT RUN RUN RUN.*'

We spent the next hour with it on a loop as we tidied up. Being silly is what Tim and I do best. The journey from Brixham took only two hours but it had been traumatic. Eventually we lay exhausted on the bed. Above our heads, hanging from the skylight, were Tim's ageing M & S underpants that I had hung to dry in Brixham.

'That's really sexy,' I said to Tim.

If we had had any energy left we would have both laughed hysterically.

Chapter Twenty-One
Darting Back and Forth

Tim and I only stayed one night at the marina by the chain-ferry. It was unbelievably expensive so we moved *The Princess Matilda* to a marina in Kingswear by the other ferry slipway. The lights of the handsome Dartmouth Harbour danced on the water in the darkness. They did not entice us to move across the river, except by ferry. I have had enough of mooring on Town Quays. Paul Crompton was arriving to discuss filming the voyages of *The Princess Matilda*. There were several reasons why we had not had Paul onboard when we left Weymouth. Most of them were contractual. Tim's agents at Markham & Froggatt have been in the business a long time. They wanted to make sure every 'i' in the contract was dotted. These things take time. Another problem in arranging Paul's time with us was our itinerary. Paul understood that we were governed by the weather and also by Tim's work and our domestic arrangements.

The three of us had lunch in The Ship, a little pub high above the harbour. We were all puffed out by the time we had climbed all the steps to the bridge that crosses the steam train line. I told Paul we had a friend, my old mate Michael Wilding, due to arrive in London from New Mexico, and that Tim had filming commitments. We intended to leave the boat in a secure mooring fairly soon. Where that 'secure' mooring was we could not predict, nor were the dates we would be back onboard.

'I feel really sorry for Paul,' I said, as we watched him get into a cab. 'How's he going to explain this to a commissioning editor at the BBC?'

Tim and I walked to the chandlery the other side of the steam railway line and bought a dinghy.

'We'll need one if we moor on a swing buoy and need to get ashore,' Tim said, rubbing his hands, evidently really excited about playing with his new toy. He spent the rest of the afternoon blowing it up with a foot pump while I hurriedly finished reading *The Mayor of Casterbridge*. I was aware we had left Dorset, the land of Thomas Hardy, behind and were heading for Daphne du Maurier country. Cornwall was beckoning, but we were in no hurry to leave the River Dart quite yet. Tim called out to me and I rushed up to the wheelhouse just in time to see him launch himself into the grey little inflatable boat. He rowed all the way around *The Princess Matilda*.

'Wanna go, darlin'?' he enquired solicitously.

'Maybe tomorrow when you hit your stroke,' I said, and went back to the Mayor.

The following day Tim and I took *The Princess Matilda* a couple of miles upstream to Dittisham. We had been told in the marina office that there were swing buoys there. Frankly I was dreading having to get hold of a buoy after the fiasco we had when we left the Medway. As it turned out it was far easier this time; there were only a couple of other boats in our way. There was no wind or ebbing tide. I was concentrating when Tim joined me on the bow. He made me jump out of my skin.

'Go back, I can manage!' I said, grabbing the ring on top of the buoy with the boathook.

He bossily took charge so I sulked and left him to it.

'You can't be in two places at the same time, Tim!' I snapped, and went to the wheelhouse to take charge of the wheel.

While he was securing our lines I saw someone else approaching another buoy. I watched their technique with interest and resolved to do it the same way next time. It was so simple; they just threw a rope around the whole thing and someone else onboard threaded a line through the ring. Tim and I went below. I had dinner in the oven and laid the table while Tim struck a match and lit the candles and a firelighter in the stove. The April nights were still chilly.

'I can't think of a single place in the whole world I'd rather be,' Tim said as he filled up my glass with champagne.

'Nor me, it's so quiet here, so lovely. I'm sure I saw a kingfisher earlier on.'

*

Midnight
My back is not strong enough. I want you to take care of me. I received a postcard from Pascale today:

'Hello everyone, hello Daddy, I miss you … we've got the best view, we can see for miles. Our room has a fridge so it's full of beer. We're going to hire a boat on my 20th birthday and have a picnic somewhere … miss you all, lots and lots xxxx'

I'm glad she's away for her birthday. I'm glad she's having a wonderful time. What's the point of us all being miserable?

For the first time ever, I cannot be bothered to think about the circumstances of her birth. She phoned from Greece and liked her presents. I'm glad she is enjoying herself. I shouted at Rafe crossing Waterloo Bridge, but I don't want to take my despair out on my children. You started another temperature after a clear day and rigored, the worst one so far. Please let it be the last. It is all so demoralising. We're both fed up. Your veins are buggered because the Hickman Line won't bleed. The beauty about a Hickman is it not only delivers the drugs into the heart but also allows blood samples to be taken, sometimes two or three times a day. The vampires now have to go into the vein manually, poking and prodding through bruises that reach from your fingertips to your shoulders. I find excuses to leave until they are done. You never complain. When you rigor they give you more pethidine. I worry. I would love a veinful. You slept most of the day but said your brain wasn't right. I tell you I am writing up notes for my thesis. You say the sound of me tapping on my laptop is reassuring ... I write to keep myself focused, to keep strong. I have to be strong for us all.

*

We went back to Kingswear briefly the following day. Miriam Jones was going to spend a night onboard. Miriam has spent more time on our various boats than any other of our friends. Tim and I relish having her onboard. She never makes a fuss unless we run out of champagne. I took our shopping trolley on the ferry and stocked up in Sainsbury's in Dartmouth. I bumped into her on my return as she was parking her car by the chandlery. We walking down the gantry as a steam train arrived.

'I thought you said it was quiet,' she said in her completely original hybrid accent.

I call it 'Welshjaw'. Miriam had lived with Jimmy Nail long enough for some of the Geordie to rub off. She had been a student in Newcastle when they met. Miriam can speak Welsh and say 'howay man' in the same sentence. But on this occasion she stuck to English.

'Howay, I hope that train doesn't run all night!'

'No. Miriam, it's Devon not Clapham Junction and, anyway, we have a treat in store. We're going to take you upstream, moor on a buoy, climb into the dinghy and go to the pub.'

'Well, I understood the last bit,' she said as she spotted Tim and waved.

'Welcome to Kingswear,' Tim yelled.

I unpacked the shopping and we untied our ropes and went upstream.

'It's so gorgeous here,' Miriam said. 'I had no idea Dartmouth was on a river and had never heard of Kingswear. You are certainly seeing Britain.'

'Apparently we could take *The Princess Matilda* all the way upstream to Totnes, but Dittisham is so charming and someone told Tim The Ferryboat is a lovely pub…'

Tim interrupted me. 'The only problem is we have to row there as we have to moor in the middle of the river.'

'I'd better not have too much to drink then,' Miriam said, filling up her glass. In many ways she is a true Welsh-Geordie lass.

'Cheers!' she said, clinking her plastic cup with Tim's. 'I love being back on *The Princess Matilda*.'

I left them in the wheelhouse and prepared to lasso a buoy as we drew closer to the picture postcard village of Dittisham. Along the small harbour-side is a terrace of the now-familiar pink, yellow and blue pastel-coloured houses. They reminded me of bookends: the taller three-storey buildings have smaller ones sandwiched between them. I took my position on the bow and signalled Tim to slow down then stop and threw my rope around the buoy. It floated off, so we had to turn around and approach it again. Tim joined me. We squabbled a bit, I lay down and snagged the ring on top of the buoy and left him to it.

When Tim finished tying up to the buoy, he joined us in the wheelhouse. Miriam and I were looking in a book, trying to work out the name of the trees on the opposite bank.

'I'm sure the green shoots have grown since we arrived. You can almost hear the leaves unfurling,' I said.

'Come on you two. Put down the book, let's lock up and go to the pub.'

He dragged our new dinghy around to the side of *The Princess Matilda* to the lowest part of the gunwale.

'You will be quite safe if you do what you're told,' he assured us as he climbed down.

'Right, Shane, you come in next.'

'And how will I do that?' I asked, trying to keep exasperation out of my voice. I still think I am 27, but my joints tell me this is not so. I rode too many horses bareback and fell off too many times when I was young. But my husband looks at me like I am still the girl he married. In one hand I had a waterproof grab bag, which held the camera and my purse. I threw it into the dinghy. Tim handed me the painter – the thin rope that is attached to the front of the little boat.

'Wrap that around the grab rail and pass it back to me,' he instructed.

Miriam watched us, amusement flickering over her countenance. She had seen Tim and I bickering many times

I sat on the side of *The Princess Matilda*, my feet searching for the wide rim of the pristine grey dinghy. I hung on to a fender and slid from the deck to the little boat.

'Your turn now, Miriam,' Tim said as he and I shuffled our backsides around to make room for her.

Miriam tightened her life jacket and, with a dogged look on her face, she took a sip out of her glass. She also had a cup of tea on the go. It took a while, but in due course she finished the contents of both and placed the empty containers on *Matilda*'s roof. She sat on her bum with her legs dangling over the side of the mother ship, Tim and I offering words of encouragement. My husband held out a chivalrous arm to help her get from the barge to the dinghy. The three of us all sat very pleased with ourselves once we had her safely aboard.

'Cast off now, Shane,' the skipper courteously requested.

'What?'

'The painter is still wrapped around the grab rail.'

'Oh for God's sake,' I said irritably, as I stood to undo the rope.

Miriam screamed, 'Howay!' as the boat rocked alarmingly and she was almost pitched head first into the river. Tim swore and we all assumed our previous positions.

After a great deal of shuffling and coarse language the painter was undone. We all breathed a sigh of relief, until I noticed something hanging from Tim's back pocket. Miriam saw it too.

'You've got something brown hanging from your arse, Timmy,' she cried.

'It's your wallet,' I called out, recognising one of his recent birthday presents.

We watched it plop into the river. Fortunately the amount of plastic within the leather case held it suspended beneath the surface of the water. Tim dexterously lent over and fished it out.

The ebbing tide took us away from *The Princess Matilda*. Tim was in the wrong position to row, so we all cautiously changed places once again. Miriam was now on one side, me on the other, and the skipper on the plank in the middle. It was all to do with balance.

'I have to sort out my rowlocks,' Tim said, with annoyance in his voice.

'What?' Miriam asked quizzically.

'It's all to do with his oars,' I replied.

'Whores and bollocks. I thought we were going to the pub, not Soho,' said my best friend with laughter in her voice.

No sooner had Tim organised himself and started to row against the tide towards the pub, than the harbour master in his little motorboat arrived to collect the mooring fee.

'You get nothing for free on the Dart,' I explained to Miriam as I pulled soddened notes out of Tim's wallet.

By the time the transaction was complete, we were 100 yards further downstream from our mooring. I took two plastic glasses out of the waterproof grab bag and half a bottle of Nicolas Feuillatte. It had been on special offer at Asda in Weymouth, so I had stocked up. As Tim began to row, the cork erupted.

'Cheers, Miriam,' I said, not wasting a drop. 'Tim can't have any or we'll go backwards again.'

'I don't want any,' he said, grunting as he fought to propel us against the outgoing tide.

Miriam and I had finished the bottle by the time we arrived at the jetty. I managed to throw the painter around a cleat and climbed off the front on my hands and knees. Miriam followed suit.

'Not the most elegant manoeuvre,' Miriam said as I dragged her to her feet.

There were half a dozen families on the small jetty, all with crab lines. No one took a blind bit of notice of two middle-aged women. Sometimes it's good to be invisible. Tim is more agile than both of us and he leapt out of the dinghy.

On entering The Ferryboat Inn, Tim went to the bar and Miriam and I found an empty table.

'If there is a pub with a better view, then I want to know where it is,' Miriam exclaimed as we looked out of the huge picture window.

A woman at the next table overheard us. 'It is beautiful, we're so lucky having this on our doorstep,' she said with a sweep of her hand. 'We have a little ferry that can take you over to Greenway, it's over there on the bend of the river. It belongs to the National Trust now, but it was formerly the home of Agatha Christie. She loved the river. Oh, I am sorry for interrupting your conversation. Do forgive me!'

'Not at all. My husband and I would like to go further upstream. Our boat's moored out there. The big blue one.'

We all turned and stared at *The Princess Matilda*.

'We had a nasty experience a couple of days ago, so we keep listening to the Met Office forecast and moderate seas feature in most of them. So we're waiting for a perfect day to leave.'

A man wearing red corduroys and a navy blue boating blazer came over to the table. I noticed he was also wearing a paisley cravat and that his nose matched his trousers. He had a coat in his hand.

'Come on my dear, let's be making a move. Mummy wants to get the last train to London. Let's relieve her of the *kinder*. The luscious little Lithuanian au pair should have 'em bathed and in bed by the time we get back from the station.'

He looked at Miriam and I and winked. His wife stood up and he helped her into her coat.

'There's a chap at the bar, evidently quite famous. He says that blue monstrosity on a visitor's buoy out there is his. I asked him if he'd brought it by sea. "No," he replied. "We brought it here on the top of a Morris Oxford." I think he was being facetious. He must have had it craned in at one of the local boatyards.'

His wife sent Miriam and I a grimace of embarrassment and we bade her goodbye.

'Twll din!' Miriam said after they left.

I looked at the bar. Tim was deep in conversation with the barman.

'Is that Welsh for twat?' I asked her.

'No, a twat is a twat in Welsh too,' she replied.

'What is it then?'

'Arsehole!'

Tim came over carrying a tray.

'I've just been talking to the governor. He reckons we should call in at Salcombe on our way to Plymouth. And we'd be stupid if we didn't go to the Isles of Scilly. It's not too far out of our way when we go around the Lizard.'

'Oh, I love the sound of that, Tim.'

We all clinked our glasses and said cheers.

'I start a job on 3 May,' Tim said to Miriam. He turned to me. 'We have to find somewhere to leave *The Princess Matilda* for two months.'

'Oh don't talk about that yet.'

We settled into the pub for the rest of the afternoon.

The dinghy row back to *The Princess Matilda* was easier for Tim. The tide was still going out and we got back to the boat in no time at all. Back on board, Miriam and I sat in our chairs wrapped up in blankets. We had run out of fuel for the stove. In true Dunkirk spirit, we worked our way through the rest of the Asda emergency rations. When it ran out we all danced and sang old music hall songs from our compilation tape. 'Howay,' we all sang.

We dropped Miriam at Kingswear the following morning. She was driving to Cardiff to visit her mother.

'Don't forget, Miriam, you have to be on board when we get to Wales at the end of the summer,' I shouted as we waved her goodbye.

'You said that last year!' she replied.

There were a couple of new boats on the visitor's mooring at Dart Haven Marina. As usual, we were all swapping stories: who had had the biggest waves and the most broken glasses. They told us horror stories about the size of the waves out on the mouth of the river. Tim and I had listened to the Met Office. A slight sea was forecast with hardly any wind.

'And a good tide to take us around to Salcombe. Come on, let's take a look. If we don't like it, we'll come back,' Tim said with a devil-may-care look. I have heard this before. We put on our life jackets and untied our ropes.

Chapter Twenty-Two
This is England

Dartmouth to Salcombe: 16 nautical miles

We left half an hour before high water, pushing the tide out of the river. A gentle nor'easterly wind was blowing. Tim said it would be in our favour.

'It's perfect out there,' Tim said. 'The visibility is good and the waves look fine.'

We settled down to our usual routine, except I had mislaid my road atlas. I picked up one of Tim's books instead. I was surprised to find it interesting.

'According to *The Shell Channel Pilot*, Salcombe is not an estuary because no "river debouches through its arms to the sea". I love the sound of that. It also says the town of Salcombe lies on a Ria, which, according to the author of your pilot book, is "a drowned valley". I always thought Ria was a character in that old sitcom *Butterflies*.'

'He's a lovely writer, what's his name?' Tim asked.

I shut the book and looked at the cover.

'Tom Cunliffe,' I replied.

'I've been reading it. He says there's a tricky sandbar at the entrance to Salcombe, so I'm shitting it a bit, in case we don't have enough water to clear it. You know what happened to Paula and Ron on *Cailin* when they came into Poole Harbour? We also have to keep clear of Skerries Bank and Start Point. Here, have a look at the chart.'

'In a minute,' I said, which meant 'no thank you'. Reading the pilot book was one thing, looking at charts another. I gazed out of the windows. All of the wheelhouse doors were fastened back. Hardly a breeze ruffled my hair.

'Wanna cup of tea?' I asked.

Tim shook his head.

I went below and checked all the catches were across the drawers and cupboards. I had carefully wrapped all the remaining crystal glasses in bubble wrap and put them away until the winter. Plastic tumblers would do. Tim had used a strap and tied the two chairs against the radiator. Everything was ship-shape. *The Princess Matilda* hardly moved as we cut through the perfectly blue, tranquil sea. I rejoined my husband in the wheelhouse and scanned the horizon.

'It's just us out here,' I said as I put my arms around his waist. 'How lucky are we my darling?'

Then I screamed.

'WHAT? WHAT?' Tim said with terror in his voice.

'Look over there, about two o'clock from the windscreen wiper.'

'OH MY GOD!' Tim cried out. 'Fuck me!'

Three dolphins were leaping in perfect symmetry out of the water about 50 yards away. We stood transfixed as they disappeared, and then in seconds they soared out of the sea and the sun caught their glistening silver hides as they arched their spines on our portside. We could have touched them, they were so near to our open door.

'Go on, baby,' I whispered, not wanting to scare them away, but our engine is so noisy, it wouldn't have made much difference.

'Go on my darlings!' Tim shouted. He knew it wouldn't matter.

Then I began to hyperventilate. 'Ohhh yes, yes, my God, ohhhhhhh my God…' I shouted as they kept changing places. First one led, then they would fly through the air and another would take its place.

They swam with us for several minutes, Tim and I dashing from one side of the boat to the other as they swam beneath the hull, and then they were gone. Tim and I both scanned the horizon in vain for another sighting.

'Amazing, I can't believe we saw dolphins. Why didn't we take any pictures? Damn,' Tim said, taking my hand.

We stood together and looked towards the shoreline. There was a patchwork quilt of sun-drenched fields on the sloping hillsides. The deep, rich chocolate of the newly ploughed earth had what looked like toy tractors turning over the soil. Seagulls swooped down, the riches of the ocean ignored as earthworms were thrown up by the ploughs. In between were fields of succulent pea-green pasture. Ancient hedgerows embroidered with spring blossom, the palest blue of the Sloe and the palest pink of the May, enclosed them all. Yellow gorse shone on the common land.

'We live in the best country in the world. It is a green and pleasant land we live in,' I said as I clicked away on the camera.

'I'm sick of the detractors,' Tim agreed. 'Look at it, it's so beautiful.'

'I understand what they fought for now. They must have looked behind them when they left the coast of England on 5 June 1944. All those young men heading for the Normandy beaches,' I said.

I looked towards the patchwork where sheep and cows were grazing. 'Ploughmen, dairymen, shepherds … my dad.'

'When did Jim leave?' Tim asked.

I thought for a few moments before I replied, but he knew the answer.

'The Mulberry Harbour was built by the time me dad got to Arromanches. Mom received a telegram from him on 5 June. She didn't hear another word until March 1945. I still have the letter; she gave it to me for safekeeping. "You're the historian, the keeper of precious things, precious memories."'

'You are my darlin'.'

I thought about the many letters Tim had received when he was ill. One sticks in my mind. It reminds me of Winston Churchill rallying the nation after Dunkirk. 'We shall fight on the beaches…', but this was from Big Clive Mantle, an old friend of Tim's.

DEAR SPALL,

FIGHT THIS BASTARD.

FIGHT IT FOR YOU.

FIGHT IT FOR YOUR FAMILY.

FIGHT IT FOR US.

FIGHT IT FOR THE FUTURE.

BELIEVE IN YOURSELF.

BELIEVE IN YOUR BRILLIANCE.

BELIEVE IN YOUR FAMILY IN THEIR ALL-CONSUMING LOVE FOR YOU.

BELIEVE IN YOUR FRIENDS AND COLL-EAGUES, WHO, WITHOUT EXCEPTION, REALLY LOVE YOU, RESPECT YOU BEYOND MEASURE, AND ARE ALL FAR BETTER PEOPLE FOR HAVING KNOWN YOU. WE ALL OWE YOU SO MUCH.

FOR YOUR LAUGHTER.

FOR YOUR FRIENDSHIP.

FOR YOUR BRILLIANCE AND YOUR INSPIRA-TION.

NOW YOU ARE BEING CALLED ON TO INSPIRE US AGAIN.

IT SHALL BE THE BIGGEST AND MOST CHAL-LENGING JOB YOU'VE EVER HAD TO TACKLE.

I'M PROUD TO KNOW YOU.
I'M PROUD EVERY TIME I SEE YOUR NAME IN
THE *RADIO TIMES*.
I GLOW.
THAT'S MY MATE, I VAINLY SAY.
FROM 4 AUGUST 1974,
OUR FIRST DAY AT THE NATIONAL YOUTH
THEATRE,
YOU STOOD OUT FROM EVERYONE ELSE.
YOUR TALENT AND PERSONALITY.
WE ALL WATCHED MIGHTY YOU.
YOU AND ONLY YOU.
YOU STOOD HEAD AND SHOULDERS ABOVE
EVERYONE ELSE.
A FIERCE LOYALTY TO YOU STARTED THEN.
AND A PRIDE WHICH HAS MAGNIFIED COUNT-
LESS TIMES SINCE.
ON *WHITE HUNTER BLACK HEART*, I WAS SO
PROUD OF YOU.
WHEN I SAW BIG CLINT [Eastwood] BITING HIS
FINGERS TO STOP HIMSELF RUINING A TAKE.
HE WAS LAUGHING SO HARD.
THE VEINS WERE STANDING OUT FROM HIS
NECK.
HE CHANGED COLOUR.
I WANTED TO RUN AROUND THE UNIT AND
TELL THEM YOU'D BEEN MAKING ME LAUGH
LIKE THAT SINCE 1974.
I AM THINKING OF YOU SPALL!

White Hunter Black Heart. That was the first job Tim had done
abroad for an extended time. He was away for weeks. I still have
one of the few letters he wrote to me in an old Filofax:

My darling, all I can say is I love you so very much, I hate being away from you and can't wait to get home. I yearn with my whole being to be with you. I love you, I miss you, I want you, and I need you, nothing more to say. Tim x

It is more or less the same letter my dad wrote to my mom in 1945.

The Princess Matilda passed safely over the Salcombe sandbar and we entered a magical kingdom. There were houses perched on the top of cliffs, with secret steps down to private coves.

'It could be the Med, look at the white beaches,' Tim exclaimed.

'Or Africa,' I replied. 'I've been reading up on it. In the seventeenth century the locals were captured and sold as slaves in Algiers.'

We didn't have time to discuss this further as I went to the bow to take photographs. I noted there was no room for us on the small harbour front, but Tim had booked us a mooring out of the town.

He shouted to me, 'I'm going to get some diesel.'

We pulled alongside the not-so-picturesque fuel barge. There was a man standing on it. Tim had radioed ahead. The man was wearing wraparound reflective sunglasses. Both of us chatted to the glasses as he filled up our diesel tanks. He wasn't impressed with my questions about the slave trade or our tales about the dolphins.

'You'd be best going on to the bag,' he said, pointing upstream. 'The bag will keep off the swells.' Those were the only words he spoke.

Tim looked at the price on the fuel pump and paid cash.

'That's just what Tom Cunliffe advises,' the skipper said as we undid our rope.

To my great disappointment 'the bag' was nowhere to be

seen but there was a pontoon with a skip. We moored up for the night. I read the pilot book as Tim threw our rubbish into the skip. When he joined me I told him we were assured of 'a peaceful berth … the disadvantage is a long dinghy ride to the town'. We ate at the Bistro Princess Matilda. It was so quiet as darkness fell. There were a few boats on swing buoys, but they were all empty. We fell to sleep listening to the hooting of an owl.

Salcombe to Plymouth: 22 nautical miles

'Oh fuck a duck!' Tim yelled, but I was already out of the door, rushing to fend off.

He and I had just untied our ropes from the visitor's pontoon. According to Tim's tide table we were on a flood tide. We didn't realise just how quickly it was coming in. The tide grabbed hold of *The Princess Matilda* and took her upstream sideways as Tim tried to turn her around. We were heading towards a group of small boats on swing moorings. I grabbed a fender, thinking we were going to smash the little boats to smithereens, but Tim managed to bring our Princess around. We missed the last of the innocent craft by inches. Once we were clear I went back to the wheelhouse.

'We didn't hit anything did we?' Tim asked anxiously.

'It was close. I can't believe how quickly that tide is moving,' I said, wiping the sweat from my palms.

'I really had to fight to bring the heavy old bitch around to seawards – that's the boat not you, Mrs Spall,' Tim exclaimed, relief written across his face.

We pushed the flow tide out past the fuel barge we had used on the way in. There was no sign of the man with the sunglasses.

'I'm really nervous about going over that sandbar, as I've only researched coming in, not going out, but I'm going to follow those two,' Tim said, pointing towards a small sailing yacht and a RIB. 'They seem to know where they are going.'

There was very little other boat traffic about once our guides over the bar turned left. We waved them goodbye and headed out to sea.

'I thought you said we were going to turn right, Tim?'

'I will when we're two miles south of the Mew Stone off Bolt Head,' he replied.

'But I thought the Mew Stone was off Dartmouth?' I said, looking at my trusty road atlas.

'I think it's a Devonshire thing, a name they give to stone islands off the headland.'

'Mew as in cats?' I enquired, peering through my binoculars at the green fuzzed island outcrops.

Tim thought for a while, zooming in on his satnav and then looking at his sea-charts.

'Or the mew of seagulls? I'm not sure, but we have to look out for a couple near Plymouth. For the time being I'm leaving this pair off our starboard side because the charts show there will be tidal rips.'

I could only imagine what damage a tidal rip could do to us.

'I'm so relieved the sea is calm again today,' Tim continued as he pulled the steering wheel around. 'I've set a course of approximately 300 degrees and we'll hug the coast now for 16 nautical miles. Just keep a look out for the Great Mew Stone off Plymouth Sound. The visibility's not great, but I reckon we should see it in about an hour or so.'

I kept taking up my binoculars and searching the horizon. Occasionally I walked on to the open back deck to check our towed dinghy. We had christened it *New Si* in memory of Simon Channing Williams. Inspecting our small inflatable also gave me an opportunity to look back to where we had come from. I enjoy this as much as looking ahead. To see things like the Mew Stone off Bolt Head gradually shrink makes me understand how slowly we travel. I don't mind this. Tim often says that air travel has made the world a smaller place. But travelling at six knots makes you understand how large our world is, and how varied the British Isles are. I joined Tim in the wheelhouse.

'Was it Robert Louis Stevenson who wrote, "To travel hopefully is a better thing than to arrive?"' I asked Tim as we crossed Bigbury Bay towards Plymouth.

'I think so,' he replied. 'I think I can make out the Great Mew Stone off Plymouth Sound.'

I looked behind me. The Mew Stone off Bolt Head had disappeared.

'OH MY GOD!' I yelled.

Tim turned around. 'WHAT? WHAT?'

'There's a puffin over there, look!'

'For fuck's sake, Shane,' Tim said sharply, 'I thought we were under nuclear attack. Please don't yell like that.'

'But it's so cute, look at it, it's like a little aquatic parrot. I've never seen one before.'

I disappeared down below to find my bird book. Once I began to turn the pages, I lost track of time. Tim eventually shouted down to me, 'Shane, can you come up here, darlin', please?'

The VHF radio was crackling when I returned.

'Did you catch any of that?' Tim asked me.

'No, why?' I replied.

'There's a navy ship about to commence firing. I tried to take down the position but the pencil snapped. I'm sure it will be miles out at sea, I mean they wouldn't be firing towards the land would they?'

He didn't sound convinced. I searched vainly for a pen in the new logbook. Then I emptied the contents out of the pencil tankard we keep in the wheelhouse. It was full of clothes pegs and Tilda's crayons.

'Why can't we ever keep a pen or pencil up here?' I complained.

Tim was looking under all the maps and guidebooks. We had no time to worry about being blown out of the water as we were too busy ranting about biros. We were both annoyed, secretly blaming each other for losing the pen.

'That's the Great Mew Stone over there,' Tim said to stamp on the slumbering monster of a domestic. Our rows always begin about silly things.

'It looks like a little volcano.' I replied, calling a ceasefire.

*

Midnight
I cannot find a pen except Sadie's crayon and I cannot find you.
I sit outside of our bedroom. I cannot imagine a life without...
> *stop!*
> *I see the moon and the roof tops. I try not to think.*
> *Concentrate.*
> *I see what?*
> *I see the moon – I cast a spell.*

It's a secret and it must already be working because I found a pen under the bed. Everyone is asleep but me. When I was having my bad seizures, sometimes I could stop them by concentrating. Spells.

Ooh I want to smash this, stop this. I hate – not good hey? I want to hit the wall with my fist, to break my hand and cause myself pain to take away the pain in my heart, but sensibly I sit on the balcony and sniff the air. It's a warm summer night. I leave the doors open and look over the rooftops towards the hill, but I

know when I go in you won't be there. Mom's snoring like a drain.
My brain, I wish it would stop. It buzzes and fizzes, but do you
know what? I know that if I indulge I'm done for. Those dogs next
door are barking. I'm barking too, I want to howl. I have to shut
the doors. Timmy, Timmy, if I go downstairs will you be there asleep
in front of the telly? If I try really hard, I can conjure you up, but
you dissolve. But I shall phone the night nurse first. Her Jamaican
voice is always so reassuring, it heads off my panic.

*

Harmony was resumed. We knew we were in no danger; we
were too close to lighthouses, batteries, breakwaters and great
big battleships at anchor. We knew they wouldn't be firing our
way. Why bomb a lighthouse?

'We're approaching Drake's Sound,' Tim explained. 'Read
me out the pilot notes, will you, love?'

I picked up the book and discovered a pencil had been
used as a bookmark. I put it behind my ear and quickly
scanned the page.

'It says you can pass east or west of the breakwater.'

I looked through my binoculars. Waves were breaking
against the breakwater. Common sense really, I thought. That
is what it is for. I turned around to see what was going on
behind us. A large ship had appeared out of nowhere. I pointed
it out to Tim.

'It's moving very quickly, maybe it's a ferry, they go to
Spain from Plymouth,' he said.

There was a neat lighthouse on one end of the breakwater.
Tim had decided this was the route we should take. Plymouth
was about a mile away. We could see ugly concrete high-rises
that overshadowed the Georgian terraces on the water's edge.
The city had been bombed unmercifully during the Plymouth
Blitz of 1941. But Tim and I stopped commenting on the view
as we realised we had a war ship chasing us.

What moments before had been a dot on the horizon was now heading our way. We heard the captain speaking to the Queen's harbour master over our VHF.

'I better get a move on,' Tim said. 'But I'll keep just outside the buoyed channel so we're not in the way.'

'It's a bit like that film, *Duel*,' I said with my back turned to Tim, 'where that driver is being stalked by that malevolent truck.'

'He was driving a red Plymouth Valiant,' Tim said as he looked behind to see how far away our pursuer was. He gave Matilda some more revs.

I watched the beast moving closer. 'It's called F931, the *Louis Marie*, and it's flying a red ensign.' I gave a hoot of delight; there were three Canada Geese swooping in formation before the sleek silver navy ship as it cut through the waves, heading upstream.

Tim knew he wasn't going to beat it. I heard the engine slow until it was just ticking over so we could let her pass. We waved to the captain on the bridge.

'Thank you *Princess Matilda*,' crackled over our radio. The sailors and the geese ignored us. The frigate went one way around Drake's Island, the geese the other. We followed the birds. We were able to relax a little now.

*

The first job Tim did after we were married in 1981 was *Remembrance*. The film was about a group of young sailors on leave. It was all filmed on location in Plymouth. We had just moved into a hard-to-let council flat in Brixton. Pascale had started a new school. It is difficult to believe now, in the days of instant communication, that we did not have a telephone in our new home. We had to wait a month for the GPO engineer to put in a line. I wrote a hundred letters and Tim sent me daily telegrams. Pas and I ticked the days off. We were going to get a train to

Vincent Oddie on his RIB in Poole Harbour, August 2008. Lord knows how they managed to sleep under a tarp.
(Photo Anne Oddie)

The SeaCat ferry coming into Weymouth just after we arrived in September 2008.

Visiting Portland Bill Lighthouse on a crisp winter's day in 2008. The sea was flat calm, but Tim's already worrying about the infamous Portland Race.

Sunset over Weymouth, as we wait for a window
of good weather to leave in April 2009.

We finally arrived on the River Dart in April 2009.
Tim's relaxing with a glass of lemonade on his brand new dingy.

Tim rowing us to the Ferry Boat Inn at Dittisham.

My best friend Miriam Jones and I making the most of emergency rations of champagne as we wrap up against the chill of the evening on a swing buoy on the River Dart.

The sublime
Helford River,
midsummer 2009.

Nick Bailey the
Helford River man
(pretending to drink
out of our recycling!)

The Helford
Patrol man giving
Tim some petrol
when *New Si*
broke down.

Tim and I leaving the Helford River in September 2009.
(Photo Paul Crompton)

A VIP aboard - our granddaughter Matilda pretends to steer *The Princess Matilda*.

With Patch Harvey and the Penlee RNLI crew in Newlyn Harbour.
(Photo Paul Crompton)

The Penlee Boathouse, unused since 19 December 1981,
after the tragedy of *The Solomon Browne*.

A seal in St Ives awaiting his dinner.

The Princess Matilda in Padstow. Tim's fast asleep on a blazing hot September day so I've hidden him away from the sun.

Tim force-feeding (a seasick!) Paul Crompton beer and lobster.

Arriving in Wales with flags flying.
(Photo Paul Crompton)

WE MADE IT!
(Photo Paul Crompton)

join him for her half-term break. Tim was staying on the harbour front in the Mayflower Hotel. Pascale and I loved it: we had a panoramic view of Drake's Island and Pas had a single bed in the corner of the room. After breakfast we would go exploring, but we couldn't go too far as she only had little legs. The hotel had a babysitting service, so in the evening I would put her to bed and then Tim and I would join the cast and crew in the bar.

This was all new to me, mixing with actors. But now, looking back, I think everyone was in the same boat. It was a young cast and everyone pretended they had worked on loads of films. Most of them were straight out of drama school. The film was a big deal as it was one of the first to be commissioned for Channel Four. It's hard to imagine that we only used to have three television channels. Gary Oldman, then an unknown actor, was cast in one of the leading roles. He played a matelot who had the shit kicked out of him. I was glad it wasn't Tim. I wouldn't let Pascale watch the film when it was shown on TV. It was very violent. She complained about the injustice for weeks, until one day she came home from school and said, 'That's not fair. I can't watch Dad as a sailor, but I can see him being a pervert!'

'What on earth do you mean, darling?' I asked her.

'We had a film today about not talking to strangers, and there was Dad looking like he was going to molest some kids!'

I couldn't really ague with that. Over the years Rafe and Sadie had to suffer the same jibes. 'Your dad's a perv!'

Don't Talk to Strangers was the first time Tim worked with Brenda Blethyn, who played a policewoman. The job paid for a secondhand Vauxhall Viva.

*

Tim and I phoned directory enquiries as we travelled into the harbour, but the Mayflower Hotel no longer existed and we couldn't agree where it used to be.

'That's it!' I would say, pointing towards a 1960s blot on the landscape.

'No, no, Shane, don't you remember it was by Plymouth Hoe?'

We agreed to disagree as Tim called our pre-booked marina over the radio. We were directed to a hammerhead in the Mayflower Marina and tied up quickly so we could survey our new home.

Across the harbour from our mooring was the grandly named Royal William Victualling Yard. Designed by Sir John Rennie, it looks more like a royal palace than a brewery and bake house. The pale shining Portland stone hid away the Mills Bakery, which housed steam engines that drove 27 millstones to grind the corn and huge ovens to bake the bread. The beer and bread had fed the Royal Navy, but it had been many years since any victualling had gone on.

'I'm surprised it's not been turned into a shopping mall or executive apartments. Come on, let's explore,' Tim said.

We found an empty flocked wallpapered Indian restaurant just the other side of Plymouth Hoe. After we got our food we understood why we were the only customers. It was pretty dreadful. But not even a poor curry could dampen our sense of achievement. *The Princess Matilda* only had one night by the Victualling Yard as a trip boat seemed to take great pleasure in speeding past us. I think the skipper did it for fun, as he left behind a wake that seemed designed to punish us for being outsiders. Tim and I would hide and watch as he crossed from Drake's Island, picking up speed as he passed just feet in front of our bow. Usually boats slow down as they pass moored boats. The wake made *The Princess Matilda* shake and my cups fall into the sink. It reminded us of our first night in Ramsgate's outer harbour. Tim phoned Yacht Haven Marina and we moved there the following day. It was not as attractive but we could sleep without being thrown out of our bed. Tim's agent had arranged for him to do a voice-over while we were in Plymouth, so we caught the ferry over to the old town. I explored while Tim went to the studio.

The old town was crawling with tourists. Trip boat operators were touting for business. I looked for our tormentor but he was nowhere to be seen. Boards with pictures and timetables were prominently displayed and just in case anyone missed them, hawkers rang bells and yelled.

'*From here, ladies and gentlemen, Walter Raleigh sent a ship to what is now known as North Carolina. The vessel left this very quay on 27 April 1584, the anniversary is just a few days hence. On 13 July the land was claimed in the name of Queen Elizabeth and called Virginia in her honour...*'

Another tout was shouting even louder. '*In 1620, ladies and gentlemen, the Pilgrim Fathers sailed from near this spot on The Mayflower. They made landfall after 66 days at sea...*'

I left them to their shouting and found The Dolphin, a pub where I had arranged to meet Tim after his voice-over. It was a lovely old boozer with some familiar pictures of large women on the wall. I sipped my cider and took a look around. The landlord joined me and pointed out his favourites. I saw Tim outside the open door speaking on his mobile, so excused myself and went outside.

'He played me!' the governor said when Tim and I went inside the warm cosy pub.

'I'm sorry?' Tim said, bemusement all over his face.

'Beryl Cook, those are her pictures on the wall, and you, Timothy, played moi!'

'Good lord,' Tim said, turning to me. 'Do you remember I did the voice-over on an animated film with Dawn French and Alison Steadman a couple of years ago?'

The landlord interrupted. '*Bosom Pals*, it was shown on BBC One. It was all about fat ladies in this very public house!'

'What a small world,' I said as we boarded the ferry to take us back to the marina after lunch.

I received a text as we disembarked. Tim walked ahead and I stopped to read it.

'WE MADE IT! WE ARE JUST PASSING DRAKE'S ISLAND. WHERE ARE YOU MOORED? x ANNE'

'Good God, Tim,' I shouted, running to catch up with him. 'The Oddies are here on the RIB.'

'Don't be so stupid, it's over 130 miles from the Solent to here. You'd have to be completely mad to do it in one go,' he replied.

'Well, that's why I took no notice of the emails when Anne said they might do it...'

We were walking past some yachts up on the hard, but something familiar caught my eye.

'That's *Cailin*,' I said.

The little sailing boat was on blocks and a long wooden ladder went from the gravel to the side of the boat.

'Hello!' I shouted. 'Anyone aboard?'

Paula's head and Ron's grizzly beard appeared over the cockpit and they both climbed down the wobbly ladder. We all slapped each other on the back and swapped stories, the kind that involve high seas, danger and running aground. We all knew they were true.

'Where to next?' Ron enquired.

'Cornwall, of course,' Paula replied on our behalf. 'The same as us. *The Princess Matilda* will have another head start, but we're hoping to get to Wales before September.'

'So are we, I've been thinking Swansea or Cardiff. But we have to get around the dreaded Lizard and Land's End first. We're leaving on the tide tomorrow,' Tim said.

'We've been worrying about the Lizard all winter...' Ron replied.

Paula interrupted him. 'Why do sailors like to scare you to death? We've heard so many horror stories! But I'm sure we'll meet again soon. It's a small world.'

We left Ron and Paula and headed back to our boat. I sent a text to Anne and told her where we were moored and invited them onboard for tea. They both looked grey when they arrived, and Anne was shivering. I opened a bottle of champagne.

'I think you deserve this. How many hours did it take?' I asked her.

She used two hands to bring one of my two remaining crystal saucer coupe glasses to her lips. For a moment I thought I had been rash to get the best glasses out of the bubble wrap, her hands were shaking so much.

'Six hours ... this is a lovely cup of tea.'

Tim and Vincent were talking ten to the dozen. Sea-charts were all over the floor. Anne and I sat silently drinking champagne. She took my hand and mouthed 'thank you'.

We finished the bottle and opened another. Tim told them we were leaving for Fowey the following day.

'But we have arranged to leave *The Princess Matilda* there for several weeks, so if you get sick of kipping on the RIB, feel free to use her while we are away,' I said to Anne, who now seemed to have feeling back in her limbs.

'A new film is it Tim?' Vincent enquired as he and Tim folded up the charts.

'Yes, it will take six weeks, but Shane has an old boyfriend coming to stay with us for a couple of days in London...'

I interrupted, 'Michael is not an old boyfriend! Well, if he was it was so long ago it doesn't count! I've already booked the flights from Newquay to Gatwick. We'll have three days to explore Fowey.'

Chapter Twenty-Three
Pirates and Pipes

It was April when we left Cornwall for London. It was mid-June before Tim managed to get back to Cornwall. I had flown down to Newquay with Sadie the week before to check everything on the boat was in order. The cab dropped us off at Fowey Town Quay. We waited for the water taxi to take us upstream to where we had left *The Princess Matilda*. Tim and I had gotten to know Stubbles, the taxi man, over the few days we had spent there after we left Plymouth. Stubbles is as about as Cornish as you can get.

'When he first picked us up,' I said to Sadie as we waited for the taxi, 'we were moored over there.'

I pointed to a place mid-river, which was empty when we had arrived in April. Now yachts were anchored thick and fast.

'There's a pontoon just around the corner. It was just your Dad and me. We had one of our rows.'

Sadie laughed. 'I'm glad I wasn't around then.'

'Oh, you know what he's like. He winds me up until I scream at him.'

'Yes, I know, Mum Chum, I've heard you enough times, and then you start slamming doors and go for a walk to cool off.'

'That's just what I did. I slammed the door and realised we were moored in the middle of the river. There was nowhere to go so that made me even more furious. I sat on the toilet with the door shut. Look, here's the taxi.'

It was high tide and Stubbles expertly tied up at the top of the town steps. Half a dozen people joined us and he helped us all onboard.

'Good afternoon, Mrs Spall,' Stubbles said as he lifted down our suitcase. 'Where's Timothy?'

'Earning the shrapnel for the Grid Iron,' I replied.

Stubbles chuckled, 'O' he'll need a few bob to pay for tha', be a couple a gran' at least.'

Sadie was tugging at my sleeve. It is amazing how my kids all revert to being ten years old when I have them to myself.

'What's the "Grid Iron", Mum?' she demanded.

I knew Stubbles would eventually answer for me. He reversed the taxi off the quay and we all looked behind us and watched the black and white skull and crossbones ensign flapping vigorously. Stubbles spun us around and we sped away from the town. He turned towards Sadie as he lit his pipe. I could tell she was thinking, 'You can't smoke when you're at work.'

'The Grid Iron, tes' somewhere the pirates won' find you. I'll be droppin' you off las',' he said, winking at Sadie.

Or maybe the pungent smoke was getting in his eye.

The water taxi has a small open cabin with side windows. Stubbles drives sitting on a stool. He rests his smoking elbow on the window frame. I am not sure if he loves or hates his job. He appeared to me now to be more sunburnt than earlier in the year, but somewhat more jaded.

Back in April he had told Tim, 'I work seven days a week, twelve hours a day durin' the season. Come October an' I've had enough. Me an' my wife go to South Africa an' come back to Polruan in February.'

Polruan is the working half of the beautiful river. On our last night he had picked Tim and I up from the village and pointed out his house. We crossed over to Fowey to pick up a passenger from the Town Quay. It was dark; the only light was the glow from the end of his cigar. He smokes a pipe during the day and Havanas at night.

'How many windows ha' lights on?' he asked us.

Except for the waterside restaurants and the snaking street-lights up the hill, we could see very few.

'Tes' because there'll be second homes. Local's born and bred can't afford to live in Fowey. Come the school holidays it'll be a differen' story all together. The whole town will be illuminated.'

I remembered this conversation as Stubbles dropped off his passengers on to their various craft until there was just Sadie and me remaining.

'How many drunken sailors have you seen safely home recently Stubbles?' I asked him.

'Besides you an' your husban'? The usual average pissed tes' all. That's why I like to give 'em return tickets. Some of 'em can't remember where they moored.'

The three of us travelled for ten minutes upstream. As the river narrowed, trees replaced the picturesque holiday cottages. I spotted *The Princess Matilda* hidden away behind some fishing boats. She was moored on a narrow grey pontoon. It looked like something an iron rests on. But I am sure years before a tin mine existed somewhere close by. Opposite was an industrial wharf with cranes.

'Welcome to Grid Iron,' Stubbles said as he helped Sadie and I off the taxi.

'I've been keepin' my eye on her,' he said, as he gave me my change for our return tickets. 'She got a bi' of china clay on her from the clay boats tes' all.'

He tapped the contents of the pipe into his hand and shook it into a bin.

'Call me on channel 6, and I'll pick you up later. I expect you'll be wantin' to have some dinner in the town.'

We waved him goodbye and Sadie and I boarded *The Princess Matilda*. I called Stubbles back sooner than anticipated. Our hot water system wasn't working. Sadie couldn't cope with a kettle of hot water and an all-over wash, so I phoned the local hotel and Stubbles took us back to Fowey. He was smoking a fat cigar.

'I can't imagine what he smokes at home, Chum,' Sadie commented as we waved him goodbye.

Tim, on his return, was made of hardier stuff. The hot water still hadn't been fixed – we needed a completely new boiler – but Tim is handy with a flannel, unlike Princess Sadie. He doesn't mind an all-over wash. Sadie flew back on the plane he arrived on. As we climbed out of the cab on the Town Quay on our way back to our boat, someone from the RNLI was coming out of the British Legion.

'I love your work. I'm the coxswain of the Fowey Lifeboat,' he said to Tim, shaking him by the hand.

'I admire the job you do too, but how did you end up in Cornwall?'

My husband has a keen ear for regional accents, but even I recognised this one. We find Geordies are great fans of Tim's earlier work. The coxswain brushed some crumbs off his oily jumper.

'It was too cold up north.' He looked behind our heads and waved. 'Stubbles is on his way. You have your boat on Grid Iron I hear. How long are you going to be in Fowey?'

'There's a high front, so I'll do my passage to Falmouth and leave the day after tomorrow. We only have ten days. I start a new job in Manchester soon. So we hope to find her a secure mooring. This one here is pretty good, but I'm dreading the bill,' Tim said as he picked up his roller bag to take down to the steps.

'Aye, it's not cheap. You want to see if you can find a swing buoy, that'll be cheaper.'

Stubbles helped me onboard, and shook Tim's hand.

'You've go' a yach' rafted against *The Princess Matilda*,' he said. 'Bu' it's a classic, a beautiful lookin' thin', I think they're leavin' for the Helford River tomorrow.'

Tim and I decided not to mind. But we were a little bit annoyed.

Our new neighbours guarded their privacy as much as we did ours. They waved and we waved and all of us disappeared inside our own boats. The first thing I planned to do was fill in the skylight over the bathroom. After we unpacked Tim and I thought the weather was too fine for us to sit indoors. Our neighbours had the same idea, so we all appeared on our decks with a bottle. They invited us aboard theirs. It seemed bad manners to refuse and the skipper insisted he show us around.

Lutine was a beautiful sleek yacht. We climbed down a steep ladder backwards to get inside. Clive the skipper was very proud of her and showed us every nook and cranny. The yacht was over 100 years old and had recently been restored. Gillian, the skipper's wife, asked us where we had come from and where we were headed.

'Well you can't go around the Lizard until you have visited the Helford River, it would be a sin,' Clive said. 'And moreover I have some swing moorings available, so if you need…'

Tim interrupted him, 'We do! I start a new job soon.'

'Does your engine need a service?' Clive asked as he took out a pen. 'I can get one of the lads to pick her up and take her up to Gweek Quay on the Helford river. We've got a boatyard at the top of the river. Do you need anything else done?'

Lutine left on the early tide the following day. We did not hear a thing.

*

I had been in communication with Paul Crompton since we left Dartmouth, and we had all agreed he should spend a day filming with us when we left Fowey. I told him to get a lift up with Stubbles. Tim spotted the water taxi heading upstream as it dropped off a couple of boys who had a sailing dinghy on the pontoon.

'We're expecting a man with a camera, have you seen him Stubbles?' I asked him.

'I saw somebody. A shifty lookin' fella on the quay, but I though' I'd better check with you firs',' he replied. 'I hear you have a moorin' in Helford.'

'News travels fast,' I laughed.

While we were waiting for Paul, I sat on the Grid Iron pontoon enjoying the sunshine. I had a book of short stories by Daphne Du Maurier on my lap. Stubbles, the mine of information, had mentioned she used to live nearby. Hearing a commotion, I stood up and saw a fat evil-looking seagull emerging out of the water. It looked hideously deformed but then I realised it had an orange starfish in its hooked beak. My book fell on the pontoon as I stood, the pages barely moving in the breeze. I picked it back up and saw it had fallen open on *The Birds*. I had not read the story, but had seen the Hitchcock film on many occasions. Who can forget Tippi Hedren having her hair messed up as she runs from the marauding gulls? I looked up and decided I should wear a hat. There were quite a few gulls circling about. I didn't want them shitting on my head. Seagulls do that. I grabbed my straw-boater out of the wheelhouse. Tim was inside swearing at the satnav.

'I've forgotten how to use it,' he complained.

I left him to his instruction manual and went back to my book.

Moored at a rickety wooden pontoon behind *The Princess Matilda* was a small fishing boat. The crew was tidying their nets. I waved to one of them and she waved back. I noticed tiny little jellyfish swimming in the clear water. A cute family of moorhens appeared from a hiding place, the newly hatched chicks squeaking and paddling to keep up. Like a bolt of lightening, the gull swooped. The smaller birds were dive bombed and scattered. The gull had gone for the hen.

'Tim!' I screamed as the seagull began to flap its wings for take-off.

The fisher-lady threw something and the cannibalistic bird dropped the prey from its cruel talons with a splash. Tim rushed out of the boat to see what the hullabaloo was about.

'Look, the moorhen, she was kidnapped,' I explained as we watched the little family taking shelter underneath the low-lying branches of the riverbank. 'No wonder Tippi Hedren had blood running down her face on the poster.'

Before I could elaborate, we noticed the water taxi coming upstream. Paul, who had a grin like the Cheshire Cat, was coming aboard. Stubbles held on to the side of *The Princess Matilda* as Paul passed us all his gear. There wasn't too much.

'How beautiful is Fowey?' Paul said in his strong Salford accent.

'Tes' pronounced Foy,' Stubbles said in Cornish, his pipe clenched between his teeth as he readied to leave.

'Welcome aboard, Paul,' Tim and I said in English.

'Wanna cuppa?' I enquired as Paul followed me down the steps.

My husband interrupted me, 'Oh get him a beer. Sorry about the mess, we've had engineers in trying to mend our boiler.'

There was a gap in the airing cupboard where the old boiler used to live. The engineers had removed the door to take it out and used my best IKEA towels to wipe up the mess. I had made arrangements for a new boiler to be delivered to Clive's boat-yard in Gweek Quay on the Helford River. I had looked up where it was on my road atlas.

Stubbles called us on the radio as the kettle came to the boil and said there was room on the water point. We had two tanks to fill up and Stubbles had pre-warned us how difficult it was to get on to the pontoon with the taps. Tim and I lost no time untying our ropes and made our way downstream very quickly. We were careful not to leave a wake, mindful of the moorhen's nests.

'Why do you need water if you can't shower?' Paul asked us.

'I still have to wash up and use the washing machine,' I explained.

'And it's ballast. It keeps the bow in the water,' Tim added.

I could see one end quarter of the long water pontoon was free. But before Tim could turn around to moor against the ebbing tide, a sneaky yacht crossed our bow. It moored dead centre of the free space. It had 25 feet ahead and 25 feet behind. The vessel was about 15 feet long.

Stubbles buzzed over to the yacht in his water taxi. We could see a discussion was going on. After a few moments a cloud of smoke appeared out of the window of the taxi, along with a thumbs up. We thanked the crew who had made room for us. While the hose was in our water tank, Tim and I walked up the gantry to pay our mooring fees in the Harbour Office. Stubbles had been right in his estimation. Tim winced a little bit. When the water tanks were full we undid our lines and left to make room for others. Fowey River in summer was so different from the one we experienced when we arrived in the early spring. Small craft were everywhere. The pirate Stubbles was crossing over to Polruan, weaving in and out of the RIBs and dinghies. We all waved to him.

Tim and I both spoke at the same time.

'I'm going to miss Stubbles!'

'I loved his accent and he's so proud to be Cornish, I just didn't realise Cornwall is a different country,' I said as we came out of the estuary.

'The Corrrnish accent,' Tim said, rolling long arrs around his tongue. 'Starrrts at the front of the mouth and ends at the back of the throat. I did a radio play not long ago and mentioned to one of the cast that we would be taking *The Princess Matilda* to Cornwall. He said, "My grandma was Cornish. She called the English egg-jellies." "What's an egg-jelly?" I asked. "You go to any pub in Cornwall and you will hear an Englishman at the bar saying *Ec-tually*, or to a Cornish ear, *egg-jelly, I'll have a pint of your best, please Landlord.*"

Tim was happy to have a fresh audience for his stories. Paul did a lot of laughing.

Fowey to Falmouth: 23 nautical miles

'I hope this isn't going to be too boring for you, Paul,' Tim said as we lost sight of Fowey. 'The visibility's pretty bad, but with a bit of luck we might see some dolphins.'

'Hey, this is great,' Paul said. 'I'm loving it. How long will it take to get to Falmouth?'

'About four hours,' Tim replied.

I went below to make some sandwiches. I was cutting the doorsteps in half on the chopping board when Paul bent down so he could peer through the doors down below. He shouted to me quite urgently.

'Shane, Tim says to come up here quick.'

I looked out of all the windows. I could see nothing that warranted any urgency. The sea was dead calm, there was no wind. It could have been Battersea Boating Lake. I took my time and took the sandwiches up into the wheelhouse.

'Emergency rations,' I said. 'What's up?'

'Over there, look,' Tim said pointing out of his open door. 'It's a war ship and it says it's going to commence firing.'

The VHF radio crackled into life again. Fortunately there was a pen in my logbook. Tim and I both had our ears next to the radio. I tried to take down the firing coordinates but the signal was weak, and whoever was giving them was not from the United Kingdom. Tim looked at his sea-charts.

'It says we are entering a target practice area, do you think they know we are here?' he asked me.

'Of course they do, now do you want a sandwich?' I replied. Tim shook his head. He can't eat when he is anxious.

'But they might bomb us out of the water!' he said as he looked through the binoculars.

I turned to Paul, 'Do you want one?' Then I remembered he was supposed to be invisible.

I sat down on the canvas chair and read the newspaper. There's nothing quite as good as reading the *Daily Mail* when the Spanish Navy is stalking you.

We arrived in Falmouth, unscathed, at teatime. Tim and I had not booked a mooring because we were only staying one night. Everyone we had spoken to had said there would be plenty of room for us; there were three marinas. Sod's law, not one of them had space for us, so the harbour master suggested we use a mooring buoy. I was used to this routine by now, so I stood at the bow armed with my trusty boathook. I don't quite understand why Tim becomes so apprehensive when I do this. He tells me that he is afraid I might fall in and drown when I lean over to grab the buoy.

'How many times have you fallen in Tim?' I have asked him on many occasions.

'Five times,' he replies shamefully.

'And how many times have I?'

I knew he would be joining me on the bow shortly. He never lets me down.

Once we were safely tied up to the buoy, we called for a water taxi, or in this case the 'Aqua Bus', to take us to the pier.

'How wonderful it is to come into a new town by sea!' Paul exclaimed.

There were kids sitting on the steps, smoking dope, and a boy playing guitar. All three of us live in South London so we all felt perfectly at home. We waved Paul goodbye. He had a long road journey ahead of him before he got to his bed that night. Tim and I were more fortunate. Aqua Man took us home. We left for the Helford River the next day.

Chapter Twenty-Four
The French Connection

Falmouth to Helford River: 6.5 nautical miles

Crossing Falmouth Bay on a calm sea was a joy. Tim turned *The Princess Matilda* into the mouth of the Helford River easily. During the nineteenth century, the Cornish coastline was infamous for shipwreckers and pirates. The wreckers lured ships on to rocks for plunder and the pirates sneaked into secret creeks. As I sat on the bow of *The Princess Matilda*, taking photographs, I didn't know which way to look. A river has two banks but this one had rocks, woods, coves, beaches, old wharves and seven creeks. The river opened to a wide pool. Putting down the camera, I gazed ahead. There was a line of yachts tied up to swing buoys. We gave them a wide berth. These, according to the *Reeds*, were visitor's moorings. Although we were visitors we had been allocated a Gweek Quay buoy. These were a different colour to the rest, and to the left of the others. But they were all taken. I phoned up the number Clive had given me and spoke to his assistant, Sarah, who said to moor on one of the visitor's buoys if there was one free. She said we could move to theirs the next day. Tim had no choice but to leave me to snag this lump of floating security on my own. The wind had picked up and he had to watch that we didn't hit anything. I felt very proud that I did it first time. But this was because the buoys had neat little floats, so no more hooking the boathook into a ring. I snagged the float out of the water. It was attached to a rope, which was attached to a chain.

Tim came up to help me haul in the heavy chain.

'So this is the Helford River,' I said as we both pulled on the clanking slimy shackles.

'There's a strong easterly blowing up the river that'll hit us broadside when the tide turns. I want to make sure we're well and truly tied up,' Tim grunted as he heaved more iron on to the deck.

'I'm going to hang some washing out, I'll leave you to it,' I said as he tied intricate knots.

Slap, slap, slap, went the waves. There were white horses galloping towards us and the wind could not make its mind up which way *The Princess Matilda* should face the breakers. Tim eventually joined me on the back deck.

'You'd better watch out that washing doesn't get blown away. I can't see us getting ashore on our dinghy today. It's too rough, we'd sink!' he said, wiping his hands down his trousers.

The wind whipped up the sheet. I added more pegs.

'It will be dry in half an hour.'

A couple of the people on the yachts looked longingly and suspiciously our way. There was a free buoy behind us, but they were rafted against yachts the same size as themselves. All of them were flying French ensigns.

'Maybe they didn't like our Union Jack?' Tim commented.

After hanging out the washing, I sat down and re-read the opening page of *Frenchman's Creek*. It seemed so relevant.

'Listen to this Tim. "*When the east wind blows up Helford River the shining waters become troubled and disturbed and the little waves beat angrily upon the sandy shores.*"'

'Well it's an easterly wind,' Tim replied, 'and the waves are beating angrily by that beach house over there. But I have to look at my script for half an hour, so you enjoy the scenery.' He was about to commence rehearsals for a film for television, *The Fattest Man in Britain*.

While Tim looked at his script, I managed to get online with my dongle. 'Hey Tim, that beach house,' I said, pointing to a house on the shore. 'Guess what?'

He looked up from his script. 'Nice place to have a house, it looks like it's surrounded by jungle,' he said.

'Well I think it must be the house mentioned on this website. It was used by the Special Operations Executive during the war and some bizarre raiding party left here in 1941...'

His phone rang.

'That's great,' he said after he hung up. 'Can you change our flights? They've put the dates back, we have three extra days.'

'Brilliant.'

I logged into my Flybe account. 'Where shall we have our lunch?' I asked him once I had confirmed our new tickets.

'There's supposed to be a pub in Helford village. The *Reeds* says there's a ferry. I'll give them a call. We won't be able to row.'

But the ferryman said he couldn't get to us as the wind was making it too difficult to get away from his jetty.

'What you going to conjure up darlin'?' Tim said hopefully.

I looked in the fridge. 'There's half a dozen very small new potatoes left over from the night before last night. Two boiled eggs, possibly on the turn. A bit of curled up ham from the Fowey butchers, some cheese from the same shop, half a tomato, some stale bread and a few leaves of an organic cabbage.'

'You're a clever enough cook to turn that into something tasty,' he said as he grabbed an egg and swallowed it whole.

Then he burped.

'That's horrible!' I complained.

'Thank you, I think it has the essence of a hot afternoon in Karachi.'

We had an elegant if somewhat rocky luncheon onboard as the waves crashed against us. I carefully unwrapped the crystal glasses and laid out our linen tablecloth and napkins. We dined al fresco. As we ate our hors d'oeuvres we watched a steady stream of French boats arriving on the last of the tide. Our table was sheltered from the wind by the wheelhouse. The doors were fastened back and we had a dining room with a view. After our main course of cheese on toast Tim showed me where we had moored on his sea-chart.

'Over there past the beach house is Port Navas Creek. We can row up that at high tide. On the other bank ahead of us is Frenchman's Creek. I can't see any of those Frenchmen rowing up there today can you?'

Our boat had swung around. The part of the river we were facing now was dyed an emerald green, taking on the pigment of the oak trees smothering the hillsides. The only break in the colour was a steel-grey band of rocks on the water's edge. Tucked beneath the trees almost camouflaged from view was a boathouse. There was a flight of stone steps and a slipway cut into the rock.

'This really is the heart of Du Maurier country,' I said.

I left Tim on the deck and went into our cabin, where I had put away my book. It was open, so I put in a bookmark and carried it back up with me. For seven days I had been rationing myself.

As I rejoined Tim on the deck he pointed to a free buoy just ahead of us. 'They must hate us, because if they were to use that buoy they know they'd get walloped as *Matilda*'s fat arse comes around with the tide.'

French yachts were rafted five abreast.

Tim took my book from me. 'You're on the last chapter. How about I row you up there when you finish it? But not tonight!'

We went to bed listening to the slap of the tide and the clatter of halyards on the Frenchmen's yachts. I read *Frenchman's Creek* and dreamt of pirates.

The trill of my phone woke us the next morning. It was Sarah from Gweek Quay. She said our buoy was now free. I lit the gas and put our battered kettle on to boil. Looking out of the galley window I saw we were facing a completely different direction. The tide was now slapping on our starboard side. The green boathouse and SOE beach house on the opposite shore had disappeared. That is the marvel of a swing mooring. The state of the wind and tide dictate our outlook. Through our port side windows the Helford River glistened upstream towards Frenchman's Creek. From our starboard windows sunbeams lit up the surface of the sea. All of the French yachts were facing the same direction as us.

'There're even more of them now,' I said to Tim.

He was still enveloped in goose down. What I love most about *The Princess Matilda* is that her galley and cabin are in close proximity. When our kids were small, Tim and I longed for space. Now it is just the two of us, we enjoy stepping four paces and climbing back into bed to drink our tea.

Tim sat up in bed. 'I'll have a quick swill after this and we'll move to the Gweek buoy. Free up this one for the Frenchies,' he said, sipping his tea.

It was a perfect summer's morning. The sun streamed through our open windows. When Tim was dressed we put on our life jackets. I took the helm while he untied our ropes from the chains. It took a while. Three yachts raced for our vacated space. It is dog-eat-dog in the boating world. I put *The Princess Matilda* into forward gear as Tim walked down the gunwale. He took the wheel as we passed our old neighbour, the stately *Lutine*. According to Sarah our buoy was beyond her.

'The tide's coming in pretty quickly,' Tim said. 'I'm going to make a wide arc ahead of that anchored yacht over there in the middle of the river and come back against the current. Somehow I don't think Clive would appreciate us getting too close to his pride and joy.'

We came around 180 degrees, but our dinghy took a short cut.

'Tim!' I yelled. 'We've lost *New Si*!'

The painter was cut as we came across the yacht's anchor chain. Like an Olympic athlete off the starting blocks, *New Si* made a break for it. The flooding tide carried our dinghy upstream. *The Princess Matilda* and *New Si* were heading in different directions like a couple of squabbling teenagers. The French yachts, I noticed, were still hovering over our old swing buoy. I don't speak French but even I understood, *Fuck me that crazy Englishman is going to kill us.* They scattered before us.

Our engine screamed as Tim put our boat into reverse gear. We did a figure of eight around banks of rafted craft with people shouting *Merde!* It took a while before we were heading once again in the right direction. We chased *New Si*, heading it off. I was at the helm whilst Tim battled with the boathook, trying to snag the little brass hoop where the torn painter had been tied.

'I've got it, but we have to swap places, leave the wheel quick,' he cried.

We exchanged places.

'I'm going to get as far away from all those yachts as I can, so for God's sake don't lose the dinghy.'

Once in the middle of the river he put *The Princess Matilda* gently into reverse so that we stayed in the same place. I found another rope as Tim dragged *New Si* to the side of the open wheelhouse door. He lay down while I hung on to the dinghy. I thought for a moment he was in danger of falling into it head first.

'It's no good,' he said as he stood up. 'I can't reach the hoop.'

'Why don't you hold the boathook and lift the front up, then I'll have a go?'

'Just be careful,' Tim said as he pulled with all of his might.

The back end of the dinghy began to fill with water but I managed to get the rope through the ring. 'Well that was fun,' I said once the errant dinghy was firmly attached to *The Princess Matilda*. 'Let's go and claim our buoy.'

After we were tied up, Tim called the ferry. The tanned blonde ferryman was built like a rugby player. Tim and I were a little disappointed he wasn't Cornish. His name was Nick and he was an ex-public schoolboy from Oxford.

'I married a local girl,' he explained.

Nick dropped us off with our recycling at the Sailing Club jetty. I left Tim in the clubhouse while I went to the Post Office and general store. Nick had told me the best way to go. The champagne was extremely expensive, but our holiday was coming to an end so I bought two bottles along with three tomatoes and a loaf of bread. I asked the postmistress why there were so many French boats about.

'Oh, it's the 50th anniversary of L'Aber Wrac'h race!' she replied like I should know what this meant.

I walked back to the Sailing Club. The tide was out so I was able to walk over the stream that flows into the Helford creek. The water was cold but my feet were dusty in my flip-flops so I plunged them into the water despite the chill. I felt like I was ten years old again. I noticed tiny transparent baby crabs and wondered how long they would last once the seagulls found them. But there were no seagulls around, just a single white egret in the shallows. It picked up one long graceful leg and placed it carefully back as if it was testing the water, just as I had done. Suddenly it spotted me. Neither of us moved. Soon the bird decided to ignore me and bent down its snowy white head. Its black dagger-like beak was barely above the surface of the water. For a moment I imagined it was studying its own reflection but then it snapped. A fish was swallowed in one go.

Tim was sitting outside on the crowded balcony when I got back to the Sailing Club. The clubhouse sits high on top of a hill. I was out of breath and whatever I had left over was taken away from me by the view.

Tim put a gin and tonic into my hand. 'We've been all over the world,' he said. 'But have you ever seen anything to beat this?' The sea on the bay was turquoise. Yachts with multi-coloured sails danced in the gold-flecked sunlight.

'That's Nick, crossing the river, look how he's having to zig-zag his ferry to keep out of the way of all the boats.'

It took me a while before I realised only Tim and I were speaking English.

'We could be in Cannes...'

'*Non, Bretagne*!' a small woman said, interrupting me as she squeezed by my chair.

'My *grand-père* helped your English RAF escape from occupied France during the war. L'Aber Wrac'h is where I live and for as long as I can remember a member of my family has taken part in The Race. There on the north shore of the Helford River the airmen were picked up before being debriefed in Dartmouth. My *grand-père* kept in touch with one of the pilots. They are both dead now, but for many years they raced each other in their yachts. Then they would get drunk around my *grand-mère's* table and talk about old times.'

She disappeared before I could question her. Out on the balcony it was standing room only.

Nick had allowed us to tow *New Si* behind the ferry so we could row back with the tide. Because of the festival there were lots of different local races going on. Four long gigs, wooden high-sided rowing boats, were on the jetty. Several bonny girls boarded their craft without giving us a second glance, not even when Tim launched himself into our boat. It was squeezed amongst dozens of others. I followed suit.

We had never heard of gigs before Weymouth. That was the first time we saw a crew rowing a long, thin boat across the bay. Now of course we know they were practising for the Scilly Isles' gig races in June. The original gigs were used to chase out to ships needing a pilot into port. It was extremely competitive and still is. We have watched teams practise on the Dart, Fowey and Helford rivers. Men, women, old men, old women, young men, young women, all kinds of crews.

Tim rowed us back with the beginnings of an incoming tide. The next few hours were spent lazing about on *The Princess Matilda*. I could not help myself; I sat in the sun and finished my book.

'Lady Dona should have run away with the pirate!' I sighed as I put the book on the step.

'Come on then darlin',' Tim said, 'let's go and take a look at the Creek.'

I grabbed the gin, some ice and tonic and threw our grab bag into *New Si*. Tim helped me get off *The Princess Matilda*.

'We're on the last of the flood tide,' he said as he began to row. 'It's about a quarter of a mile to the entrance to the creek.'

Tim sat rowing backwards. I faced the way we were heading. 'Take us by the boathouse, I want to have a look.'

'No,' Tim replied, 'I'm staying midstream.'

Swish, swish went his oars. Grunt, grunt, grunt went his lungs.

'Here, let me help you,' I said as I shifted to join him on his plank.

We had one oar each. Splash, splash, splash, my oar went. Swish, swish, swish went his.

'We are going around in circles,' Tim complained. 'Give me back the oar darlin'.'

And this is how we entered the fabled Frenchman's Creek, where pirate ships with red sails hid from sight. It was 7.30, but close enough to the summer solstice to be one of the longest days of the year. I shivered under my life jacket. I wasn't sure if it was the ghost of the swashbuckling Jean-Benoit or simply the lack of sunlight. The high, densely forested banks screened out the rays of the sun. Honeysuckle clambered up the ancient oak trees, as if searching for warmth. The creek was silent except for the slap of Tim's oars. Slanting trees on the shore dangled lichen-clad branches into the emerald forest reflected in the water. The two banks drew closer as we travelled further. I could almost reach over and grab a branch. Eventually Tim stopped rowing and we let the tide take us up the creek until a fallen tree trunk stopped our progress.

The water now was sluggish and smelled of salty must and mud. We whispered to one another, not wanting to break the spell. There were 20 shades of green in the water and the trees. A nightjar called out and, as if by a pre-arranged signal, a black-bird began to sing. Tim lay back in the dinghy as I poured out our cocktail.

'I will remember this for the rest of my life,' I whispered as I passed him our shared plastic cup. 'Will you read me something?' I asked as I reached for my book in the grab bag. 'Close your eyes and open it anywhere.'

This is a game Tim and I often play. Tim opened the book randomly and began to quietly narrate.

'The solitary yachtsman who leaves his yacht in the open roadstead of Helford, and goes exploring up river in his dinghy on a night in midsummer when the nightjars call, hesitates when he comes upon the mouth of the creek, for there is something of mystery about it even now, something of enchantment. Being a stranger, the yachtsman looks back over his shoulder to the safe yacht in the roadstead, and to the broad waters of the river, and he pauses, resting on his paddles, aware suddenly of the deep silence of the creek, of its narrow twisting channel, and he feels – for no reason known to him – that he is an interloper, a trespasser in time.'

He handed me the book and took a swig of gin.

'That's us,' I said wistfully. 'Interlopers, trespassers.'

Tim scratched his balls, farted and said, 'That's easy for you to say, but I'm sweating like an old orangutan. Rowing up here was murder. But do you know what? I've loved it too. We're a couple of mad inseparable sods who've taken to the waters, brackish, alcoholic and wave infested. Top me up me darlin'.'

When the gin was finished we sat side by side, Tim teaching me how to row. It was 10pm when we got back onboard *The Princess Matilda* and still light. We could not see anyone on any of the French yachts.

'They must all still be at the Sailing Club. I picked up a programme on the way out,' I said, showing the booklet to Tim. 'It's party night, the race to Brittany starts in the morning. I heard somebody say it's about 98 miles to L'Aber Wrac'h.'

Just as I finished reading the programme, fireworks exploded into the darkening sky.

*

Miriam had arranged a black cab on Jimmy's account to pick up my mother, Rafe and Sadie to take them to see Oliver! *at the Palladium. I'm at the hospital so much, I hardly see them. It makes me happy that they can all go out and enjoy themselves. My mom is no spring chicken, but they are good kids and don't give her the runaround. Rafe said she panicked when she got in the cab because the meter was running. My mother has worried about money all of her life. She was born into a world of poverty, so it's not surprising really. She has an ache in her heart that will never be resolved. Her father left shortly before she was born. She never knew him. All she has are the sepia photographs that she passed on to me. They say history repeats itself … but Pascale has you as a father and she loves you so much.*

I watch as you become weaker by the hour. I cannot write my midnight notes any more, I am afraid to write what I feel. Instead I take out the sepia photographs and wonder what happened to the man who left my grandma with two children to raise on her own. With the photographs are certificates: births, deaths, marriages and baptisms. My mom was born in 1920. She was raised by Polly, her granny, so my grandmother Nance could work. Nance had two jobs. Hers was the only income. My mother was a little girl during the General Strike of 1926. She knew what is what like to feel real hunger. Her uncles and grandfather were miners.

I am reading Oliver Twist *again. I sit by your bed and the lunch tray is taken away uneaten. As was your breakfast and dinner too. Food glorious food, scraped into the bin. Krissy stopped eating. Her mother used to strain carrot juice through muslin. I walked to Heal's on Tottenham Court Road and bought a juicer.*

*

When we awoke the following morning, all our French neighbours had left. The crowded mooring buoys were all empty. We saw Clive and his crew were aboard *Lutine*. 'I've given them all a head start, I'll still beat them!' he shouted as they unshackled their lines from the buoy.

Tim called Nick to pick us up and take us to The Ferryboat Inn on Helford Passage.

'The Ferryboat's a busy place today,' Nick said when he arrived. 'It's the weekend, people drive here for a day out. The kids can play safely on the beach while their parents eat the local Helford oysters outside the pub.'

Nick has a jetty with wheels that he pushes up the beach with his ferry as the tide comes in so his passengers don't get wet feet. He has a noticeboard that tells you what time he operates. On the opposite shore of the river is the Sailing Club.

'I'd suggest you leave your dinghy by that house over there,' Nick said pointing to a place upstream from the Sailing

Club pontoons. 'It won't be so far for you to row if you need to get some shopping from Helford Post Office. I'm doing myself out of a future fare telling you this, but you really should get an outboard Timothy.'

'Well you've got another fare tomorrow,' Tim said. 'We have to get back to the real world in the morning. Can we pre-book you to pick us up?'

'Just call me on the radio. I'm the Helford River equivalent of a London mini cab,' Nick replied.

'So when I call you, someone will say, "He'll be with you in a minute, he's just at the lights"?'

'No, she will say, "He's just coming around the lobster pot"!'

Tim and I had lunch sitting outside the pub and watched kids building sandcastles on the beach.

'It's all the fresh air that gives us such an appetite, hey Tim?' I said, smothering my chips in homemade mayonnaise.

Tim was tucking into locally caught sea bass. He nodded and stole one of my chips. After lunch we took a walk up the cliffs and watched the fishing boats heading home to the safe haven of the Helford River. It would be many weeks before we would do so again.

Chapter Twenty-Five
The Old Boiler

The Princess Matilda was taken upstream to Gweek Quay while we were away. We had arranged for Clive's boatyard to do some work. When I got phone calls from Sarah I would tell her what I could see in Manchester and she would tell me about Gweek.

'Hi, Sarah. It's pouring with rain and I'm sheltering under a canal bridge.'

'What colour is the water Shane?'

'Sludge brown. What about you?'

'It's low tide, so we have sludge brown too. The sea has disappeared. *The Princess Matilda* is sitting on the mud.'

'That sounds nice. I can see a sign on the canal bridge that says "*Please refrain from any lewd or obscene behaviour.*"'

'Good lord!'

'Well I'm in the cruising centre of Manchester and I'm not on about canal boats, more Canal Street. Tim and I cannot wait to get back.'

'Just let me know what time to expect you and I'll make sure Paul, the marina manager, is here to meet you. *The Princess Matilda* is all shipshape. You now have a new calorifier boiler and, as requested, an autopilot. Rick lifted and serviced the engine, packed the stern gland and filled the greaser.'

'That will all come cheap then.'

'Just a bit,' Sarah laughed.

'I've got a bit in the kitty for that, as long as Tim keeps working, but I just hope we have a bit in the weather kitty bank to get us to Wales this summer,' I replied.

Tim had a gruelling six weeks of working twelve-hour days in Manchester. He gives everything to a part. He was playing

Georgie, a wonderful fat man. The prosthetics alone took two hours. One of the best things about the job was he was working with Frances Barber. He and Frank had met in 1981, when they had both worked on one of Mike Leigh's films for the *Play for Today* series. So Tim has known Frank as long as he has known me. She is godmother to one of our kids. We can never decide which one it is, but it doesn't matter, Frankie is family. Sometimes instead of writing my midnight notes when Tim was dreadfully ill, I used to phone her instead and sob down the phone.

'He's on diamorphine Frankie. He's in so much pain, sometimes he doesn't know who I am. His eyes look through me...'

'Stop it, just stop it! The doctors know what they are doing. That's what chemo does. It half kills you to make you better. Timothy Spall will not leave you. Do you hear me! He will not leave you or the kids. He loves you all too much. Just remember that...'

But sometimes I could tell she was crying too.

As promised, Paul, the marina manager, was waiting for us when the Newquay airport cab dropped us off at Gweek Quay.

'I'm afraid she's rafted against a yacht,' he said as he helped with our bags.

I remembered the fuss I had made the first time we saw *The Princess Matilda* moored at the bottom of a ladder in Brentford. That ladder was a piece of cake. The ladder leading down to the yacht was a rickety old portable wooden thing, the kind that window cleaners used in the 1950s. Paul climbed down first and Tim followed behind. They both looked up at me. I was wearing flip-flops. I took at deep breath and put a tentative foot on the ladder.

'Come on old girl,' Tim said, aping some pompous colonel. 'You can do it.'

'Fuck off Tim!'

Paul laughed, 'Four more rungs.'

They both took an arm as I reached the deck and dragged me from the yacht to *The Princess Matilda*. This obstacle course was made even more difficult because the tide was out. The water was oozing away from the mud, which was bubbling with air pockets. Swallows swooped down on the little water that remained, snapping up flies.

Gweek must be extremely bleak in the winter. It lies in a valley and Sarah had told me it suffers from heavy frosts. Even on an August day the creek at low tide felt abandoned, melancholy. It reminded us of the Medway creeks.

I re-climbed the ladder, reluctantly, to go to the chandlery later that day. There were several people there but I recognised Sarah by her voice. She wasn't anything like I had imagined her. She is very pretty and much younger than I expected. I had pictured her as being a headmistress, but she looked like a head-girl. And like a couple of schoolgirls, we were both shy.

'Paul's got your new outboard on the roof,' she said as we shook hands. 'And unless I'm mistaken that's your Tesco delivery on the wharf.'

We left Gweek that evening after eating fish and chips bought from a mobile chip van which parks once a week by the creek. Tim and I ate them sitting on the grass by the lichen-encrusted arched stone bridge. The Helford River trickles down over a tiny weir from a small and shallow brook above. Mesmerised, we watched the tide trickling up the creek, the salt and the fresh water mingling.

'I could sit here all evening,' I said to Tim as I finished my chips.

'Tide and time wait for no man,' Tim replied, pulling me to my feet. 'We have to leave soon.' He looked at his watch. 'Paul said there should be enough water to get us back down to Helford Pool by eight.'

It was a dingy, drizzly evening when we cast off. We rounded a sad buoyed bend of the creek. To our right was some kind of concrete industrial site. Tim's face was creased with anxiety. He was afraid we might run aground. But the creek opened up to banks vividly green with oak trees that would have been saplings during the reign of Charles I. It is a vista that has not changed for hundreds of years, or so I thought until we passed the Seal Sanctuary. One of the rescued beasts was howling and the haunting sound was carried on the stillness of the air for miles. We saw no other boats until we passed Frenchman's Creek. It was coming up to 9 pm by the time we reached the Gweek mooring buoys.

The light was going very quickly, which made it a little more difficult to get the boathook into the floating ball. Tim and I had words because he insists the way he does it is better than the way I do it. But we managed to do it in the failing light.

'I'm going to put the central heating on,' I said.

I left him on the bow. He joined me in the saloon a few minutes later.

'I thought you were going to put the heating on,' he said as he poured himself a drink.

'I did.'

'It must be broken then, because it's not fired up.'

Our heating comes from a diesel-fired system that sounds like a jet about to take off when it fires up, then it settles to a hum. Tim kept turning the switch on and off. The motor coughed and spluttered then turned itself off.

'We've not had any hot water since we left Fowey. And now we've got a brand new boiler, 'cos the other one sprung a leak and we still haven't got any fucking hot water. The engine at least should give us some,' he said running the tap.

Our engine is water-cooled and the heat transfers to the water tank.

'It's stone cold. How much has all this cost us?'

'A fortune. Come on let's go to bed, we've got to be up at seven,' I said, putting on the kettle for a wash.

'I'm not getting up at seven and then having to wash my bollocks in tepid water with Tilda's hand puppet frog flannel! I've just spent the last six weeks hauling my arse out of bed at 5:30.'

'Well if you want to be taught how to use the new auto-pilot, you will have to. Chris, who fitted it, is coming on his RIB from Falmouth. Sarah says it's the only time he can do as he's racing in a regatta tomorrow.'

*

Following our early morning sea trial with the autopilot, which Tim seemed to understand more instinctively than technically, Chris left us and we pootled about on the estuary for a little while. Tim tried out the new gizmo while I phoned Sarah and said the Webasto central heating wasn't working. She gave me a number for a local dealer as it was a specialised job.

'But you should be getting hot water from the calorifier,' she said, 'your engine is water-cooled. Can you wait until tomorrow? I'll send Rick, our engineer, down at high tide.'

'Thanks Sarah. I'll give the Webasto man a call now.'

I joined Tim in the wheelhouse a few minutes later.

'Set your autopilot for Falmouth. I called the specialist. He said he would be there at noon.'

We arrived in Falmouth at 11. There were no swing moorings free because it was regatta week so we anchored. I put the kettle on and saw the Aqua Bus heading our way. It slowed right down so I opened the window in the saloon to see what it was up to. On board I saw two familiar faces and rushed up the steps to the wheelhouse. It was Paula and Ron, our old neighbours from Ramsgate, Poole and Plymouth. We all waved like mad.

'How long are you staying in Falmouth?' Paula yelled as the bus came closer.

'A couple of hours, we're on the Helford,' Tim shouted back. 'How about you?'

'We're just around the corner, plucking up the courage to get around the Lizard!'

'So are we, we're going to the Scillies,' I yelled. 'But have to get some more work done on the boat first.'

I could tell Aqua Man was getting tetchy, so we all wished each other fair weather and waved goodbye.

'Maybe we'll see you on the Helford?' Paula shouted.

'Maybe!'

My phone rang soon after they left. It was Webasto Man who said he had arrived.

'Where are you?' I asked.

'I'm parked on the quay. Are you going to pick me up?'

I don't know why I thought he would be arriving by boat, but it was high tide so we decided to take *Matilda* to Webasto. It was the easier option. Our dinghy was on the roof of the boat and the outboard was still where Paul had left it the day before. Webasto Man took a line from me and one from Tim and helped us moor on the quay. He then passed me his tool-box and came down the iron ladder. Tim told him the problem, and opened the hatch to the engine room. The man disappeared beneath the deck for a few minutes.

All we could hear was, 'O' dear, o' dear, o' dear! You don' ha' a gooseneck, the salts go' in!'

Eventually he climbed out of the engine room carrying a rusty piece of machinery that he placed on the deck.

'My name be Kevin by the way,' he said as he looked at his watch. 'I'm on an hourly rate.'

He was a small wiry man and I was sure I saw him rubbing his hands together, much like Scrooge, expecting a windfall. We were relieved when he took the motor away to be fixed. He said he would finish the job on the Helford River. Tim meanwhile had put the dinghy in the water and, with lots of difficulty, the outboard. He had several attempts at starting it. Kevin, as he climbed up the ladder to the quay, thought the engine was flooded and to leave it for a little while.

'You'd better be off now, 'afore you ge' hung off this here wall, the tide be goin' ou' quick in these parts, I'll throw down your ropes,' he said.

As we were leaving Falmouth, with our dinghy in tow, I became worried that the outboard might fall off.

'It won't,' Tim said, but I had planted a seed. He threw himself into the dinghy, much the same way as toddlers do when they throw themselves on to a bean bag. As he sat himself upright, a trip boat sped by. The dinghy bounced up and down as it was caught in a tidal wave from the wake. I fought with our steering wheel to keep *The Princess Matilda* steady.

'Do you know what, Tim?' I said once the sea had calmed down again. 'I think they do it on purpose to allay the boredom of doing the same trip day after day. They try and cause as much havoc as possible.'

Tim nodded, but I could tell he wasn't really paying attention. He was kneeling and staring at the outboard.

'Pass me a sturdy rope will you darlin'? I'm going to tie it around the engine, so if I do drop it we can pull it out.'

I could see another trip boat heading our way. We waited for it to pass before Tim unscrewed the motor.

'It must weigh 45 pounds,' he complained.

He now had the whole piece of apparatus laying across his lap. The long metal rod that had been sitting in the water with the little propeller was dripping all over his linen shorts. I made a mental note to pre-soak them to get rid of the oil. I am pretty good at getting rid of stains. The bulbous fat head of the engine was full of petrol; I could smell it.

'OK, get on your hands and knees, Shane.'

'I've not heard that for a while.'

'It's not funny Shane! We should have left it exactly how it was. It wouldn't have fallen off. So just remember if I do drop it into the sea, it will be all your fault!'

'I've not heard that for a while either,' I whispered under my breath.

The gunwale was two feet higher than the dinghy. I bent down on my hands and knees and Tim heaved the propeller part up towards me.

'I've got it,' I cried.

Tim hoisted the rest on to the deck. His face was purple. I leant forward and held out my hand to help him onboard.

'I love you,' I said, giving him a kiss.

He kissed me back then ran his oily hand all over my face.

I cuffed him, 'Let's get back to Shangri-La. I'm going to get that Gweek buoy on the first attempt, and if you get involved I shall kill you!'

*

I'm going to swing for that nurse. All the other nurses are lovely, but this one's a nasty piece of work. Why go into nursing if you hate it? Opinionator you called her at first. 'If I say black, she will say white,' you complained. I wish you would complain now. I sit by you and talk. I don't know what you hear. You are attached to a machine that delivers diamorphine into your Hickman Line.

'Why does he need fucking heroin? When's Panos back?' Panos would explain everything to me. He doesn't mind if I swear. Doctor Rye just raised an eyebrow and pretended not to hear. I know all about heroin. It killed two of my friends. Poor little Sue-Sue. I abandoned her. I ran away from London and the filthy junkies, but she stayed. 'You have to give it up, Sue, come back to Wales with me. I'm going to get a little cottage, we can make bread and grow vegetables.' The good thing that happened after

I gave up drugs was Pascale. I was fit and healthy when I found out I was pregnant. Sue did stop for a while. She got a job in an office and phoned every day after Pas was born. 'Tell me about the baby, I want one. I've been clean now for six months…' Then I had the dream. She was surrounded by fire and she kept calling me, 'Shane, please help me I'm burning please help me!' But the flames were too high, I couldn't get to her. I sat up and wrote her a letter, lest I forget the dream. I put it in the post the next day, but thought I would tell her when she rang me in her lunch break. The phone call never came. I caught a National Express coach to London and knocked on her door. She lived in a squat in Brixton. The door swung open. The house was abandoned. I knocked next door. This too was a squat. A girl I knew answered. Before I said a word she said, 'Have you heard about Sue? She OD–ed. She was cremated today at Golder's Green.'

After all these years, tears fall down my face. Sue was 19 when she died. Her husband, Chad, gave her a hit she couldn't refuse. She used to complain to me, 'I get home from work and there's always stuff on the table. I do find it hard…' Krissy didn't like Sue or Chad. She blamed them for getting me into drugs. But that was my fault, not Sue's. But you, Timmy, you don't have a choice. Rye says you will not get addicted, but I know better. Opinionator is back in the room. I ignore her and hit my keypad harder to show my annoyance. She picks up a card at the side of the bed that Sadie had given me this morning before I took her to school. I cannot believe this woman. She reads it out loud in a little girl voice.

Dear Dad,

I'm in your bed till you come home because I'm scared of Ghosts, when you come home I'll go back in to my bed.

Love Sadie xxx

Chapter Twenty-Six
Mechanicals

'Why am I totally useless at anything mechanical?' Tim said the following afternoon.

My husband was sitting in the dinghy with his huge toolbox open before him. He was even reading the instruction manual. Three kids in a dinghy went by. A nine-year-old was at the tiller of the outboard, which looked just like ours.

I pointed to them and said, 'Even kids can do it, why can't we?'

Nigel, the bewhiskered Helford patrolman, had just towed us back to the barge. He had found us tied up to a buoy to stop ourselves being taken out to sea. It was raining, what the Irish call soft rain, but it was still wet. The trip to the Sailing Club, where we had had a really enjoyable lunch, had been perfect. Our motor hadn't cut out once and Tim seemed to think he had cracked the art of outboarding. It stopped four times on the return trip and eventually he gave up trying to restart it, thinking we'd run out of petrol, and began to row instead. This was pretty difficult against a swiftly ebbing tide. So we tied up to the buoy. Nigel had come to our rescue and, taking on our painter, he took us back to *The Princess Matilda*.

As if the tow wasn't help enough, Nigel also gave Tim two measuring jugs of petrol, out of his spare jerrycan. Fortunately we had a one-and-a-half pint jug, but I have put a funnel and petrol can on the shopping list. But it seemed we had not run out of petrol so Tim had to give half a jug of fuel back to Nigel and they both discussed what else might be the problem. The white knob on the top was stuck fast, maybe that was it? This knob apparently lets the air out. Tim gave Nigel a pint bottle of Chablis from our Tesco booty to show our appreciation. Our kindly Captain Bird's Eye patrolman left us to it and Tim read the manual. I think it was the sight of the nine-year-old that gave him the impetus to unloosen the white knob, the one that lets out the air. He got the motor working again. He was very pleased with himself and gave the kids a derisory look as he cast off. My husband was gone for about 20 minutes and came back beaming.

'Yes, I've cracked it this time, wanna come for a ride?'

'At low tide,' I replied. 'When the tide's right out!'

It had been raining most of the day and the weather appeared to be brightening up when we left for the pub. We both agreed that we were perfecting our method of getting in and out of the dinghy. Tim tied up to the ferry jetty to let me off. It's not a graceful manoeuvre but I did it with as much style as I could muster. My skipper beached the dinghy and just about managed to get off without getting his shoes wet. We pulled it up on to the sand. The tide was coming in slowly so we thought we would have time for a drink before the water reached it. I placed a couple of big stones over the painter just in case, recalling how the pirate had used a stone as an anchor when he took Lady Dona fishing in *Frenchman's Creek*.

The pub and restaurant were busy. Every table was taken, but there was a high stool free by the open window, looking out on to the beach. Tim helped me on to my perch and stood behind me. Next to us were a couple ordering food from a waitress.

'Fancy some oysters darling? Let's have half a dozen. Actually make that 12, let's push the boat out!'

'He just said *egg-jelly*! They are all so posh in here. I think only we two and the waiting staff are working class,' I whispered to Tim.

But before he could respond, the waitress said to the couple, 'So ya. Would you like the Duchy natives or the Helford rock oysters?'

Tim smiled at me and leant over so we would not be overheard. 'Most of the kids who work here are from public schools. Don't you know the middle classes are tight when it comes to allowances? They have to get jobs. She'll be working as a chalet maid in Chamonix during her Christmas holidays, saving up for her gap year.'

I sipped my working-class glass of champagne and Tim his proletariat Chablis, and the restaurant and bar filled up.

We clinked our glasses and said, 'Power to the people.'

Groups kept arriving the same way that we had done. I realised that it wasn't just me that looked like a beached whale when getting out of a rubber boat. We watched other people's technique and thought it was a little bit dumb the way that we had done it. Next time we determined that we would both get off and pull the dinghy along the jetty side to the beach.

When we got back to *The Princess Matilda* we found a note in the wheelhouse. The Gweek engineer had been. 'I forgot to turn the valve on, so if you run your engine for half an hour you'll have some hot water.'

Tim and I were having a cup of tea on the back deck the next day when we saw the ferry heading our way. We had not seen Nick since June when he had dropped us off at The Ferryboat to get the cab to the airport. He was tanned then but now he was the colour of mahogany. He had Kevin, the heater man, with him.

'Hi Nick,' Tim and I both shouted in unison.

'I heard you've been talking to the blonde bombshell about getting parking for this man here?' he said as he came alongside.

He saw our look of incomprehension.

'Sarah, my missus!'

'Sarah from Gweek Quay Sarah?'

'No!' he laughed. 'Helford Passage Sarah!'

'Ah, yes. Have you got time for a cuppa?' I replied.

'No, I'd love to but it's regatta day, so everything is a bit manic at the minute.'

We all helped get Kevin's stuff from the ferry to *The Princess Matilda*.

'You'd better give me the keys to your van, Kevin,' Nick said, 'in case I have to move it.'

Nick went back, leaving Kevin and numerous boxes and tool kits with us. But Kevin had something more besides tools.

'Here you are my dear,' he said with relish, handing me two paper bags. 'Real Cornish parhsties.'

They were still hot. I thanked him. I hadn't the heart to tell him I didn't eat meat.

'We'll have them for lunch,' I said and took them inside where Tim was making him a cup of tea.

When I went back up top the whole of the wheelhouse floor was covered with open tool- and cardboard boxes. Carefully I picked my way across the deck. This was difficult on an undulating boat with restricted space.

'I now know why sailors dance "The Hornpipe",' I said as I manoeuvred myself around the open hatch to the engine room.

Kevin's head poked out. With a flourish he grabbed a carrier bag and took out what looked like a loaf of bread. 'A real Cornish Cake,' he said. 'You can' ge' it anywhere else. Cornish Saff-rron Cake, bew'fu' with lots of budder my handsome.'

I thanked him heartily for his thoughtfulness and when Tim brought up the tea, Kevin chuckled. He pointed at Tim's head above the lid of the open engine room. 'He'll enjoy tha' he will.'

He disappeared back down under the deck. He was eating a sausage roll; there were several more in his carrier bag.

Kevin was with us for over three hours. In the boxes he had three metres of exhaust pipe. Ours apparently needed replacing. Plus three metres of exhaust lagging, four new exhaust clamps, one new thermo burner, one new glow pin, one new thermo ninety flame sensor detector, one exhaust silencer with bracket and one burner tube. I know this because he told me so. He gave me a running commentary. I also noticed he was getting more and more annoyed, even though I kept bringing him more tea and saffron cake.

Nick came back at about 12:30 and asked if it was OK to move Kevin's van up to the car park, as they needed to bring down the St John's Ambulance. Kevin said that would be fine and went back under the deck muttering. It occurred to me he was happiest when I gave him my total attention, for I noticed my saffron cake was still uneaten. I thought this a bad sign, so I stopped reading and even stopped looking at the scenery. When we had first met him in Falmouth, Tim had christened him Dame Edith Kevins, and now I realised how insightful he had been. I think Kevin was giving a performance and it wasn't working out the way he had planned. He couldn't get the fucking heater to work.

'Tes' no' workin', I'll 'ave to come back with some techn'al back up for this here 'puter.'

Our Dame assured us this would clear the faults on the brain of whatever he was doing under the deck.

After the ferry picked up Kevin and his numerous toolboxes and computer, Tim and I took *New Si* to the visitor mooring in Helford. It is *egg-jelly* a private jetty but the owner has an honesty box where you are supposed to pay £2.50 a go. We had moored there before. It is a short walk up to the pub and Post Office. We needed a loaf of bread and to get rid of some rubbish. The flimsy jetty was full of kids who immediately spotted Tim. They all nudged each other, squealing and shouting,

'IT IS! HE'S IN HARRY POTTER! PETER PETTIGREW!'
Meanwhile I was doing my beached whale impersonation
getting off the dinghy on all fours.

'He's Popeye the sailorman at the moment,' I said, but
they ignored me, only having eyes for Pettigrew. By the time
Tim had tied up and got off the dinghy himself they had gone
ahead to tell anyone else in the vicinity that Ron's rat had just
got off a dinghy. Pettigrew went to the rubbish bin while I
went to the Post Office. I bought a paper and the bread and
we returned to the boat. In all we were away from the mooring for 7 minutes. It had cost us about 37 pence a minute
to park.

Tim said, 'Expensive loaf that hey?'

*

*I just had a to-do at Sainsbury's. I had to park the car on the
main road because a huge lorry had blocked the entrance to the
car park. All I wanted was some organic citrus fruit just in case
you fancied some juice and to get some groceries for home for the
kids. I tried to pay with my brand new Switch card that apparently hadn't been activated, so the checkout girl pressed a button.*

I said, 'Is there a problem with the card because I can pay cash?'

She said, 'No you can't!'

'I would like my card back please,' I said, looking at my watch.

'You can't have it,' she replied.

*I was becoming visibly upset because I didn't want anything
delaying my getting to the hospital.*

'So what's the problem?' I asked. 'I need to go!'

*'It says phone the bank,' indicating that anonymous machine
behind the till.*

*Two men appeared and took my card, saying 'Follow me', as
if I was some bloody shoplifter. People were staring and I became
even more upset and angry. My life was so out of control that I
could not even buy a fucking grapefruit or a toilet roll. You are*

*in hospital fighting for your life and I'm being dragged through
a supermarket in south-east London. It is surreal.*

*'Excuse me!' someone yelled from quite a distance. I ignored
the pompous voice because I have a name on the card, it's Mrs
Spall. He comes to me.*

*I try to calm myself and explained I was worried about my car
on the main road, because of the lorry blocking the car park. The
manager rushed off, not to see about my car I suspect, but rather to
see what was happening with the traffic jam that must have been
three miles down Lordship Lane. I should be writing up my thesis
now, as I sit by your bed. If I could tell you about what happened
you would laugh, but you just lie there. The grapefruit sits in a bowl.*

*

We scrambled back into *New Si* and headed over to Helford
Passage to the pub.

'But the beach is packed, I don't want to go there, Tim,
let's go back to *The Princess Matilda*. The jetty is thronged and
the pub is heaving,' I grumbled.

For years we have avoided regattas and festivals, but for
some perverse reason Tim wanted to go to The Ferryboat Inn
that day. He kind of wedged the dinghy under the jetty. I
climbed off the front and stepped up while half a dozen under-
five-year-olds in wetsuits were lined up ready for a swimming
race. I did this really elegantly, inasmuch as I wasn't on my
hands and knees. This was because there was a railing that I
could grab on to. I edged my way along the outside. It wasn't
very far, maybe about six feet before I got off on to the beach.
Tim, meanwhile, with great agility, leapt off *New Si* and up and
over the railing.

'Not bad for a fat girl,' he said as he pulled the boat to the
end of the jetty. I helped him to drag it up on to the sand. The
refreshing thing is, no one took a blind bit of notice of us.

Absolutely no one. We walked up the beach and the MC man kept giving his commentary, calling out the races.

We had an astonishing afternoon sitting outside the pub watching the races. Tim and I had never been to a regatta before.

'There's something so quintessentially English about it,' Tim observed.

'Dunno if the Cornish will approve about you calling them English. Stubbles won't like that at all!'

A pretty girl called Alice, a local girl and not a Sloane Ranger, served us. I had put Kevin's pasties in the freezer. Nick and his wife Helford Passage Sarah came over. We had not met her before. Her husband was quite right: she was a blonde bombshell. It appeared everyone knew them, patting Nick on the shoulder as they passed and waving to Sarah. By no means was it a perfect day; the rain fell but the races continued. Alice kept out of the way of the sailors in the pirate's hats. They obviously thought they might have a chance, but I think they had drunk far too much cider and Alice definitely knew they had.

The tide had gone out some way by the time we were ready to leave. We had to carry the dinghy down the beach to the shore, and then we set off back to *The Princess Matilda*. We were about halfway when the engine cut out. Tim kept trying to start it.

'Fuck, fuck, fuck,' he shouted. 'This time we really have run out of petrol.'

Captain Nigel Bird's Eye was nowhere to be seen. He was no doubt busy patrolling the regatta so Tim rowed back against the tide, grunting and cursing with every stroke.

We took *The Princess Matilda* down to the Sailing Club to take on some water the following day. I walked up to the club to book a table for lunch. It is quite a steep and arduous climb up the hill but the spellbinding view across the river is always worth the effort. Our boat looked huge and blue in total contrast to all of the grey dinghies moored to the jetties. I asked Alli, the stewardess, if she knew where we could get petrol for the outboard. 'Helston' was her reply. This was no good for us without a car. When I got back to the boat I told Tim and we decided we would get the ferry back to the Sailing Club after we were tied back on our buoy. I was becoming quite an expert at getting that swing mooring now. While Tim was tying off the chain, I called the ferry on the radio but got no reply. Tim had a go and he got no answer either, so he rowed us down to the club with the tide. I had a couple of empty beer bottles in my bag to put in the recycling, and the measuring jug, just in case. As we walked up the pontoon we passed a chap with a can of petrol. He very kindly gave us a jug full.

'Thanks my friend, you've saved me the agony of rowing back to our boat against the tide,' Tim said, shaking his hand.

The Sailing Club car park was packed.

'I'm glad you booked us a table, Shane.'

Tim fought his way to the bar while Alli showed me to our table. The interior of the Sailing Club is not particularly attractive. The names of all the commodores are written up on the wall in gold leaf. I noticed the last name was a woman's.

'Nordic log cabin style circa 1979,' Tim said as he joined me at our table. 'But the view makes up for it.'

Alli came over to have a chat with us once the tables began to empty.

'That's the best Sunday lunch I've ever had,' Tim said.

I shot him daggers.

'Besides my wife's of course. Who's the chef?'

'My husband, Greg Laskey,' Alli replied. 'He used to work at the Trelowarren Estate. He received two AA rosettes when he was there,' she said proudly. 'We've only been here since April.'

'Well he's got a third rosette now from *The Princess Matilda*,' Tim said.

After lunch we clambered into the dinghy and Tim started the outboard. It worked first time.

We flew to London early the next morning. Tim was doing publicity for Jimmy McGovern's highly acclaimed BBC drama, *The Street*. It was a short but stressful visit to the metropolis and when we returned to our Cornish paradise we organised a driver to meet us at the airport. I asked him if he would mind stopping off at a garage. Tim fell asleep as soon as he got in the car and when he woke up we were back at Helford Passage with two 5-litre cans of petrol that Gary, the cab driver, had very kindly filled up for me.

Paul Crompton was at the pub when we arrived. The documentary series about the voyages of *The Princess Matilda* was now green lit. He had spent the day filming up at Gweek and around Helford Passage. We had a few drinks and dinner with him and discussed our plans about going around the Lizard the next day. The weather forecast was ideal.

'The Lizard has turned into the bogeyman now,' Tim explained to Paul. 'I asked a Falmouth pilot if he had any advice about getting around it, he replied, "Yes, don't!"'

I left them to chat while I phoned Kevin. He had promised to work on the boat while we were in London. As people do in isolated areas, I climbed on to a wall to get a signal, but Kevin's phone went through to answer machine. Oh I do hope you are aboard *The Princess Matilda*, I thought as I watched the ferry approaching the jetty. Then my phone rang. Not wanting to lose reception I stood still. It was Kevin.

'I'm jus' at Helford Passage now,' he said, 'but I can' get dow' to *The Princess Matilda*, tha' damned ferry's no' runnin'.'

'Oh, really?' I replied as I watched half a dozen people boarding.

'So I'll come dow' in the mornin' if tha's OK.'

'Yes, Kevin,' I said with frost in my voice.

I joined Tim and Paul, who were sitting in the sun outside the pub.

'I'm afraid we're not going anywhere tomorrow. Kevin says the ferry's not running so he went home.'

We left Paul at The Ferryboat. Tim would have liked to have stayed longer but I insisted it was time we went back to *The Princess Matilda*. My husband was tanked up on more than the two gasoline containers. Kathy, one of Nick's summer assistants, was on ferry duty. She was very patient. Tim asked her name three times and spoke with passion about Charles Bukowski. Kathy had read American Contemporary Writers at Cambridge.

Nick brought Dame Edith Kevins up at about 9:45. I didn't put the kettle on. He just had the one toolbox and his computer this time. Tim stayed in bed. Goodness knows what the Dame did but the Webasto fired up. I called Nick on the radio to come and collect our errant electrician and studied the invoice he had just given to me. It was for over a thousand pounds. Nick arrived and took the toolbox off Kevin.

'Kevin said he drove all the way from Falmouth last night and couldn't get up here Nick,' I said.

Nick looked at me quizzically and Kevin sheepishly boarded the ferry. I felt rather sorry for him; I don't take prisoners.

'But Kathy said she dropped you and Tim off at 9:30 last night,' Nick said.

'She did.'

'I thought you were going to leave this morning?'

'We were but we had to wait for somebody,' I said, staring at Kevin. 'And now we've missed the tide.'

Kevin looked at me with pleading eyes. 'Will you let Webasto in England know we do a good job here in Cornwall, me handsome?'

'I'll think about it, Kevin,' I told him as he got on to the ferry.

Chapter Twenty-Seven
The River of Entrapment

Tim had a sore head as we listened to the Met Office forecast.

Outlook for the following 24 hours.

Wind. East or southeast 6 or 7, increasing gale 8 at times.

Occasionally severe gale 9 later.

Sea State. Rough becoming very rough.

Weather. Rain later.

Visibility. Good, becoming moderate later.

'Maybe it's just as well we didn't go today,' Tim said, guzzling water like a camel. When he drew breath he continued, 'We wouldn't like to get stuck going around the Lizard in a Force Six.'

And so for the next two weeks we got into a routine. A cup of tea and the Met Office forecast. '*Gales imminent. Rain later*'.

'How unusual. Why don't they change it to gales permanent,' Tim growled on day 12.

'The Cornish climate is on a par with Manchester weather,' I replied. I had just handed Tim a brew before joining him under the duvet. The weather was starting to cheese us off. 'I mean, you expect it to rain up north, but I thought Cornwall had this magical microclimate. It's cold down here, really cold. I'm going to have to put an extra blanket on the bed tonight.'

Later we took the dinghy over to the visitor mooring in Helford. The rain held off long enough for us to get there without getting wet. A teenager called Georgie helped to shove dinghies aside to make room for ours. Phil Shotton, a cameraman and colleague of Paul's, was there to meet us. Tim had worked with him before and liked him.

'Is this place for real?' Phil said as he shook Tim's hand, then mine.

'Helford Village is like something off a box of chocolates with all of those thatched cottages that hug the creek. It's about as perfect a place as you can get,' he said in his Geordie drawl.

'But you must be freezing,' Tim commented.

'No man, I'm from Newcastle,' Phil replied.

Tim and I were wearing waterproofs. Under the macs we wore jumpers. Phil seemed to be dressed for the summer. He followed us up the now-familiar path, past the picture-postcard houses. A man appeared out of a thick hedge that was high up on the shore of the creek. He reminded me of the rabbit in *Alice in Wonderland* as he hurried in front of us.

'Where did he come from?' Phil asked.

'He's a local fisherman. He's in a hurry because he has to get his catch ashore. The local fishermen don't have it easy here, they have to moor on a buoy in the centre of the river and load their fish into a tender. That's what that guy has just done. He's now rushing to get his van,' I explained.

'Why don't they build them a jetty or some kind of pier like?' Phil enquired.

'According to what I've heard on the grapevine, it's a contentious issue. The locals who own some of these cottages don't want one. They say it will change the area.'

Tim and I stopped and took off our macs and jumpers. The sun shone for about 30 seconds and then it began to rain again, so we put everything back on. Tim's feet squelched in his pink Crocs. We all traipsed down the hill that leads to the pub, The Shipwright's Arms.

'I'd be happy to spend the rest of the day in there,' Tim said looking at his watch, 'but it's only 10:45 and it doesn't open till 11.'

'I don't care what time it is, Timmy, I want to find that church.'

I had been nagging him for a couple of days about walking to a village called Manaccan. Someone had mentioned a church with a fig tree growing out of the wall, and Sarah the blonde bombshell had said there was a restaurant almost next door. Unfortunately she had not told us how to get there, just 'it's a lovely walk'.

'I'm going to pop into the Post Office and ask Colin,' I said before turning around and coming straight out again.

'It's packed,' I complained.

We carried on walking down the lane towards the bridge over the creek. The postman was in his van waiting for one of the fishermen to pull out from where they parked by the red phone box.

'Everyone else has to park at the top of the hill on the other side of the creek, Phil,' Tim said.

We all watched as the fisherman drove his van along the beach.

'He's going to pick his fish up now,' I explained to Phil while Tim asked the postman the best way to go.

'He says to turn right at the footbridge,' Tim said as he crossed the narrow lane.

We crossed the bridge. Well, Tim and Phil did, I paddled over. This is arguably the prettiest part of Helford Village. The stream below the footbridge swells at high tide, but at low tide it trickles through grassy banks embroidered with wild flowers that scent the air. Tim led, and Phil and I followed him up a gentle hill. All the rose-covered cottages have doors that open directly on the lane. Each had an advertisement: 'This cottage is for rent.' Phil and I stopped outside every cottage to see how many bedrooms and bathrooms the property boasted. Tim walked ahead of us then turned and came back.

'I don't think that road goes anywhere. I'm not sure now if the postman said right or left. Look, there's someone walking down the hill from the Sailing Club. Let's ask them.'

'Excuse me, do you know the way to Manaccan Village please?' I asked.

'No, sorry,' came the reply.

I noticed an open stable door on one of the tiny cottages that look out on to the creek, so I knocked. A lady came to the door.

I asked her the same question.

'*Egg-jelly*, we only arrived this morning, so I'm afraid we don't have a clue but this holiday cottage has mice,' she replied.

Tim and I were in a real quandary about which way to go. Then it began to rain again, this time quite heavily.

'Surely there must be a local person who knows the way to Manaccan,' I grumbled.

There was an open door to another cottage, and a man came out.

'Do you know where Manaccan Village is?' I asked him.

'I have no idea, we only just arrived.'

'Let's go and ask at the Sailing Club,' Tim said, 'then at least I can have a pint.'

Half way up the hill we passed a couple, so I asked just in case.

'I'm not sure,' one of them said, 'but I think we saw a sign-post by the tea room.'

We all tramped up the steep hill.

'This a complete wild goose chase!' Tim protested. 'Let's go to the Sailing Club.'

'No I want to go to Mannacan!'

'And what about poor Phil, lugging all his gear.'

Phil interrupted. 'It's fine with me, but I wouldn't mind stopping so I can light a tab,' he said in his Geordie lilt.

I walked ahead and found the sign. It pointed to a muddy public footpath.

'We'll need Wellingtons to walk up there,' Tim objected

when they caught me up. 'I'm only wearing Crocs and they are made of flippin' polystyrene.'

'Pink poly Crocs, very fetching,' Phil purred, puffing smoke through his nose. There was something both camp and butch about him.

We walked over a couple of fallow fields and then stopped when we got to the brow of the hill. The three of us stood looking down on to the Helford River. The sky and the water gave the impression of being drawn with charcoal that had been smudged across a page.

'How many shades of grey can you get in an English summer?' Tim asked as we hiked through the drizzle.

'We're in Cornwall, Tim, not England.'

The signs ran out as we came back on to a lane.

'Which way now?' Tim asked crossly. 'Right or left? There's no one about to ask. We're in the bleeding middle of nowhere. We should have stayed at the pub!'

'Let's turn right. It's downhill,' I said, ignoring him.

The fine coating of drizzle turned into a downpour so we all made a run for it to take shelter under a tree.

'I can hear machinery,' Phil drawled as he wiped the lens of his camera. 'There must be someone nearby.'

I looked at Phil quite closely now as we sheltered under a dripping oak tree. He was late-thirties with dark hair and heavy eyebrows that framed his face. The baggy denim jeans had been washed a thousand times; they had not been professionally distressed. He lit another cigarette.

When the rain stopped a little, we carried on walking. The noise was coming from a farm. I left Tim and Phil on the road and picked my way over rivulets of farmyard mud. It had been mixed into a soup with cow manure. I spotted a man in a Land Rover listening to an iPod. When I knocked on the window, he jumped a little before pulling out his earplugs.

'Do you know the way to Manaccan?' I asked after he wound down his window.

'Op daz hill,' he said. 'To mizz it, is an impossibility!'

I went back to Tim and Phil, who were deep in conversation on the road. 'The man from the farm was German. Do you think anyone around here is Cornish?'

So we all trudged up another slope. Cornwall is full of hills. And there was a sign that read MANACCAN. For a few seconds it was an Eldorado moment, then it began to hail. Lumps of ice bounced off the tarmac. We took cover in a bus shelter that smelt like a urinal. Used condoms littered the floor.

'This must be the youth club,' Tim said, kicking broken bottles out of the way.

'I feel completely at home here,' Phil laughed as he put his fag end into an empty can of Red Bull.

The rain stopped after a few minutes and we walked by a council estate.

'1960s architecture has a lot to answer for,' Tim said, 'but I feel at home here too.'

Then we saw a sign, 'SOUTH'. We all made a dash for it; it was a restaurant.

After an excellent lunch, the sun came out so we asked if we could leave our stuff while we took a look at the fabled fig tree in St Mennaccus, the village church.

'Look at the size of the trunk coming out of the wall,' Tim said, pushing back enormous fig leaves. 'The waitress said the church is over 200 years old. And look at that tree over there,' he said, turning around. 'I've got to give that a hug!' My husband loves trees.

I read inscriptions on the gravestones. 'Come and have a look at this one, Tim,' I said when he finished communing with the yew. 'It has a pirate motif on it. I'd love to get to the bottom of that.'

'What, you want to get to the bottom of the grave?' he asked, taking my arm.

We didn't expect the church to be open. It really used to piss me off that Fowey Church was shut at certain times, but the waitress at South said the verger in Manaccan locks it every night using a large key. Tim tried the handle and it opened into a truly spiritual space, beautiful, still and empty. All of us spoke in hushed voices. It was quite dark. Only the drizzly light from the stained glass windows cut through the gloom. I found a light switch, but it didn't help much. The high wooden ceiling was carved but there wasn't enough light to examine it properly. I left Tim sitting on a pew. This is what he does in a church: he says a little prayer to thank God for sparing his life.

Phil and I went outside and sat on the bench by the fig tree.

'We had a visit from a local man the other day,' I said, 'who was interested in our boat, so we invited him onboard to take a look around. He told us a story about this church. The vicar was away and his wife saw a suspicious-looking fella lurking about, and supposed he was a French spy. It was the time of the Napoleonic Wars so there was quite a bit of spying going on. When her husband came home she told him and the spy was arrested and locked in the coal cellar of the vicarage where he remained unfed for a couple of days. The spy's name was Bligh, Captain Bligh of The Bounty.'

'That's fascinating that,' Phil said. 'But what was he doing around here?'

'I think he was promoted sideways after the mutiny, doing Admiralty research around the river.'

'How much longer are you going to be in Helford?' Phil asked as he felt his pockets for his cigarettes.

'Sometimes I think we shall never leave. I've asked if we can winter up at Gweek Quay. They say they can find room. The summer's almost over. We thought we'd be well on our way to

Wales by now. When we left Weymouth in the spring we made such good progress...'

Tim interrupted me as he closed the church door behind him. 'We are calling the Helford River "the river of entrapment". Come on, let's go and have a drink back in The Shipwright's.'

On the way back to the Helford visitor's mooring we heard someone shouting to us.

'Hello, hello!'

We looked up above some rose bushes and an elderly lady appeared.

'My name's Kit, do you fancy a tomato, come on up.' Her Yorkshire accent was at odds with the surroundings. 'I've just picked them! Come and have a look at the view from my garden, oh you have someone with a camera,' she said, looking at Phil suspiciously.

'It's OK, I won't film you if you don't want me to. Can I try one of your tomatoes?'

'Of course you can,' she said as she rubbed one on her sleeve before she handed it to him.

'This is some view you have up here, Kit, and look at those egrets feeding on the mud. I'm a bit of a twitcher,' Phil said.

'Oh, we don't usually have this many. There's a really bossy one who lives up in that dead tree, really bossy, I'm surprised he's let them feed here!'

'Do you know what, Kit?' Phil said. 'You are the first person I've met that actually lives in Helford Village.'

'Me too,' I said, swallowing a tomato. I would like to say it was warmed by the sun, but it was not.

Chapter Twenty-Eight
Cabin Fever

For about four minutes the next day we thought we might leave the Helford and go around the Lizard to Newlyn. But after I checked several different weather websites, and Tim his charts, we thought it would be really stupid.

'By the time we got there the wind around the Lizard would be gusting 28 knots and the waves would be at least eight feet high, which would get us broadside,' Tim said. 'Now, I'm going for a shave.'

While he was in the bathroom a small sailing boat came alongside us. They asked if we had a pump they could use for their dinghy. They didn't have an adapter on theirs, so I lent them ours. They tied up to a visitor's mooring buoy behind us. About half an hour later I saw them climb into their pumped up tender and come towards us. Just as they reached *The Princess Matilda* their outboard cut out. The sensible thing would have been for one of them to have grabbed on to the side of *New Si* to stop themselves being taken away by the tide. Tim re-joined me on the deck and we watched them as the flow took them up river. The man was desperately trying to start the outboard while the girl tried to row. They got further and further away.

Tim shook his head and said, 'He's going to flood it. I'd better go and give them a tow!'

By the time Tim had rescued the pair and delivered them back to their small vessel, I noticed a large yacht had anchored ahead of us.

'Look, those newcomers are swimming off that yacht,' Tim said, pointing as I helped him onboard *The Princess Matilda*.

He handed me the retrieved pump. 'The woman's not hanging around.' We watched as she quickly hauled herself out of the water and back on to their yacht.

'He's a pro though, look, he's towing a red flag from his ankle,' I said.

'I think that's so he won't get decapitated by any motor boats,' Tim replied.

'It must be freezing, that water,' I said, wrapping myself up in a fleece.

Tim and I both watched as the man swam and swam.

'Or maybe it's the tide taking him upstream? Do you think I should go and bring him back?' Tim asked.

'I think his girlfriend has the same idea.'

We watched her in their dinghy, trying to start the outboard without any success.

'What is it with outboards?' Tim said, putting on the life jacket he had only just discarded.

I shouted to her, 'Do you need help?'

'No thanks!'

'She means yes, Tim.'

We watched as the man made absolutely no headway trying to swim back to his boat. Tim was in our dinghy, starting up the outboard.

'It's OK,' I said. 'There's another boat going by them. Stay where you are, love.'

I heard someone shout to the girl, 'Do you need help?'

'No, no thank you!'

The swimmer breathlessly said the same. It took him 20 minutes to swim 20 yards. By which time numerous people in various boats were all nervously on standby to go and get him out. His girlfriend meanwhile was throwing a rope to him, but he kept missing it.

'I'd throw a fucking hammer at him if he was my boyfriend!' I said as eventually he hauled himself back aboard the yacht.

*

Once again we awoke to rain and howling wind.

'We can't get to shore today,' Tim said. 'It would be complete madness and I don't think the ferry is running either.'

'God help anyone at sea this morning. I'm coming back to bed,' I said. 'But we're running out of grub. You're down to the last tin of Fray Bentos Chicken & Mushroom Pie, and that went out of date last month. We need to get in some shopping.'

'See if you can get a Tesco delivery to the Sailing Club.'

'What a great idea, I'll have to wait for low tide though.'

I had tried to get a signal with my dongle in most places on the boat but with little success. However, after more than three weeks being moored in the same spot, I finally found the wheelhouse at low tide hit the mark. Fortunately low tide happens twice a day, but not necessarily at a time convenient to me. We battened down the hatches and waited for the tide to go out.

'Cornish weather stinks,' I said as I stole from the warm cocoon of our bed two hours later. Tim and I love our boat so much that we go into a Zen mode when we're onboard – as soon as we start complaining, we stop and instead say how lucky we are. 'We have a safe remote mooring, we have lots of books, numerous games in the drawer. But fuck me, Tim, my teeth are chattering.'

'The day that the Scrabble board comes out will be a very bleak day. There are still lots of DVDs we've not watched,' Tim replied. 'And I'm glad the telly signal is shit. It's given me so much time to cross-reference my charts.'

'Yes and I've cleaned the oven, the shower and tidied the store cupboard, which wasn't too strenuous. But we need victualling. The dried yeast is out of date, but I can always make bread if we have flour. The low-sugar marmalade's mouldy, the cream crackers are soggy and once I cook that Fray Bentos for your lunch that will be it. I have a wrinkled potato with green eyes for mine.'

Wrapping myself in blankets, I took my laptop into the wheelhouse. Sheets of rain howled by. I tried half a dozen times before I got online and immediately went to Tesco.com and changed the delivery address to Helford Sailing Club. I was very patient and managed to order everything we needed and chose a delivery time. Our tide table was next to me, so I made sure there would be enough water at the Sailing Club for us to come alongside. Tim was still in bed when I went back inside. I stripped off all my clothes and joined him. It was better than playing Scrabble.

The Tesco driver called me on my mobile the next morning. He said he wasn't far away. I looked out of the window, but I could tell the weather had calmed down considerably.

'What a bugger. Come on, Tim, quick we have to get there before he does so I can get him to reverse down that hill to the head of the jetty.'

The driver had been and gone by the time we got there. Absolutely nothing is plain sailing at the best of times. Tim and I have learnt we have to make the best of every situation. Greg, the chef, had very kindly put our Tesco order in his stock room above the car park. Helford Sailing Club is about 40 feet above the river. The hammerhead where we moor is about 200 yards away from the steep hill that goes up to the car park. It took exactly one hour to bring down our victuals. Seven times I climbed that steep, torturous hill. Tim was at the bottom with

New Si. He put the shopping in the dinghy and took it around to *The Princess Matilda*, thus saving several journeys up and down the jetty.

'We have to hurry, Shane,' Tim said as we got the last bag onboard. 'The tide's going out really quickly and we don't want to get stuck on the mud.'

We quickly cast off and went back upstream. While I was below unpacking the shopping Tim shouted down to me.

'There's something on our buoy, I think it's the Gweek maintenance boat.'

Tim and I had a few sharp words as we made a tricky manoeuvre to raft up alongside it. The tide and wind didn't help us much. I was knackered from heaving all of the shopping.

'Throw the fucking rope around something,' Tim yelled.

A squall had blown up from nowhere. I missed on the first attempt and had to drag the sopping rope out of the water. I ignored Tim and reached for the boathook.

'There's nothing to tie against,' I shouted over the wind. Somehow I managed to hook my pole on to something, but the tide was dragging us upstream. Like Rudolph Nureyev without the tights, Tim leapt from *The Princess Matilda* on to the maintenance boat. I threw him the rope and he tried it around the derrick.

'Well, that was a pain in the arse, but at least we are secure now,' he shouted as he finished tying up the ropes. I went inside and made us lunch.

After we cleared the table, we went a bit barmy. This is something we do really well. About every half an hour or so we both yelled CLIVE at the top of our voices. Everyone knows someone who is called Clive. It is a wonderful name. CLIVE. No one could hear us. The wind was blowing too hard. It was like letting steam out of a boiling kettle. We went to bed and listened to the groaning of the ropes rubbing against our new neighbour. The waves slopped under and over our bow. Hail on the roof almost deafened us. 'CLIVE!!!!!!!!!' we both yelled. This was so hilarious, we laughed until we almost wet the bed.

Chapter Twenty-Nine
The Voyages of New Si

'I think we have to give serious consideration to finding a winter mooring in Falmouth, Tim. I think our journey is over for this year.'

'But Nick says the weather improves in September. We had a great September last year, if you remember, we didn't leave Poole until the 24th! We can still get to Cardiff. We've just been unlucky,' he replied.

'I'm going to book us some tickets to go home. You have to be in Berlin on 5 September, for *The Desert Flower* premiere, then it's Tilda's fifth birthday on the 8th.'

'We'll drive back,' Tim replied. 'Let's make the most of it. I mean those cottages in Helford cost over a thousand quid to rent, and it's raining for them too. It's Helford Village Regatta tomorrow, then the next day we've been invited to a barbeque over at the secret boathouse. Do you know what the most amazing thing has been for me so far?'

'Kind of, I feel the same too.'

'It's just been me and you. I didn't realise how much that *Fattest Man* job took out of me. It's been so amazing here, even though it's rained every day. What decisions have we had to make? One. Shall we leave today? No! Two. Where shall we have our dinner? The Sailing Club, The Ferryboat Inn or The Shipwright's Arms or Bistro Matilda? It's been an enforced rest!'

The sun came out the next day for the Helford Village Regatta. This regatta was so different to the one we watched over at The Ferryboat. There was a bunch of young, well-spoken Londoners all dressed up as American sailors. They got pissed and entered races and fell in and all in all had a wonderful time. They made us laugh. We chatted with some of our new local friends: Kit from Rose Cottage, Colin from the Post Office, Nick the ferryman, Sarah his wife, and Phil the Geordie cameraman. He had flown down from Manchester to cover the regatta.

'It's so amazing, there's not a copper in sight!' Phil said.

When the races ended Tim and I walked up to the Sailing Club. We sat on the balcony, as we did that first weekend.

'It seems so long ago,' I said to Phil. 'This balcony was full of French people who had come over for a race back to Brittany.'

There was a bird's nest in the eaves of the clubhouse. I pointed to the swooping swallows catching flies in the air and taking them to squawking chicks that poked out their greedy open beaks a few inches above our heads.

'That's the second lot of chicks they've raised in there,' I said.

'And they will be going back to Africa in a couple of weeks,' Phil replied.

'It will be dark soon. The nights are drawing in so quickly. We rowed up Frenchman's Creek on an evening close to Midsummer's Night and it was still light at 11pm,' I looked at my watch. 'Tim and I better get back to *The Princess Matilda* before it gets dark. I forgot to bring a torch and we don't want to get mowed down by any RIBs.'

Tim and I waved goodbye to our new friends and left them on the jetty where everyone had gathered to watch the fireworks. We came alongside *The Princess Matilda* on *New Si* and as usual I seized a hanging fender to hold us to the side. Then Tim made a grab for the rim of the gunwale while I threw our painter around the cleat on our deck. We have done it so many times, but a couple of days previously I hurt myself as I climbed on to *The Princess Matilda*. I have sore joints at the best of times, but the Cornish damp had seeped into my knees. One gave way as I got onboard.

'Just be careful,' Tim said as I gingerly hauled myself on to the deck.

Then it was his turn. Usually I hold on to the grab bar and give him my hand to help him step aboard. He does this really easily, not on his hands and knees as I do. He simply steps up from the wobbly dinghy. But this time he missed and I heard his rib crack on the rim of the gunwale.

'Fuck me that hurt,' he said, rubbing his side. 'I've bloody bruised my ribs again.'

Tim wasn't the only person feeling under the weather the following morning. We decided to leave the dinghy where it was and call the ferry. A curly haired summer ferry assistant, also named Nick, picked us up and he looked as seedy as Tim. This Nick helps out during the summer months but runs a 100-acre cattle farm.

'We had the end of the season staff party at the Sailing Club after the fireworks. Alli chucked us all out at 2am,' farmer Nick said.

Kathy brought us back to *The Princess Matilda* after we had lunch in The Shipwright's. She had a hangover too. Tim showed her his bruised rib. Kathy tried to squeeze out a sympathetic smile.

'That's called a *drinjury*,' she said. 'That's what we call it when you've had too much to drink and you hurt yourself getting out of a dinghy.'

'Quite right,' I said as I paid her. 'And now we're going to spend the rest of the day reading the Sunday papers and have an early night.'

Tim and I sat on the back deck. I fetched him ibuprofen and a glass of wine. We flicked though the papers.

'Everything sounds so remote and far away from us, like none of it counts,' Tim commented as he threw his paper on the deck.

'No, listen to this, Tim. This is a summary of last week's weather in the *Telegraph*, listen! *Monday 24 August 2009 to Sunday 30 August 2009. Ex-Hurricane Bill turns up. The week begins with a band of rain swinging east across England and Wales, the remains of the weekend's heavy rain in Northern Ireland and Scotland. What follows is a few days of sunshine and showers before the arrival of the next Atlantic depression in the west around midweek.*

'*What is interesting about this one is that it was once Hurricane Bill over in the western Atlantic, but as it tracks towards the UK, it will move over cooler waters, lose its intensity and become an ex-tropical system. It will retain certain characteristics though and looks set to bring rather wet, windy and humid conditions to our shores.*'

'Oh great,' he replied, 'it's going to carry on raining.'

It was August Bank Holiday Monday the next day, so, being British, we expected it to rain. We were not disappointed. Tim and I dressed in our waterproofs and took the dinghy over to the secret boathouse. For more than three weeks we had been watching the comings and goings from this place. On warm evenings we had seen people sitting around a large table underneath the green awning by the water. A bearded man, who introduced himself as Greg, had rowed over to us one day and invited us over for a drink. We had already booked a table at the pub, so regretfully we had to decline.

The actual boathouse was a little higher than the water level, to protect it from the floodtides. Its grey gabled roof sloped down over three large windows. We drew alongside the slipway, and the bearded and amiable Greg came down to help us tie up.

'The tide's going out, so we'll pull it up here,' he said.

He helped me off, and he and Tim hauled *New Si* up the slip.

'We're neighbours now, you've been moored there so long!' Greg said.

Already present were a few people standing under the green corrugated roof. I saw the boat shed housed some kind of a workshop. There was machinery in the corner by a wall. Two sides were open to the elements. A roaring fire spat in a brazier, and a large barbeque with a chimney heated the space. The floor was uneven and well-trodden, the same grey stone as the slipway and walls. There were several people sitting on home-made rustic furniture and a young man in a wheelchair. Gosh, I hope he has the brake on, I thought, for the edge of the high wharf was just behind him.

'Welcome!' Katie, our hostess, said as she came out to meet me. 'Come in here, get warm by the fire. Let me introduce you. This is Henrietta and Michael and their sons, Freddie, and this chap here is Henry.' Henry was strapped into his wheelchair. Henrietta shook my hand. She was a small, dark-haired woman with a handshake of steel.

'We're the Spinks, call me Heni,' she said.

I looked out across the grim, steely grey Helford River. Torrential rain was splashing on the surface and tumbling down the corrugated iron above our heads. Heni and I had to shout over the din. She told me that Henry was severely disabled and that Freddie had problems too. I saw him being led into the boathouse. Heni, like a hawk, watched my eyes and she turned to see what I was looking at. The boy shuffled and moved clumsily.

'Freddie's 17. He was born with half his diaphragm missing and has massive scarring in his oesophagus from years of constant vomiting. He has autistic tendencies,' she explained. 'We have two carers here with us today, which is just as well. Go and take a look inside the boathouse when Freddie's finished in the bathroom. Be careful though, he projectile vomits!'

Freddie was sitting next to Tim when I finished exploring the boathouse. The boy seemed to be playing an imaginary drum kit.

'Freddie loves drumming,' Heni said by way of explanation.

'Me too,' said Tim and he began to sing, 'Da da da tickka da da da da tickka da da da da…'"

When he does this he sounds like he is playing tabla drums and his hands knock out the beat on the table. Freddie stared at him for ten minutes, long after Tim finished his impromptu recital. Suddenly he stood up and threw his arms around Tim's neck.

'Wow,' said Heni. 'I have never known him to do that before!'

Heni and I swapped email addresses before Tim and I left. On our way back to *The Princess Matilda*, I said, 'Heni's a cross between Catherine Zeta-Jones and Joyce Grenfell. Did you get to speak to her husband, Tim?'

'From what I could gather he's some kind of specialist in Islamic art. They have an awful lot on their plate.'

We had to strip off all of our clothes when we got back onboard our boat as were soaked to the skin.

It rained all day the next day too. The wind blew shire horses up the river but about 5pm the weather cleared so we took *New Si* to the visitor's mooring. We put £2.50 in the honesty box as the charming tousled-haired Georgie had gone back to school and wasn't there to help. There were no other boats tied up, so we had lots of room.

'No more shoving tenders and dinghies out of the way to get tied off,' said Tim. 'Come on, Shane, we'd better hurry, the Post Office closes at 5:30.'

We walked quickly past the hedgerows, now heavy with scarlet and black berries. In June, when we first arrived, the hedges were full of elderflowers, foxgloves and honeysuckle.

'The seasons have changed so quickly.'

The Post Office was shut. A notice on the door said they were back to winter hours.

'No toast for us in the morning, our bread has gone mouldy and I can't be bothered to make any,' I said to Tim.

'Let's go to the Sailing Club,' he replied.

We took the dinghy around the corner and walked along the empty pontoons and up the hill. A notice on the door informed us 'We shut at 3 and open at 6', but Greg, the chef, saw us through the kitchen window.

'I'll let you in,' he said.

While we waited I turned to Tim, 'I feel like someone has turned off the lights after a party, and we are the Billy No Mates who have nowhere else to go.'

We followed Greg into the bar and he opened up the shutters and got us a drink. The club slowly filled up with locals. Tim and I were on nodding terms with so many people now, and on first name terms with many, too. We ate our dinner then bade everyone goodbye and walked down to the jetty. The rain was still holding off, so we pulled the dinghy out of the water. Tim tugged out the plug and let out six inches of rain that had fallen that day. We then set off back to *The Princess Matilda*.

'Oh fuck me,' Tim yelled as we came out of the protection of the Sailing Club bay. We got a face full of salty seawater with every wave we went over. My waterproof coat was letting in water and I began to tremble with cold. Every muscle tensed as I held on to the painter and the side of the dinghy. It occurred to me that if I fell in, I would never get out again. Even though I was wearing a life jacket, I knew my clothes would drag me down. In my mind's eye I saw Tim jumping in after me to save me. Then we would both die. The waves were enormous and we would probably get separated and drown. I saw the buoy, the one we had tied up to when our outboard had broken down, the day that Nigel, the harbour patrolman, had come to our rescue. But now the season was over, and it was just Tim and me on the river. Three-foot waves were breaking over the front of our dinghy. *New Si* filled like a paddling pool, the icy water steadily rising up to my knees. I keep a plastic pint glass in my waterproof grab bag, which was on my lap. I managed to open it and find the glass and frantically tried to bail us out, but the nose of the little boat would rise with a wave and then crash into the next, scuppering my efforts. A rolling wave hit us from the side and I dropped the bag and the glass as I hung on for my life. It came to mind that we might sink. I put this from my thoughts, intent only on the next wave, and the next. A little voice inside my head was saying, 'What if the outboard cuts out?' I had my back to Tim, but I know he was thinking the same as me. Both of us heard the motor glug and miss a beat a couple of times. *New Si* fought against the outgoing tide but we didn't seem to be getting any closer to *The Princess Matilda*. I tried to remain calm, my inner voice reassuring me, 'We are passing the empty visitor's buoys. We are definitely getting closer.' But another voice inside me was saying, 'If the engine fails, Tim will not be able to row.'

We were making slow progress. Forked lightning lit the sky and hailstones the size of ping-pong balls hit me, stinging any bare skin. My negative inner voice carried on nagging, 'When did he last fill up the petrol tank?' Closer and closer we came. The hailstorm passed but the wind was screeching. I was almost blinded by the spray of the breaking waves. Desperately I tried to breathe through my nose. My mouth was clenched shut so I would not swallow any seawater. A couple of waves sent me toppling from my perch. I was aware of Tim's hand grabbing my life jacket as I fell forwards. The next wave sent me reeling back.

It had been half an hour since we set off. This journey usually takes seven minutes. My hands and my legs in the rising water were numb. I realised that I was suffering from hypothermia. I tried to look up to see how far away we were from our boat, but felt unable to breathe. Almost instinctively, I tucked my chin down as low as I could to find some respite from the storm. I still don't know how Tim managed to get us against *The Princess Matilda* but we both automatically made a grab for the side. My arm felt like lead as I stretched to grab a fender. By a miracle I secured our painter on the first attempt. I had never done this before; usually it takes three tries. My teeth were chattering and I was shivering. Snot ran down my face from the cold. I knew I had to get aboard as quickly as possible.

Tim and I had both hurt ourselves recently getting out of the dinghy and back onboard our boat. I felt as if my wet clothes were dragging me down and knew we wouldn't get a second chance. The storm caused *The Princess Matilda* to roll and buck. *New Si* began to pull away. I could feel the painter cutting through my fingers. Where I got the strength from, I don't know. In a flash I was up and out of the dinghy like a sea lion, holding on to the grab rail to help Tim, with what we suspected was a broken rib, get off too. Both of us were thoroughly drenched. Trembling, we stripped off our wet clothes in the wheelhouse, I was quicker than Tim and went below and put on the Webasto central heating. It fired up first time. I wanted to phone up Dame Kevin and tell him, 'THANK YOU!' My husband joined me inside the saloon. I tossed a white bath towel at him and we rubbed each other dry.

'Thank God we are safe! I thought we were going to die, Timmy.'

'Me too darlin', but we didn't, we're alive!'

*

Midnight

I stopped writing in my notebook on the 11th. It all goes back to why do it? I know Sylvia writes her journal every day, 'Oh dear Lord let him be well'. Naturally, she is your mother, and she weeps and cries as she writes. But it's all about one's own pain and frankly I don't need a reminder of that. Over two weeks have passed since last I wrote and you have been desperately ill. You are so heroic. Last week I held your hand as someone did a bone marrow biopsy. To think of the fuss I made the first time. You were heavily sedated but you still flinched. How vulnerable and helpless one is. How brave you are. You had your Hickman Line removed because it wasn't working properly. Your veins, therefore, are in a hellish state. What pissed me off most was that the line bled one morning but no one thought to take a culture until it was too late. I was furious with the nurses. Someone got a bollocking. So the line was removed in case it had an infection brewing. I haven't asked if this was the case; I am guessing. A central line was inserted into your neck through which more drugs were pumped for the pains in your chest. You are still on diamorphine because the pain is so severe. They just told me the last CT scan has shown up a fungal infection on your lung, which may need surgery. How can they possibly operate on you? Your platelets are zero. You would bleed to death...

Chapter Thirty
Hello and Goodbye

Nick, our friendly ferryman, picked us up and took us to Helford Passage the following morning. I noticed he was wearing long trousers and boots now, instead of his shorts and sandals.

'That was some storm we had last night,' he said. 'You've got a cab waiting for you to take you to Truro Station. How long are you going to be away?'

'About ten days,' I replied.

The Ferryboat Inn was shut and all the tables piled up, ready to be put away for the end of the season. I felt melancholy seeping into my soul. Tim had packed us a picnic for the long train journey back to London. Once onboard the train, he spread it across a table. This cheered me up. I far prefer his sandwiches to mine. The Penzance-to-London railway in part hugs the Kennet and Avon Canal, which was the first big trip we ever did on our old rust-bucket narrowboat, *Cassien*.

'Do you remember, we listened to Princess Diana's funeral on Radio 4 when we were doing that flight of locks?' I asked Tim as we both gazed out of the window.

'I do remember my love, and when we got to Bristol, I got *Our Mutual Friend*. It was one of the first jobs I did after being ill. I had to give you a masterclass in driving *Cassien* that involved the Wiltshire constabulary,' he laughed.

'I was steering past some moored boats and that man shouted at me to slow down. You shouted to him, "She's learning and we have a problem with the engine, it's running too fast."'

'He was having none of it,' Tim said. '"What's the name of your boat? I'm going to report you!" I yelled back, "F!"'

'And the man shouted back, pretending he had pen and paper, "F!"'

Tim began to giggle. 'Then I yelled, "U!" And he yelled back, "U!"'

Tim's eyes began to water with laughter. He could hardly speak. '"C!" I shouted and he yelled back, "C!"'

I noticed several people changing theirs seats as our mirth filled the train carriage.

'He had his little pretend pen writing it all down,' Tim gasped.

'And when you got to K he threw his pretend pad away and shook his fist at us and called the police!'

After we had recovered from our fit of giggles, Tim said, 'Do you miss the canals?'

'Yes,' I replied. 'I think I've almost had enough of this, Tim. For God's sake, we could've died last night and frankly it's put the shit up me. What on earth do we think we're doing?'

'Do you want to sell the boat?'

'No, but I wouldn't mind doing something that won't kill us. I enjoyed the canals. If and when we get to Cardiff, that will be it. I think reaching Wales, another country, will be enough, don't you? We can winter there and take *The Princess Matilda* up the Bristol Channel to the River Severn and back on the inland waterways.'

'Let's see how you feel when we get back to Helford Passage. We'll drive, so we can gauge just how far from London we have travelled by sea.'

It took us seven-and-a-half hours to drive back to Helford Passage, a nightmare journey with motorway contraflows, traffic jams and B roads.

'You know this means we will definitely leave Helford now?' Tim said as he locked the car.

'Of course, that's why we've done it, just to make every-thing more difficult. If we do get to Wales, then you have to come back here and collect the car, right!'

Nick had told us to park the car above the pub. It was shut so we sat on the wall and waited for the ferry. It was a glorious afternoon, so it wasn't a problem, even though the ferry was gone a long time. When it came back to the jetty about a dozen people got off. Young women with children in pushchairs, elderly folk with walking sticks, middle-aged men with beer bellies. They all quietly alighted and walked up the beach, the young men helping the older ones and the babies.

'Sorry for keeping you waiting,' Nick said, 'but they're a local family and I've just taken them up to Frenchman's Creek so they could scatter some ashes. They opened a 16-year-old bottle of whisky to make a toast. It was extremely moving.'

I turned my head away because I began to cry. Tim saw me wipe my eyes and took my hand. He knew I was thinking of my mom and dad, not to mention feeling some empathy for whatever that family had been through.

'We had a pod of dolphins on the river while you were away. I think the weather drove them in, but the last three days have been amazing, and the high front is here to stay for a couple of weeks,' our ferryman said as we went upstream.

'I can't believe we missed them,' I replied.

'You also missed me swimming across from The Ferryboat to the Sailing Club with my son for charity. It was quite warm.'

'This looks like it will be our last night on the Helford, Nick. We're going to go for it! Why don't you bring Sarah up when you knock off and we'll have a farewell drink?' Tim said as we came alongside *The Princess Matilda*.

'I'd love to. I'm sure Sarah can get a babysitter.'

We made our last night on our swing buoy a celebration of the summer. Sarah and Nick had both worked so hard while we had lazed about. They have three children. The baby was only two and Sarah also runs a shop. Tim and I love their story.

'I fell in love with her down here in Helford on New Year's Eve a few years ago. I had a job in Oxford and she was a single mum with two kids.'

'You were lucky to ge' me, Beef!' she laughed as she punched him.

'You were a wild child. My own gorgeous buxom Cornish girl,' he said, rubbing his forearm.

'Yes and I take no shi' from anyone, especially you, Beef-cake!'

Tim and I waved goodnight to them as they boarded the ferry.

We could hear Sarah saying, 'I feel sick…'

'I think he might have to carry her ashore,' I said as Nick started the engine.

A full harvest moon had risen over the hill above Greg and Katie's secret boathouse and the river was bathed by its silver rays.

'The full moon means we shall have spring tides to get us around to Newlyn,' Tim said.

'You keep going on about spring tides but it's early autumn,' I complained.

'Oh, Shane, I keep telling you, the gravitational pull of the moon and the sun are strongest just after a full or new moon.'

'We wouldn't have to worry about that if we were on a canal. I'm going to bed. I just got a text from Paul. He's in Falmouth; he's getting the ferry up with Nick in the morning.'

Paul joined us bright and early and we unhooked our swing buoy for the final time.

'Do you really think this is it?' Paul asked.

'Oh yes, the sea state is calm and there is hardly any wind, we're just going to go down to the Sailing Club and take on some water and I'm going to say goodbye to Alli and Greg,' I replied.

Paul was standing on the bow with me. I lay in the sun for a few minutes before sitting up. I saw a familiar yacht and started to wave. Tim slowed down; he recognised it too. It was *Cailin*, our old neighbour from Ramsgate. Paula and Ron were aboard and we stopped and chatted for about ten minutes, sharing our news. The weather had scuppered them too. They were going to spend a few days on the Helford before going back to Plymouth for the winter.

'Fair sailing,' Paula shouted as we pulled away. 'We hope you make it to Wales! That will be amazing!'

I looked back at them in their little yacht and an over-whelming feeling of sadness enveloped me because we probably would not see them again.

'I love them,' I said to Paul, 'they are so sweet. Such sweet and good people.'

'How do you feel about leaving the Helford River?' he asked me.

'I feel sad. Look at it. It's so beautiful. We've had such a marvellous time. Don't forget we've spent a whole season here. We arrived in Midsummer. I think I'm going to cry.'

Chapter Thirty-One
The Bogeyman

Helford to Newlyn: 34 nautical miles

We came out of the Helford River feeling like we had left a special place, but once again Tim and I settled into our routine.

'Are you nervous, Tim?'

'Of course I am, we're going around one of the most potentially dangerous places in the world, in a barge! Lizard Point is infamous for wrecking ships. What you have to remember is the land doesn't just stop, it goes out into the ocean. So that's why it's called the Lizard, it has a tail of rocks, the reef stretches miles out to sea, and these will cause overfalls. I've had three months to worry about this next journey. Sometimes I have periods of thinking, "What am I doing?" No one has shown me how to do the calculations or checked that what I am doing is right.'

'You doubt yourself too much, Timmy. We'll be fine.'

'That's not what you said on the train to London. You were all for throwing in the towel,' he said accusingly.

'That's what you love most about me. My inconsistency. How long will it take to get to Newlyn?'

'About six hours, but at least we have the autopilot now, so I can take a leak!'

I went below to put the kettle on. Tim was chatting to Paul when I came back into the wheelhouse.

'We're three miles out to miss the worst of the overfalls from the Lizard. Three thousand miles away,' said Tim, pointing out to sea, 'is the next piece of land, America.'

I didn't have America on my AA map book put I did have the Lizard. It did look like we were at right angles to the rest of the world.

'This is Britain's most southerly point,' Tim continued. 'It's the bogeyman to me, some dreadful mythical creature, something that has to be conquered...'

'What's that black line out there, Tim?'

But I knew the answer. The blue of the ocean was changing. The sun was shining, there was little wind, but we knew we would have to cross some turbulent water. I went below to double-check everything was put away. Tim and Paul were looking at Lizard Point when I came back up the steps.

'We don't like you,' Tim said, play-acting like a five-year-old. 'We're over here!'

The boat began to rotate and bounce and Tim almost toppled out of the open door.

'Oh my God, don't do that, Timmy!' I said, slamming shut all the doors.

'I didn't do it on purpose.'

'You could have fallen in, that would have been fun. I could imagine the headlines, "Actor drowns rounding the Lizard!"' But before I could finish my tirade I was almost knocked off my feet.

'Hold on, Paul!' Tim yelled as a wave picked us up.

The sound of the sea crashing against the hull was almost deafening and then all was silent, except for the noise of the engine. Tim looked through the binoculars.

'I can see Mount's Bay. We're right at the tip of the Lizard now. I'm really tempted to cut that corner but I don't think I should for some reason. I'm not saying anything to tempt fate, but we have just come round the Lizard!'

'Was that it?' I asked him as I let go of the grab bar.

'Was that it, skipper?' Paul joined in.

I don't know who sounded more disappointed. Tim, on the other hand, was delighted.

'Dear little Lizard, the scary little reptilian bastard. And there it is! Look at it! The benign thing that it is. It's only a piece of land,' he said with a huge smile on his face.

I sensed an actor moment coming on and, sure enough, he got into character.

'I'm not gonna get smug. I bow before you,' he said like the genie falling at the feet of Aladdin.

'You've got to be wary of it,' he said, looking now at me. 'Don't let fear hold you back. After all those weeks of worrying we passed it in moments.'

I went below to make some sandwiches. It was calm once more. The sea through the galley windowpane was a joy to behold, the purest of blues. Usually I don't open windows when we are at sea, but I slid open the reinforced glass. Looking down I saw white froth on the surface of the sea. It was mesmerising to both watch and listen to the melodic *swish, swish, swish* that was caused by our bow cutting through the gentle rippling waves. I sensed someone joining me. It was Tim. He stood next to me and looked down at the sea.

'Isn't this amazing? It's what's it's all about. I've left Paul keeping a lookout, but there's just us out here. If only the sea was always so kind. I think Paul's hungry, how are those sandwiches coming on darlin'?'

Tim shut the window and we took our lunch up to the wheelhouse.

We spent the next few hours enjoying the sunshine and chatting. My map book was on the table in front of me. Mount's Bay, I saw, was the largest bay in Cornwall. It took us three hours to cross it. A small island, St Michael's Mount, is the major landmark. We had had it in sight since we rounded the Lizard.

Tim kept calling the Newlyn harbour master on our radio, but he didn't respond. We had been in communication with him for weeks. I had left him several messages on his mobile, but he hadn't got back to me.

'I hear Newlyn is the fishing capital of southern England,' Paul said.

'Well let's hope we have somewhere to moor,' I replied. 'I'm going down the front to take some photos.'

I gave Tim a kiss and he pulled me back to him as I drew away.

'Love you darlin',' he said as I left him and walked down the gunwale.

It felt good to be away from our trusty but noisy engine and just sit and look at the vista of the perfectly formed half-moon bay. The sea glistened and twinkled in the sunlight. I had once heard it being described as one of the most beautiful bays in the world. Even this does not do it justice. My eyes were drawn towards the medieval buildings on top of St Michael's Mount. It looked like a film set, more Disney than Disney. It is said that the Archangel St Michael appeared to a fisherman on the island in the fifth century. A church was built on the summit after the Norman invasion in 1066. This island is joined to the mainland by a granite causeway and it is only accessible at low tide. Beyond the Mount I could see a halo of golden sand that lies below the ancient market town of Penzance. Directly ahead of us was our destination. Newlyn Harbour with its red-nipple-topped white lighthouse beckoned us to enter. Once safely through the green seaweed-encrusted outer walls of the harbour, I saw a high, open jetty with long pilings going down into the water. Two refrigerated lorries, one from Fleetwood in Lancashire and one from Spain were being loaded directly from trawlers that were berthed alongside.

I walked back to speak to Tim. There appeared to be several free places on pontoons opposite the open jetty. Tim was calling the harbour master again. I noticed someone on the dockside.

'Is he the man up there?' I said, pointing him out to Tim.

'He looks like a security guy. I think he wants me to pull alongside that old tug.'

'I think you are right, Tim, he's climbing down the ladder. I better go up the front.'

'Well it's not an ideal mooring, especially if the tug ups and leaves tomorrow,' Tim said as I left.

The security man was standing on the bow of the tug and I threw him a rope.

'Hello, hello,' I shouted. 'What a beautiful day.'

'Welcome to Newlyn, you'll be safe and sound here for the nigh'. I'm Steve.'

He went to the stern to get a line off Tim. I went back into the wheelhouse.

'It's really strange, this is where we now live,' I said to Paul.

Fishing boats, all running generators, surrounded us. Up ahead was a lifeboat.

'I can't believe we got here. All I have to do now is get off!'

Tim and I embraced. We were the relieved vanquishers of the Lizard. Well, maybe not vanquishers: the Lizard had been a pussy cat.

After locking up the boat, Tim and I stood on the side of *The Princess Matilda*. Massive black juggernaut tyres hung down from the tug. This meant we were pushed at least two feet away from our new neighbour. There was no one aboard her, it being a Sunday afternoon. I managed to climb over the tyres and over the high rail on to the deck of the rusty old tug. Then I took a rest. The deck of the vessel went uphill, so we followed it around and came on to the inside edge of the tug by the ladder. This was not just a ladder. It was an instrument of torture. I looked up. It rose 16 feet above me. There was no wall; the ladder was open to the water.

'How are you going to get me up there, Tim?'

Paul went first with all of his camera equipment thrown over his shoulder. He ascended the ladder like a steeplejack, as if this was something he did every day. Tim took my bag from me. We both knew if I didn't get on to the bottom rung soon, I was done for. The ladder at Gweek Quay was the straw that had broken the camel's back.

'You can do it darlin',' he said gently. 'Just don't look down.'

Because of his encouragement I stepped and grabbed the cold metal and just climbed. I didn't think about anything. Breathing slowly I concentrated on just putting one foot above the other. Eventually my head was above the quay. I clambered up higher and then on to my hands and knees. Paul looked worried as I tried to stand up. My legs had turned to custard. He made a grab for me as I swayed backwards. I brushed sea-gull shit off my shaking, sweaty hands, pretending everything was fine. Tim had come up behind me. I fell into his arms and buried my head into his shoulder. He had to hold me up. I get vertigo on the top deck of a bus.

*

There is a lounge at the hospital for patients who are well enough to leave their room. You have not left your room, except to go for X-rays, for seven weeks. As far as I can tell the other room is used by the nurses for their tea breaks. They sit chatting and smoking fags. I don't like to go in there in case I disturb them. Sometimes I just wander up and down the corridor, just to stretch my legs. I keep checking you through your window, but you lie as you always do now, with your head propped up on the pillow. Occasionally you wake up from your drug-infused world, your eyes are sunken in your face, your lips are pulled back over your teeth. You look like you are starving to death. They don't seem to feel this is a problem, but you are wasting away before my eyes. I overheard one of the nurses in the patients' lounge talking about a woman who also has a fungal infection. My ears pricked up and I stood closer to the shut door. Cigarette smoke was coming out from under the gap. It's one of the Irish nurses. I couldn't tell which one, they are all mainly from the west coast. 'Well it's in her brain now,' one of them said. A chill ran through my bones. You have a fungal infection in your lung and if it were to spread...?

*

Two young fishermen approached us and asked Tim for his autograph.

'Do you wan' a lobster?' one of them said to me.

I was unable to speak, so Tim answered for me, 'That's very kind of you but we're off for a curry.'

We began to walk away. I watched them climb down their ladder like a couple of monkeys. Tim gave me my handbag.

'They must think I'm a right poof carrying that,' he said.

'No, love, I think the pink Crocs are the giveaway. Come on, let's go and find a Ruby Murray.'

We waved goodbye to Paul. Unfortunately there was no curry to be had in Newlyn, but Tim and I didn't care. We found a pub called The Swordfish. I drank cider and we sang along to the jukebox.

The tide was in when we got back to the quay. The tug was almost level with the jetty. Tim and I thought this would make it easier for me to get back onboard *The Princess Matilda*, but the tide had pushed the tug out from the ladder. It was cleverly tied to several bollards, so Tim tried pulling on a few of the ropes. Nothing happened. Finally he found one that pulled the tug close enough to the ladder for me to get on. I had to do it all on my own as Tim hung on to the rope.

'Get on your hands and knees and go backwards,' Tim said.

I was in no mood to make jokes as I manoeuvred through the seagull shit, inching my way backwards. I grabbed on to the bar of the ladder and climbed down.

'A bit further, Shane, down a bit more, one more rung, now turn around,' Tim cried. 'And hurry up, because I don't know how much longer I can keep it held in by the ladder.'

I turned and saw the opening to the deck was to my right. To my left was a tyre. I knew I wouldn't be able to climb over that. It hung several feet above the sea. I prayed and moved an arm and a leg outwards. I must have looked as if I was about to be crucified. Tim kept heaving and I saw the tug inching towards me until I knew I could make a grab for the rail. Sweat ran down my back. It was a warm evening. I managed to drag myself like a sack of potatoes from the ladder to the deck. Tim was already climbing down, so I pulled on the rope and kept the tug as close to the ladder as I could. I closed my eyes as he jumped.

'I'm never ever going to climb another ladder!' I said as we got back onboard *The Princess Matilda*. 'I need a large gin!'

Chapter Thirty-Two

A Matter of Life and Death

The sound of our neighbours doing heavy welding on the tug woke us at 7am the next day. Tim and I didn't mind, we were just so happy to be in Newlyn. I was brought up in the industrial Midlands; I like to see men at work. Fishing boats had been in and out of the harbour all night long.

'It's like a fishing factory,' I said to Tim when I gave him his tea in bed. 'I'm going to see if the fellas doing the welding want one too, I won't be long.'

The man on the bow of the tug was wearing welding glasses and sparks were spraying all over the place. I saw a few landing on *The Princess Matilda*, but thought it would be OK as long as they didn't get into the gas locker. Eventually he stopped and took off his goggles.

'Wanna cuppa? I've got a pot inside.'

'Tes' very kind of you, tha' would be nice, I'm parched,' our new friend said.

I noticed someone coming down the ladder. He looked official so I called Tim, who had just got out of the shower. He hurriedly dressed. The official-looking chap, who had a tidy mustache, knocked on our wheelhouse door from the tug.

'Permission to come aboard skipper?' he asked.

'Yes by all means. Are you Mr Munson, the harbour master?' Tim enquired.

'Yes I'm the harbour master for my sins.'

I poured him a cup of tea, too. We all chatted for about 20 minutes. Tim explained that we were hoping to get to the Isles of Scilly before going on to Wales.

'Don'do wha' the las' ones did,' Mr Munson said. 'Wha' were they doin'?'

He scratched his head, and continued, 'They were doin' a trainee for Atlantic rowin', they didn't get the tides or the weather right. We had three lifeboats after 'em,' he laughed.

'Wonderful,' I replied.

'Are we too big for any of those pontoons? My wife's a bit scared of the ladder.'

'No. I have to give priority to the fishing boats because they're paid for with an EU fisheries gran',' the harbour master replied.

'Would you like a biscuit with your tea, Mr Munson?' I asked him, obviously trying to bribe him into breaking EU regulations.

'Thank you,' he said dipping into the tin.

'Now tell me, Mr Munson, if we get stranded here by the weather, would you be able to put us up for the winter?'

'O' goodness, no!' he responded. 'No, you wouldn't like it here. No, not one bit, we have gales blowing righ' over the wall. No.'

I wondered if I had misheard his name. Mr Noson suited him better.

No sooner had Mr Noson climbed back up the ladder, than we had two more visitors asking permission to board. These two were wearing RNLI jumpers. They looked like rugby playing mountain climbers.

'Come aboard,' Tim said.

'Wanna cuppa?' I asked.

We introduced ourselves.

'I'm Patch Harvey, the coxswain of the lifeboat and this is Spencer Robertson, my helmsman.'

Patch and Spencer were hunks, both with a strong hand-shake. They looked us straight in the eyes. I could imagine them swimming out across the surf to save someone's life. Both had an air of strength but humility about them. From the first you could tell Patch was a leader. Tim and I knew absolutely nothing about him. Instinctively we understood that before us were men who would be willing to go the extra mile. Spencer had a shorn head and brooding eyes; he reminded me of Corporal Jase from Chatham. I am sure the trenches in the Great War were full of men like these. Patch had an easy laugh, a lumbering gait and a hand that was the size of my frying pan. His eyes took everything in, he missed nothing at all.

'I expect you'll be here a couple of days,' he said. 'The weather's not looking so good, so why don't we take you both out on the lifeboat in the morning on an exercise? Show you what a proper boat can do! Do you know anything of the history of the Penlee Lifeboat?'

'I thought you were the Newlyn Lifeboat?' I asked him.

'We moved here after the tragedy of 1981, we'll show you the old lifeboat station in the morning. It's not been used since the night of 19 December 1981.'

He paused for a few seconds, as if he was remembering something. I realised then what he was speaking about. I had seen the boathouse on the news shortly after Tim and I were married. The lifeboat that was launched that fateful night was called the *Solomon Browne*. Patch rubbed his hand across his face. For a moment he looked like a schoolboy. And that is just what he would have been at the time of the disaster. All the crew were lost.

'That would be great to go out on the lifeboat, Patch,' Tim said, 'if I can get Shane ashore. She refuses to go up the ladder.'

'I don't blame her,' said Patch. 'I don't much like them myself, but don't tell anyone. Row Shane over to the pontoon on your dinghy.'

'I think I've fallen in love with Patch and Spencer,' I said after they left.

'I think I have too,' Tim replied. 'I can't wait to go out with them in the morning.'

Tim took me over the harbour on *New Si* the next day. Patch got us fitted in to life jackets and we boarded the lifeboat.

'Do you ever get scared, Patch?' I asked him as he showed us around the engine room.

'No, you don't really think about it. We all have jobs to do, so we don't have time to be afraid. We trust the boat and we trust each other, we work as a team.'

There were eight crew onboard with us, all dressed in yellow all-weather gear with heavy-duty scarlet life jackets. Tim went up to the bridge with Patch and I stayed on the bottom deck with the others.

Once we cleared the harbour, the lifeboat lifted up at the bow and we all lent backwards. The brooding Spencer told me to hold on so I grabbed on to a bar. He kind of lay back and splayed his feet. I felt the engines throb and the speed of the boat left a wake of spume behind us. I had to shout to be heard. Most of the guys, I discovered, were local fishermen, except for Spencer, who was a carpenter. He said they were all unpaid volunteers.

'Peter over there with the beard, we call Two Kit. He works offshore on the rigs, but when he comes home he's on the lifeboat. He used to be a fisherman, but times are hard.'

'Why do they call you Two Kit?' I shouted.

'You can call me Peter. Two Kit's my nickname. It's short for 20-stone. As you can see I'm no lightweight,' he laughed.

Suddenly the boat slowed. Spencer pointed to a lonely looking boathouse with a slipway going down into the sea.

'You may want to go up on the bridge, you will get a better view from up there,' he said.

I climbed the steps to the high, open bridge of the lifeboat. Tim and Patch were talking.

'That's the old Penlee lifeboat boathouse,' Patch explained. He looked towards the slipway. 'We steam past every time we go to sea. Things can go wrong but I've got total faith in this boat and the lads. The crew from that boathouse went out in gale force winds and 60-foot breaking waves to go to the aid of a ship that had lost its engines. The skipper had his wife and her daughters onboard and four crew members. Time and time again Trevelyan, the coxswain of the *Solomon Browne*, came alongside the stricken vessel, his crew all trying to get lines on her. At one point a wave picked up the lifeboat and left it stranded on the deck, before another wave swept it back into the sea. Trevelyan's men managed to get four people onboard the lifeboat before their radio went dead. A Navy Sea King helicopter pilot helplessly watched the whole thing from the air. He said it was the greatest act of courage he had ever seen. No one on the ship or the lifeboat survived.'

Patch put more revs on the lifeboat and we moved slowly past the old boathouse.

'That's *Mowzle* over there,' he said, pointing to the picturesque village of Mousehole sheltering behind a tiny island. 'The village is a small place, and the tragedy affected almost every family. I'll introduce you to Janet Madron when we get back to Newlyn. She was married to Stephen, the Second Coxswain Mechanic. Janet was left with two small children to bring up. She'd taken one of them to a birthday party that afternoon and left the baby with her husband. The maroon had just gone up when she got back home and her husband was half way out the door. She never saw him again.'

I stood next to Tim and Patch high up on the bridge as we came back into Newlyn Harbour. As we passed by *The Princess Matilda*, it occurred to me that if we lost our engine then it would be people like Stephen Madron, Patch, Spencer, Two Kit and Little Ray and all the other volunteers who would self-lessly come to our rescue. They would leave their families in the Co-op or the pub, or children's birthday parties or a warm bed to come to our aid. Tim and I solemnly followed the crew up the gantry to their headquarters. I noticed a smart, attractive middle-aged woman standing outside the door.

'This is Janet,' Patch said.

We shook hands and I looked into her eyes and she looked into mine.

'These are my boys now,' she said, patting Patch on the back, and we followed the crew inside.

I asked Janet if she minded talking about her loss. I felt we shared something that had been life changing. But my husband had survived his crisis and Janet's had not. She looked at me very carefully.

'I get a lot of people coming to the lifeboat shop and some-times I hide. After the tragedy the whole village was filled with cameramen and news reporters. As if I didn't have enough to contend with, I was afraid to leave my home. For three days, I stayed in. I couldn't put on the TV or open a newspaper, it was headline news the world over. But then I thought, "You live in this village, Janet, go out and lift your head high," and that's what I did. I went around to Trevelyan's house to see the old lady. She was the mother of the coxswain. "Well, Janet," she said, "what are we going to do? We'd better get a new lifeboat."'

'And you've been getting donations for the RNLI ever since. Patch says you have an award because you've raised thou-sands of pounds.'

'Yes I have,' she said proudly. 'It makes me feel that Stephen didn't die in vain. I remember going up to London to receive his posthumous bronze medal. I stood on the stage in front of all those strangers and thought, "I don't want any medal, I want my Stephen back." But then I thought, "You do, Janet, you have two children, they are part of him too."'

Janet spoke very quickly and quietly. 'I remember it like it was yesterday. We lived in the mechanic's house in *Mowzle*, it was owned by the RNLI then. It overlooks the bay; it was a few steps down to the harbour from our back door. The cottage is called "*Lowen Chy*", which is Cornish for "Happy House'. And it was a happy house for many years. Stephen loved his job. He used to spend more hours in that boathouse than he did at home. *Solomon Browne* was his life. We had put the Christmas tree up that day. As Stephen was rushing out of the door, that horrible night, I begged him not to go. "I have to, Janet," he said. "There's women and children out there!" I drew the curtains so I wouldn't see the lifeboat going out. I knew I wouldn't see him again. Sometimes when I go to a funeral I look at the coffin being lowered into the grave and think, "You are so lucky!"'

Janet took my hand as if to comfort me. I shall never forget that moment. She is one of the most gracious and courageous women I have ever met. Her husband's body was never recovered.

*

Midnight
I keep thinking about funerals, about my mother and how she suddenly hissed, 'I want to punch the wall!' at the crematorium when my dad's coffin was carried in. I know why now. You were a pallbearer … you wore his shoes, my mom gave you his shoes, you said you would be proud to step into them. My dad loved you, he was so happy I found you…

When Tim and I got back onboard *The Princess Matilda*, I told him about Janet.

Tim thought for a while and said, 'In this age of false celebrity, the lifeboat crews and their families are the true stars of our maritime nation. I really admire them all, especially Patch. He said to me, "I've been looking at your boat. I think you'll be all right in her. You must know something: you got her here all the way from London. That's a fair achievement!"'

'And so it is,' I agreed.

I went to the fridge and opened a couple of beers and asked, 'So what are our plans? And don't forget you have to do some more *Harry Potter* dates soon.'

'We have two choices. We can go across to the Isles of Scilly – it's about 25 miles off Land's End. But if any gales blow we'll be stuck there all winter. There are no marinas so we'd have to have the barge craned out of the water,' Tim said.

'And the second choice is?' I asked.

Tim had his charts open on the table. 'Patch thinks we should go to Padstow but stop over in St Ives. He knows a couple of fishermen there and is going to give the harbour master a call. They don't usually let recreational craft in. However we have to get around Land's End first. At the moment this is our next challenge. We need perfect conditions to do it, but Patch reckons the weather will be fine in the morning.'

I took a sip of beer. 'Once we turn the corner at Land's End we'll be on the home straight, almost in Wales,' I said hopefully, looking at my map book.

Tim took the map book off me. 'Look at the charts, Shane! OK, this is what we are going to do. Newlyn to St Ives is 36 nautical miles. St Ives to Padstow is 34. Padstow to Ilfracombe is 56. Ilfracombe to Swansea is about 30 and then it's a short hop up the Bristol Channel to Cardiff.'

'But that's almost 200 miles, and nautical miles are longer then proper ones too! Did you not notice the leaves on the trees in Newlyn are dropping and changing colour? We'll never make it before the winter gales blow in!'

Chapter Thirty-Three
Tide and Time

Newlyn to St Ives: 36 nautical miles

Patch and his crew came down to wave us goodbye. Two Kit was there with his wife and they followed us out of the harbour on a motorboat. I had thrown some suntan lotion to Mrs. Two Kit; the sun was burning down from the clear blue sky. Tim and I waved until our arms hurt. Paul Crompton was with us. I showed him a bag of freshly caught and filleted mackerel that a fisherman had given to us that morning.

'And look,' I said, opening the fridge door, 'you have some lobster for your lunch too. Thankfully Patch gave it to me already dead!'

I could see Paul salivating. We joined Tim in the wheelhouse.

'How are you feeling, Tim?' Paul asked.

'It's a beautiful day and I have a deep sense of terror rumbling beneath. We're about to go round Land's End. Every time we go out to sea I am in a state of high anxiety. The elements are the elements and they're unpredictable. Patch told us about groundswell. This is what's left after or before a storm hits this coast. When there's a storm in the Atlantic it produces huge waves. These waves keep moving until they hit the next piece of land. Land's End. I think we are lucky with the weather today, but we're still going to bounce around.'

We had passed the forlorn old Penlee boathouse and Mousehole Harbour. I thought of Janet drawing her curtains against the raging December storm that had begun off the east coast of America. I looked towards the horizon and recognised a sea-change that meant we would shortly be passing over troubled waters. Tim had seen it too.

*

'Why didn't you realise his lungs were contaminated with fungus earlier?' I asked one of the doctors. There are so many of them now, I can hardly keep track. This one is a large man; he's filling in. 'It's a matter of elimination. Your husband is immune compromised. We are using every antibiotic available to eradicate it, but nothing seems to be working. All we can hope for is Tim's immune system to kick in. That will be the best way of beating it. His own immune system…'

I stopped listening to him. I knew what he was saying. He didn't have to spell it out. For weeks I've walked down the long hospital corridors. I have witnessed people coming out of rooms weeping, seen the comings and goings and then the name on the door changing. The porter arrives and the ex-occupant is taken to the morgue. Just after you were diagnosed you were wheeled through the subway that goes under the road to the main hospital. It's a maze down there, a secret world. Traffic trundles above, buses, black cabs, cars and vans. Our world has shrunk. You asked one of the porters what else was down there in the subterranean zone. Your porter changed the subject. The subway ceiling has plaster hanging from it, open-air ducts and wires, and a secret room. Every morning I used to park the car and walk through this subway, by the morgue. Eventually I walked to the ward a different way. You lie in the bed, breathing oxygen from a machine. I look out of the window. The view never changes. I do not believe in God.

*

Behind and to the side of us the ocean was deep blue and relatively flat. Before us was the telltale scaly black line. I went below to make lunch. Paul joined me. He saw me staring out of the window. Both of us felt the motion of the boat change.

'I went to Land's End when I was a little girl.' I turned my head away from Paul as I remembered my dad giving me a piggyback and running with me towards the lighthouse. The memory made me catch my breath. I had all but forgotten about it until that moment.

'I never thought I'd go round it this way.'

'So how do you think *Matilda*'s doing?' Paul asked me.

I felt the boat roll a little. 'Oh, she's fine. She's doing absolutely fine, *Matilda* likes a bit of wave. It's Tim that gets a bit anxious. I'll bring lunch up soon.'

I joined them in the wheelhouse. Tim was talking to Paul.

'When you're in charge of a boat that is bobbing around you don't have a chance to think about anything else. You don't worry about the past or the future. Your anxieties are completely in the present.'

Tim pointed. 'That's Longships over there, Land's End. It's like a fantastic loony conquest to be skippering a boat around a world-famous landmark.'

'So is that it then Timmy?' I asked, getting out my map book. 'Have we turned the corner?'

'Yes, we've turned the corner and now we're heading north for the first time. In just four more hours we'll be on the home straight to St Ives. Now get some lobster down Paul's throat, he looks famished.'

'Wanna beer, Paul?' I asked him.

'Better not, I'm working.'

'Sure you are, Paul. Do you want mayonnaise with that lobster and mackerel?' Tim laughed.

We came into St Ives on an emerald green sea. Just off the rocky headland were mackerel boats, fishing. At first Tim and I thought they were waving at us, but they were throwing out lines. As usual, everything was a rush as we came into the small harbour. There was a familiar face on the quay. I recognised the chap who had filleted us some mackerel before we left Newlyn.

'Tie two of your longest ropes together,' he shouted, 'and throw it up to me.'

But before I could do so I saw a seal and almost fell in the water with glee. I screamed at Tim, who was on the gunwale by the wheelhouse.

'It's a seal! Timmy there's a seal, look, look.'

But he was too busy to take any notice of me. The sea wall was thronged with people enjoying the Indian summer. I pointed to the seal and said to anyone who cared to hear, 'I've never seen one before.'

There were actually two seals, I noticed, as I tied the two heavy, thick black ropes together and threw them to the fisherman on the quayside. Surprisingly, I managed it on the first attempt. I think it was more to do with his catching than my throwing. He had patiently waited while I enthused about the wildlife.

He secured my ropes up and shouted down to me, 'You're going to need a lot of slack when the tide goes out. Do you want to feed the seals?'

'Oh yes please, come aboard!'

He climbed down the rusty ladder; it wasn't too long. I walked back to the wheelhouse along the gunwale, which now had a brown sandstone wall running alongside it.

'Tim, this is Ian, he gave us the fish this morning.'

'I've got you something else too,' he said.

'Oh what?' I asked him.

'A couple of crabs,' he replied.

'Live ones?'

'Oh yes,' he said. 'But if you've got some of that mackerel I gave you this morning we'll go and feed the seals.'

'They're half frozen, will that be OK?'

'The seals won't mind!'

I went below and took four fillets out of the freezer, grabbed a chilled bottle of champagne and some plastic flutes and put the lot on top of the roof. The bustling town of St Ives, I noticed, was about 200 yards away. The sandy beach was full of people. There were many young children paddling in the sea. I could hear them squealing with excitement as they jumped over the gentle waves. Their cries mingled with the screech of the seagulls that followed the mackerel boats into the harbour. It was hard to tell which was which. I opened the bottle of champagne.

'Cheers my darling,' I said to Tim. 'Congratulations, you got us around Land's End, and this chap here has got you a couple of crabs for your dinner apparently, but first we're going to feed the seals.'

Ian and I left Tim and took the fish to the other side of *The Princess Matilda*. I handed him a fillet.

'Do it like this,' he said as he bent down low, 'because if you throw it the seagulls will get it before it hits the water.'

I watched him carefully as he held the fish over the sea and one of the seals snapped it out of his hands.

'Now it's your turn,' he said, 'get right down.'

'Come on baby, come on baby,' I said in a high-pitched voice, much the same way I did when our children were small. But then at the last moment I gave the fish to Ian.

'I'm scared, I can't.' I am from the Midlands for goodness sake. The only wildlife I came into contact with was our menagerie of domestic animals, not creatures like these. The grey seals had soulful eyes that did not blink and their pointed noses stuck out of the water. They looked almost human, like a couple of bewhiskered colonels that had been stuffed into skintight leather bags. I could see the rest of their plump bodies pointing downwards in the crystal clear water. They appeared to be standing to attention with their flippers next to their sides. But when they dived I saw their backs were covered in scars. Ian said it was because they follow the fishing boats in and get cut by the propeller blades.

Tim was talking with the harbour master when I went back to the wheelhouse. I urgently needed to wash my fishy fingers in the bathroom. Ian disappeared up the ladder.

'This is my wife, Shane,' Tim said, introducing me to Steve.

He was a smart-looking man in a crisp short-sleeved white shirt with epaulettes on the shoulders. I suspected he might have been ex-navy. He had a military air about him.

'Steve says we'll dry out and sit on the bottom tonight, and we'd best leave first thing in the morning and anchor outside and wait for the tide to turn to take us around to Padstow.'

'With the tide behind you, you'll make good time to the Camel River,' he said.

'Can I get you anything Steve, a beer or a cuppa?' I asked him.

'No thanks, I'd better get back to the office,' he replied.

No sooner had he gone than Ian returned. He was holding two crabs. I had hoped he had been joking.

'But I don't know what to do with them,' I said, thinking I may throw them in the sea once he had gone.

'Just get me a bucket of tap water,' he said, taking a seat on the back deck and making himself comfortable.

I filled the mop bucket up and returned to the deck. He dropped the crabs into it with a splash.

'We'll just leave them there for a while and they'll get hypothermia. Have you got any large pots?'

I must admit I wasn't happy with the way things were turning out. I had been looking forward to exploring the old town that is built around the harbour. It was a glorious afternoon, not a cloud in the sky. We don't get many days like this in late September. Instead we were stuck with two live crabs and a fisherman who didn't seem to be in a hurry to go home for his tea. Indeed, he was determined to stay and cook Tim's. I made my excuses and rushed into the bathroom and didn't come out for quite a while.

'Righty-oh,' Ian said as I came back into the galley. 'Give the crab another ten minutes on the boil. I'd better be off, the wife'll be wondering where I am.'

Tim saw him out and Paul left too. I waved to them both through the open window.

'Thanks for the fish Ian! And see you tomorrow Paul!'

The pans were bubbling away. I lifted the lid, relieved to see both crabs were well and truly dead. Tim grabbed me from behind. 'I'm starving, how much longer before they're cooked?'

'Three minutes, go and get your hammer out of your tool-box,' I replied.

I took out my heavy duty chopping board from above the fridge and filled two mixing bowls with cold water. The crabs were transferred to cool, but Tim couldn't wait. He picked one out of the bowl and burnt his fingers, but he was unperturbed as he brought down his hammer and smashed away.

'You are not supposed to do it like that! You have to lift off the shell and take out the deadmen's fingers. It says so in my copy of *The Wild Food Year Book*.'

Tim reminded me of Charles Laughton playing Henry VIII. Although I am sure the Tudor Monarch never said, 'Fucking beautiful!' before licking his fingers clean.

I had beans on toast for my dinner.

The ladder had lengthened while all this was going on.

'Let's have a night in,' Tim said. 'I'm cream crackered, but let's just check the lines before we relax.'

Ian the crab-boiler had told us to let our lines out as the

tide ebbed. I went to the front and Tim did the back ones. It was twilight and it had begun to rain. We could hear noise from the town, a band tuning up and laughter. I heard a couple of pissed girls staggering down the harbour wall. They stopped and watched me as I wrestled with ropes.

'I like yer boat,' one of them said. 'Can we jump on it?'

'If you do that,' I replied, 'I will have to kill you, so best not, hey?'

The seals reappeared, which distracted them, and Tim and I disappeared below. He shut the curtains and I lit the candles.

Tim said, 'Tomorrow we go to Padstow. The only trouble is, we have to go past Newquay, which is the surfing capital of the UK. I've got a lot of homework to do tonight. I was almost a gibbering wreck this morning. I can't believe we've come around the Lizard and Land's End!'

I poured him a glass of wine. 'That's quite an accomplishment. I'm going to leave you to it and type up your notes.'

Tim has dreadful handwriting, and we like to keep our logbook up to date.

I was up in the wheelhouse for a couple of hours. Suddenly I realised *The Princess Matilda* was not swaying any more. For a while I had watched the tide going out and the little fishing boats turning on to their sides on the sand as the sea disappeared. The *slip slap* of the outgoing tide had pushed *The Princess Matilda* against the sea wall. Then all movement ceased. This is an odd sensation when you are used to perpetual motion. The last time this had happened was when we ran aground on the Swale, a couple of years earlier.

I called to Tim, who was down in the saloon still, worrying about our next passage.

'One of our ropes is extremely taut,' I said through the open door.

I could tell my husband was a bit cranky and despondent

when he joined me on the deck. He is always like this when he works on his charts. Our spotlight was on the step and he shone it down the side of the boat.

'We're already on the bottom,' he said. 'We ain't going to go any further.' Then he went back inside. Experience has taught me it is best to leave him alone at times like these.

I sat enjoying the darkness. Our boat was now surrounded by glistening wet sand that sparkled like jewels in the moonlight. I marvelled at the pull of the moon that commands the landscape to alter so drastically. Just a few hours previously seals had swum around us. The swish of the waves on the other side of the sea wall was becoming fainter. From one of the many harbour-side pubs I heard a bass guitar. After locking up all of the doors, I went below.

'That bass guitar is really boring. Whoever's playing can only do two riffs. Come on darlin', let's go to bed, we've got a busy day tomorrow,' Tim said, blowing out the candles.

St Ives to Padstow: 34 nautical miles

Tim woke me up a few hours later.

'There's somebody walking on the roof,' he said, jumping out of bed to investigate.

I turned over and went back to sleep.

'There was a drunk bloke up there,' Tim said, shaking me awake again. 'He said he liked the boat and just wanted to have a look. I told him to clear off!'

Sleep was impossible after that. I lit the gas and filled the kettle and settled in to watch the night turn into day. The ropes were creaking and the incoming tide slapped under our hull. We could hear the fishermen parking their vans. I opened a window and looked out towards the town. Taking a sweet lungful of air, I could smell the Atlantic Ocean. But it was mingled with an interesting cocktail of seaweed, seagull shit, salt, fish-guts and bilge oil. The pre-dawn air was chill and damp; my breath left vapour clouds.

My view of St Ives Harbour was totally different from the one I had left when I had gone to bed. I felt I had witnessed a once-in-a-lifetime miracle, but it happens twice a day. The pubs were all shut and a road-sweeping lorry was the only sign of life. On the water, half a dozen small, open fishing boats passed me by. I waved to each of them. Some returned my wave, others wished me good morning, and a few just ignored me. I couldn't blame them really. It can't be an easy life, fishing from an open boat. Ian the crab-boiler motored by.

'Another early start,' he said.

The kettle was whistling so I made the tea and took the milk out of the fridge. One and a half crabs wrapped in cling film greeted me. I went back to bed.

'At least I didn't have to boil the tea bag to death. Those poor crabs!' I said to Tim as I handed him a cup.

'We'll leave in an hour or so,' Tim replied, 'then anchor outside the harbour for a few hours in deeper water before picking up a fair tide to take us around to Padstow.'

Paul Crompton climbed down the ladder as Tim and I made our final preparations to leave St Ives. He told us all about the wonderful restaurant and hotel he had stayed in. I said he had fresh crab for lunch. Paul likes his food. Tim used the bow thruster to push us away from the wall. A bow thruster is an engine that powers a small propeller in a tube. It sits at the front of the boat just below the waterline. In theory you press a button and it makes the bow go right or left. What we have learnt about bow thrusters is similar to what we have learnt about outboard motors. They always work when you don't really need them, but never when you do. However, the bow thruster worked that day. It was just as well as the tide seemed determined to keep us against the wall. Tim had to keep his hand on the button for longer than usual.

It was quite choppy when we left the haven of St Ives Harbour, but it wasn't too worrying. Once we were out, Tim went to the bow to drop the anchor. I kept my eye on the sea wall and the rocks behind us, lest we get too close. He was up there for an awfully long time. I listened carefully for the hum of the motor and the rattling chain of the anchor.

'It's not working!' Tim yelled.

Paul asked me what was happening.

'The electric motor to let down the anchor's playing up, so he'll have to do it manually.'

'Do you think I should go and help?'

'Yes please, Paul, because I can't leave the wheel. I have to keep clear of the rocks or we're buggered. I think you're officially crew now!'

Paul left me in the wheelhouse and I heard chains jangling. I kept poking my head out of the door. Ian the friendly crab-killer came by. His boat, I noticed, was lower in the water. It was full of mackerel.

'I'm on my way back into the harbour before it dries out, that's the harbour not the fish,' he yelled over the noise of his outboard motor.

'Our anchor's not working,' I shouted back to him over the din of our engine.

'Well whatever Tim's doing up front, he's using a hammer,' he bellowed.

This was a little worrying. Tim thinks brute force will solve everything. Paul came back to the wheelhouse.

'So what's going on, Paul?' I asked him, but didn't wait for a reply.

The tide was going out and I knew we had a few minutes

to decide what we should do next. I looked longingly at St Ives harbour wall and phoned Steve, the harbour master. He said the wind was going to change and that it wouldn't be a good idea for us to go back in there.

'St Ives is pretty unforgiving in a nor'westerly. You would end up being pummelled against the wall. I think you'd be best pushing the tide and going on to Padstow,' was his advice.

Paul, I noticed, was a little bit anxious. 'Are you all right, Paul?' I asked him.

'Well it's a bit choppy up the front there. I helped Tim lower down the anchor, and we pulled it up again with our bare hands. It weighs a ton. Then when the anchor was back in place we had all the chain in a pile on the front deck. I picked the camera up to do a bit of filming and Tim said, "This is a technical term, it's called giving it a fucking whack!" and then he walloped the anchor with the hammer. His foot was millimetres away from the chain when it spun out. I filmed it for a few seconds then realised this is for real. That chain could've taken his foot off. We've pulled the anchor up again.'

'I don't know why we are doing this!' I said with vexation. 'It's time he took up golf and me, bingo.'

There was a seagull sitting on the roof of *The Princess Matilda*. Its wings were being ruffled by a stiff breeze. I left Paul to man the wheel and walked along the gunwale to speak to Tim on the bow.

'Steve says we should go on, push the tide.'

I noticed the tangle of chain on the deck. It usually lives in a neat metal box in the forward hold.

'We should have a spare anchor,' Tim said with annoyance. 'I'm a complete dick!'

'I'll put it on the shopping list. But you'd better let Falmouth Coastguard know what's going on, just in case,' I replied.

'Ooh, I don't know,' Tim said in his slightly camp northern Alan Bennett voice. 'It's a different story every day.'

Just for a second he was Georgie, the character he had played in *The Fattest Man in Britain*. I laughed; I knew we would be all right then.

It took us nine hours to do 34 miles. If the tide had been with us it would have taken five. As usual I had my map book in front of me and the binoculars around my neck. We had a rolling swell on our broadside for almost two hours and didn't make any progress. Tim had the throttle down but we stayed in the same place. The undulating swell ends up as hollow surf waves that break on Newquay's Fistral Beach. Surf fans from all over the world come to the old pilchard-fishing town, which now survives on tourism as well as fish. The tourists still eat the less-than-sexy-sounding pilchards because they have been re-branded as Cornish sardines.

'At least we're not going backwards,' I said as I fed Paul one of Ian's fish.

Tim and I knew we were using up valuable fuel. The last time we filled up was in Falmouth. I went below because I had forgotten to put away a couple of glasses. For a while I had been hearing ominous sounds. Two glasses were broken – not good ones, but I was annoyed with myself. I placed them on the bed, then a rolling wave caused me to fall to my knees as if I was praying. We didn't have an anchor and we were low on fuel but I was more concerned with the survival of my glassware.

Chapter Thirty-Four
Getting the Hump on the Camel

Tim steered *The Princess Matilda* into the Camel Estuary. The tide was with us and took us upstream at a tremendous pace.

'I'm going to slow right down,' Tim said, 'in case I get us up to Padstow too quickly. We need enough water to get us over the infamous sandbank, the Doom Bar, into the harbour.'

'It's so beautiful, I feel like we are in another country,' I replied.

'Those are two of the most stunning beaches I've ever seen!' Tim said. 'We could be in Hawaii or the Caribbean.'

On both shores of the river were sand dunes and white empty beaches. I sat on the front of the boat. It is my favourite place when we come into a new port. The sun was hot and I was pleased I was wearing a hat. Behind us I saw a couple of small boats following us, and ahead were dinghies tied to large, bright yellow swing buoys. It became fairly clear to me that Tim had not seen them. He seemed to be determined to take a short cut. I turned and started to wave my arms to get his attention.

'TIM!' I yelled, 'YOU ARE GOING TO HIT A BOAT! TIM! TIM!'

But I shouted in vain. Fortunately the little dinghy was swept to one side. We did not hit it, but we hit the buoy, which disappeared. I quickly made my way back to the wheelhouse.

'You sunk the buoy!' I said accusingly.

'I did not!' Tim replied.

'You did, and moreover that dinghy over there is loose – you cut through the mooring!'

'Are you sure?'

'Of course I'm sure! I saw it happening. Did you not hear me yelling and waving my arms like a demented windmill to attract your attention?'

'We've got to try and get the dinghy.'

I already had the boathook at the ready. Fortunately we had experienced a similar situation with *New Si* on the Helford River, so between us we managed to grab hold of the errant little boat.

Tim and I both noticed a large, open-topped, tourist-filled speedboat coming towards us. I saw it was painted with shark's teeth and it became obvious the captured dinghy belonged to them. The skipper took the painter and took it under tow.

'We're very sorry about that,' Tim was saying to the skipper of what I could now see was a trip boat called *Jaws*. 'The tide took me. If there's anything to pay, we'll do it. Sorry about that pal!'

Jaws left us and I turned on Tim.

'It was the biggest buoy I've ever seen in my life and you missed it!'

'I love your loyalty, Shane, the way you blame me…'

I interrupted him, anger rising in me. 'You should have seen it, Timmy! It was a huge yellow thing!'

'All right!' he snapped. 'I did it, but what's the point of shouting about it?'

This is usually the point where I slam doors and leave. I did not have that option, so I just turned my back on him and walked to the rear of the deck.

I noticed the water was brown. In fact I could see mud being kicked up by the propeller. I called a truce.

'It's very shallow here,' I said.

'I think we have run aground,' Tim replied.

'Yep!'

Tim put the engine into reverse gear, but *The Princess Matilda* refused to budge.

'At least the tide's coming in really quickly, Tim,' I said.

'Yes I know the tide's coming in quickly, that's what drove me on to the buoy!'

I could see the water swirling and felt the boat lifting.

'Eh-up! We might be moving,' Tim said as the reverse gear bit and the boat edged backwards.

I moved closer to him at the steering wheel. He turned and hugged me before calling the harbour master on the radio.

'*The tidal flap's open, come on in,*' crackled over the VHF.

I went to sort out the fenders, and of course they were all on the wrong side. This is something else that is a contentious issue between Tim and me. No matter which side I put them, he will turn *The Princess Matilda* around and I will have to move them. While I was unpicking my knots I realized Padstow's tiny picturesque harbour was right in the centre of the town. Shops and pubs with tumbling cascades of pink busy Lizzies and scarlet geraniums surrounded our new home. The ancient fishing hub of the Camel River was also heaving with tourists. Long, lime-green park benches lined the quay. I noticed pale, sun-bleached wildflowers growing out from the arid gaps in the rough, ragged slate just above the waterline on the salty sea wall. The berth where we had been instructed to moor had children's legs dangling down next to a short, dumpy ladder. I just hoped Tim had noticed the limbs too. There were a few people on a yacht just ahead of us. They looked at us nervously as 35 tons of *The Princess Matilda* came alongside their vulnerable-plastic-looking vessel to reverse into our space. There was no wind blowing and our bow thruster worked. This made it much easier.

'Where have you come from?' one of our new neighbours asked as I tied off my bowline to a wooden capstan.

I did it carefully, not wanting to damage the wildflowers with a dangling rope.

'London,' I replied proudly.

There were people sitting next to our mooring on the lime-green benches, eating ice cream. A couple of them overheard our maritime discussion.

'What, you came from London today?' one of them asked as he sucked melting drips out of the bottom of a Cornetto.

'Goodness, no!'

The lady skipper on the neighbouring yacht ignored him and said, 'We hope to get to Fowey. That's about 117 nautical miles by our reckoning. We have a winter mooring there. Do you know it?'

'Yes and believe it or not, it's taken us three months to get from Fowey to Padstow! But my husband's been working and the weather's been crap,' I replied.

'The weather's been really bad. But we're going to push on and, given the tides and the weather, we hope to do it in two days. But the sea is a dangerous place and unpredictable...'

I sensed a little bit of doubt creeping into her voice, so interrupted her when she paused.

'Well good luck with that and fair sailing, and please say hello to Stubbles on the water taxi and give him our regards,' I said.

I noticed Tim was busy chatting to the tourists on the benches too. They were all laughing. I joined him in the wheelhouse.

'That was a palaver wasn't it? I think this is what's called keeping a low profile,' Tim said to me. 'What a journey. And we had a barney.'

'Do you still love me?' I asked him.

'Of course I still love you, you are my life. Give me a kiss.'

I ducked. He had a manic look in his eye.

'I'm going to send Patch an email to let him know we got here … eventually.'

Tim slapped me playfully on the arse as I went below.

We went to bed listening to a Tom Jones tribute band playing in one of the pubs.

'Warner Brothers are trying to pin you down on dates for *Harry Potter*,' I said as I reached for my earplugs.

'I'll phone my agents on Monday morning, I can't think about that now.'

We were tired and slept for eight hours. The sun woke us up early the next morning, so after breakfast we went exploring. It was low tide and we saw the sandbar. JCBs were loading sand into skips. The Camel River was a puddle. The tiny harbourside shops were awash with signs. *Real Cornish Pasties*, *Real Clotted Cream*, *Real Homemade Scones*, *Real Cornish Crab*, *Real Cornish Ice Cream*. And of course there were signs for the *Real Local Chef* who put Padstow on the tourist map. People waved to Tim or asked him for his autograph and most of them asked, 'Are you doing any more *Harry Potter*? I bet you would get a table at Rick Stein's!'

The sun was beating down on *The Princess Matilda* when we got back to the quay. We had little privacy. The harbour and Rick Stein are why tourists come to the little Cornish town. It must have been creeping up to 90 degrees Fahrenheit and we had no shade except for the wheelhouse. We have a fold-up camping sofa that we keep on the back deck. Tim stretched out his legs while I went below to fetch him a glass of wine. The lime-green benches were crowded with people all enjoying the last few days of summer. They were fishing for crabs, eating ice cream, scoffing fish and chips and having domestics. Tim was fast asleep when I came back up the steps.

The sun was swiftly moving around and I knew he would get burnt. I reached inside the airing cupboard just by Tilda's cabin and grabbed a purple king-sized sheet. My clothes pegs were in the crayon tankard and a few were still on my washing line above the back deck. I pegged the sheet to the line and draped it behind Tim's camping sofa. It blocked out the rays of the sun from behind, but light still streamed through half of the windscreen and our side door to the wheelhouse. There was an umbrella by the fire extinguisher. We keep the extinguisher in case of a fire in the engine room, and the brolley in case it rains. On this occasion I used it as a parasol to keep out the sun. We have stable doors to our wheelhouse, I shut the bottom half and left the top half open for fresh air. I used Blu-Tack to fix up a couple of my shawls, but one of them fell down. As I bent down to pick it up, I saw a bearded Viking with a child on his shoulders.

'I've got a boat over there,' he said, pointing across the harbour. 'Maybe we'll have a chat in the morning when this lot's gone home.' He indicated the munching throngs with a nod of his head.

'I'm Rick. No, not that Rick, I'm a sailor!'

'Hello,' I said as I stuck my shawl back up above the door-frame.

Tim was sleeping peacefully in his sheik's tent. He was hidden from view and the sun. Padstow Harbour is like a goldfish bowl and my husband's welfare is always uppermost in my mind. We are all vulnerable when we sleep, and Tim sleeps like a child. When he was ill, I sat guard by the side of his bed like a tiger. It still worries me when he sleeps for a long time in the afternoon. His endless naps were a symptom of AML. But I knew here in Padstow he was genuinely tired because of what we had just done. I let him sleep 45 minutes longer than usual. Even though he naps, Tim always goes to bed before me.

*

You must wake up, Timmy, you must wake up. I want to tear the mask off your face and the tubes and wires, I want you to talk to me, look at me. You are in a dark and dangerous place. I told them to take you off the diamorphine. You phoned me at 2am. You were crying. No, not even that. You sounded like a trapped bird. My first instinct was to leave the house and drive to the hospital but I called the night nurse on the other line and she managed to calm you down. The next day, the doctor said you will have to come off the opiates gradually. Of course you will. Not only do you have AML and a fungus eating up your lung but you are now addicted to heroin. I drove home after yet another day watching you waste away and realised you may never recover. There, I've written it! The only sound in your room is your rasping breath and my laptop and the endless beeping of the equipment. Whatever you found within you to pick up the phone beside your bed and call me has sapped you. The red and green lights on the pump flash as it delivers drugs into you. Sundays, I've always hated empty Sundays. Sundays at the hospital are a nether world. I didn't have enough strength to go home and face the kids so I stopped off at Brenda's house. I sat outside for a while, unable to get out of the car. Bren must have noticed me. She opened the door and took me by the hand and led me up her garden path. I couldn't speak at first. She sat me in a chair in the living room and poured me a drink.

'He's dying Bren, Tim's dying.' And then I howled like an animal.

Chapter Thirty-Five
The Old Sea Dog

We were woken at 7:30am by a roaring noise.

'It sounds like a huge ship's coming into port,' Tim exclaimed, sitting up in bed.

I got up and looked out of the bathroom window. I couldn't see anything so put the kettle on.

'The noise is getting louder,' I said, now looking out of the galley window. I saw the noise was coming from a street cleaning hoovering machine.

'What a racket. A broom would do a better job,' I complained as I took our tea back to bed.

'Padstow is a totally different place on a Monday morning. There's no one around except for the street cleaner. I'm going to get some fresh milk and a paper, do you want anything?' I asked Tim as I dressed.

'Only an anchor,' he replied. 'I'm going to find a chandlery while you're out.'

I got back to *The Princess Matilda* before Tim. He wasn't far behind me.

'So I saw a couple of blokes the other side of the harbour,' he said breathlessly. 'I asked them if there was a chandlery or anyone that had local knowledge of the coast. "Wha' can I do to help?" one of them said. He was a small man, hard to say his age. So the long and short was I said we needed a spare anchor and he took me to his hut – it stank! There was a tank full of water with a couple of lobsters crawling around. There was all manner of bits and pieces to do with anything nautical. He disappeared up a wooden ladder and came down with a rusty old anchor. "Will tha' do you?" he asked. I nodded. "An' you'll be needin' some rope and some chain. Come wi' me," he said. And we walked to some kind of touristy shop, but it sold ropes as well as crap. "You'll be needin' about 20 fathoms of chain, I'm guessin'." And he grabbed the chain and stretched out his arms behind his head and measured. "One two three," until there was a pile on the floor. Then he did the same with the rope. I paid and he winked at me. He was just like your dad when he was doing something a bit dodgy! He say's he's going to bring it all around later.'

'Did you give him cash for the rusty old anchor Tim?' I asked.

'Why yes, yes I did.'

'And did you ask his name?'

'Pete, and he reminded me of your dad!'

'Quite so,' I replied and went back to the *Daily Mail*. My dad was a wheeler-dealer.

'Ahoy there!' someone said from the quay.

It was the Viking from the previous afternoon, not my father's doppelgänger.

'I heard you los' your anchor? Can I help in any way?'

We invited him onboard.

'This is Rick, I met him yesterday, while you slept in the tent,' I explained.

Rick was over six feet tall, with strawberry blonde curly hair and a beer belly. He was sunburnt and we could tell he spent most of his time out of doors. His vessel was a beautiful wooden sailing ship moored by the ice cream van. We had noticed both as soon as we moored up.

'Wanna cuppa?' I asked the Viking.

'A beer would be nice, if you have one, but let's see if I can sort out your anchor first,' he replied.

I could sense Tim thinking, 'This is a man after my own heart.' The three of us walked along the gunwale to the bow and Tim told the Viking what had happened the previous day.

'What's down there?' Rick asked, pointing to the closed hatch on the forward deck. Tim lifted up the hatch and we all peered down into the hold. The coal scuttle, hose, carpet and old bits of stuff live in there, as well as our anchor chain, when it behaves itself, and the bow thruster.

'Well, let's get the chain back down where it belongs for a start off,' Rick said. 'I'm going to need some rope.'

Tim had some in his pocket. He saves things like this for a rainy day. Rick put the rope under the tangled chain and lifted it up, and as if by magic the chain unfurled and went back down the capstan hole into the hold. Tim and I were both impressed. They chatted for a while. People had begun to walk around the harbour and a couple of motorbikes sped by.

'Do you run your engine when you use the bow thruster or anchor?' the Viking enquired.

'Yes I do, come to think of it. I used the bow thruster a lot when we came out of St Ives. It must have tripped off!' Tim replied. He climbed down the ladder to the hold and looked around.

'There must be a trip switch down there somewhere,' Rick said.

'Yes!'

Tim climbed back up the ladder and pressed the anchor button on the deck and it worked.

'Show me where the trip switch is, Tim,' I said as I looked down into the depths of the murky hold.

'Why?'

'In case you get hit on the head and I have to find it!'

'Look on the bright side why don't you?'

We heard laughter behind us. The Viking, Tim and I

turned around. There was a large couple on the bench. For the last hour we had been the cabaret. We scuttled back inside *The Princess Matilda* and drank beer.

'I come out of Bristol,' Rick explained as I opened another bottle of Becks. 'Do you have charts?'

'I was hoping to get some,' Tim replied, 'but there's not a chandlery around here.'

'No matter,' Rick said, 'I've got some spares. I'll let you have 'em for what I paid for 'em. I'd better go, I've got guests arriving soon and I'm taking 'em back to Bristol. The days are getting shorter and the tides getting later. You want to watch you don't get trapped here this winter.'

Rick saw my laptop on the marble work surface. 'Can you get the weather on that?' he asked.

'Yes, do you want to look?'

'Do you use Magic Seaweed?'

'I've used magic mushrooms. Does it grow locally?'

'No, it's a website!'

I had already Googled and passed the laptop to him. He stared at it for a while.

'It's going to be a bit too breezy for you in the morning. That's perfect for me, I need the wind, but it looks OK for you to leave the day after!'

No sooner had Rick left then we heard someone shout, 'Ahoy there!'

Tim jumped up and I followed him into the wheelhouse.

'Welcome aboard, Pete,' he said.

I watched a slight man climb down the ladder. The water level does not change much in the locked harbour, so it was only a few rungs. Even I could cope with that. But this chap had a huge rusty anchor over his shoulder. He dropped it on the back deck and climbed up to the quayside to a trolley. I heard him grunting as he picked up five hundredweight of chain. I may be exaggerating, but it sounded heavy as he heaved it to the bow.

'Got any ol' carpet?' he asked us.

Tim went down the forward hold and reappeared with some offcuts from our cabin.

'Tha'll do,' Pete said as he threw it on the roof. The anchor was placed on top of it. 'Save your paintwork from gettin' rusty,' he said.

Pete was about 5 foot 6, but as a young man he would probably have been 5 foot 8. His back was slightly bent from years of hauling on heavy nets. He had piercingly blue eyes and skin like leather. With quick expertise he lashed the spare anchor to the roof. His hands were gnarled and the blue veins stuck out. His fingers were scarred and misshapen with rheumatism and his oily fingernails were split. This was a man who had worked all of his life. But at the moment he was using his calloused fingers with the dexterity of a Belgian lacemaker as he tied complicated knots.

'You probably won' need this anchor, but there it is if you do. And you don' wan' it banging about the roof in storm. This won't be going anywhere,' he said with a flourish as he cut the end of the rope with a well-used pocketknife.

'I knew it would come in handy one day,' he said with a great deal of satisfaction in his voice.

'What, the anchor?' I enquired.

He rubbed his hands together. 'I've had it in my loft for years!'

My dad never threw anything away either.

'Who taught you to splice those knots?' Tim asked him.

'I was taught by an old sailor,' Pete replied. 'He'd tell you something once, show you how to do it. If he had to tell you a second time, he gave you a bollocking. If he had to tell you a third time, he'd lay you out on the deck with a big punch. You'd never get it wrong again.'

I looked at Pete's face. His nose had been broken a few times. He looked like a man who had thrown and taken a few punches in his time.

Tim asked him if he would take a drink.

'I'm out early in the mornin',' he explained. 'Go' to check my pots.'

'I'll put the kettle on shall I?' I asked.

Tim and Pete followed me down the gunwale and we went below. They chatted away like they had known each other for years. I understood now why Tim had trusted him. I instantly warmed to him. Tim's phone rang. I could see his agent's number on the screen.

'Excuse me, Pete,' Tim said, 'I'd better take this, it's work.' He disappeared into the bedroom.

'I bet you've never had a day off sick in your life,' I said as I gave Pete a cup of tea.

'Can't afford to,' he replied. 'Now what are your plans? Padstow's a grand place, don't get me wrong, but it's a hell of a long way back to London, and if your man there needs to drop everythin' to work, you'd better find yourself a winter moorin' by an airport or a railway station. Cardiff's your best bet.'

'That's what we've had in mind since we left London in 2005. We're so close but so far, do you think we can make it?'

Pete rubbed his chin, but before he had time to reply Tim joined us.

'Sorry about that, Pete. Did you get your tea?'

Pete lifted up his cup and said, 'Have you got any charts?'

'Some bloke called Rick's going to drop off some for the Bristol Channel later...'

'I know Rick,' Pete interrupted. 'You know that channel

can get nasty. Just remember if you don't like it in the first half an hour it won't get any better. You'll be putting in to 'combe I expect?'

Both Tim and I looked puzzled.

'Ilfracombe. It's a fair old way and you'll have to push the tide for a good while. You'd better fill your fuel tanks up. And now I'd better go, got jobs to do, people to see,' he said, winking. 'I'll let them know on the fuel barge you'll be coming out at high tide. I'll give you a hand to tie up.'

Tim and I watched him climb the wooden ladder.

'Isn't he great?' Tim said. 'Think of all the arseholes we come across and then we meet men like Patch, Rick and Pete. They are like marine angels.'

Padstow to Ilfracombe: 56 nautical miles

The Princess Matilda left Padstow on a dawn tide the day after Rick left. It was still dark when we got up, but I already saw a light on in Pete's little fishing boat. He waved and I mimed, 'Do you wanna cuppa?' He put his thumbs up and started his engine, undid his ropes and pulled alongside. Tim was still in the shower.

'You are going to have a long day of it,' Pete said, 'and it's going to be fresh out there. Have you tied everything down?'

'Oh yes, we've learnt the hard way!'

Tim came up to join us and put on the Met Office forecast. A Force Six with a moderate sea was predicted. Pete saw Tim and I exchange glances.

'Take no notice of tha',' he said. 'Tha's a general forecast.'

He drank his tea quickly. The sun was rising, but it was a dingy and grey day.

'I've got to go, the tidal flap's open.' He gave me a kiss and patted Tim on the back, climbed into his boat and left us.

There was no sign of him when we came out on the river. We noticed a boat anchored close by.

'I think that's the fishing bait boat,' Tim said. 'Maybe he's gone there.'

Tim and I didn't speak for several minutes. I kept looking behind. There wasn't much to see; the visibility was appalling. Ahead we saw breaking waves at the mouth of the estuary. Frankly, they looked terrifying. I knew Tim was thinking the same as me, and I sensed he was about to abort our trip and turn around. But then I saw a fast boat coming from behind us.

'It's Pete the old sea dog! He's been hiding behind the bait boat to see how Matilda handles.'

He cut across our bow and waved to us as he headed fearlessly out into the surf going southwest.

'We're going to be fine,' Tim said, 'he wouldn't let us go else. It's such a shame he's going in the opposite direction to us though.'

The Princess Matilda lurched as she hit the surf, but she ploughed through the waves like a combine harvester. The breaking waves covered the wheelhouse and water dripped down the side doors. Pete had been a mine of information the past couple of days. He had told us many stories, not all of them printable. But one came back to me as Tim gave our passage to Falmouth Coastguard.

'On fishin' boats there is always repartee,' he said. 'Lots of chitchat, teasing and jokes, but as soon as things become difficult, no one speaks, just concentrating on the job in-hand.'

Corporal Jase had said much the same thing to us.

Tim and I didn't say a word for three quarters of an hour, and then I fell asleep.

I still had half a cup of tea in my hand when I woke up. I was sitting wrapped up on our green camping sofa. Tim smiled at me as I sleepily tried to work out who and where I was. This is something I have been doing for years. I used to have a type of epilepsy that mostly struck when I woke up. Not a good thing to have with three children around. I felt the motion of the boat first of all, and I looked at Tim and saw the sky dipping down and then disappearing to be replaced by sea. I knew we were going over big rolling waves. I stood up carefully, but it felt safe to move.

'We've had a 15-foot swell chasing behind us,' Tim explained. 'You made me feel more confident when you fell asleep. You wouldn't have done that if you'd been scared! The visibility is still bad, but at least I can see land now.'

Every half an hour Tim gave me the coordinates of our position to put in the logbook. I filled up four pages.

'It feels like we've had Lundy on our portside for hours. We don't seem to be making any progress, I swear we're going backwards,' I said to Tim at one point.

'That's because we've been punching the tide for five hours, but it will turn soon.'

We both looked towards Lundy Island but it kept disappearing behind the waves. I turned and gazed behind us. Every 12 seconds a hill of water disappeared under the boat, lifting up her nose and then coming out the other side. Our bow almost went right into the water. But along came another and another: big, long, smooth, undulating waves.

'We've only seen one boat since we waved goodbye to Pete,' Tim said. 'You do realise that when we get to Ilfracombe we shall have to hang around outside the harbour for a couple of hours?'

'Why?'

'You can't float on sand. The sea doesn't care about how tired you feel. We have to wait for the tide.'

The Princess Matilda has a shallow draft so, despite his earlier warning, Tim took a risk and went in to the small harbour at Ilfracombe sooner than he should. But the gamble paid off. He had to climb a ladder up to the quay to tie us alongside the wall. I could see he kept tying and retying ropes. We needed enough slack to let us down on to the bottom because the harbour dries out at low tide. Several fishing boats followed us in. I stood on the deck watching them. Fishermen have gone up in my estimation since we began our trip around the coast. The tide was coming in quickly and *The Princess Matilda* was now almost at the top of the wall. I locked up and climbed three rungs of the ladder. Tim held out his hand as I stepped on to the quay. It had been 12 hours since we left Padstow. I sent a text to Pete to let him know of our safe arrival. He replied, 'IT WAS A ROLLY OLD SEA BUT YOU ARE ALMOST IN WALES NOW SO BE BRAVE, THE SKIPPER KNOWS WHAT HE'S DOING!'

Chapter Thirty-Six
My Nemesis

A fishing boat called *Our Josie Grace* was unloading fish when we came back with a Chinese takeaway. Tim checked our ropes again while I climbed aboard *The Princess Matilda*; she was almost level with the wall now.

'Have you had a good day?' I asked one of the fishermen.

He laughed. 'Day, I wish. We've been out for 36 hours.'

I knew the skipper would not have slept. Pete never does.

Tim, however, fell asleep almost as soon as I had cleared away the takeaway. I thought about getting rid of it in a bin on the harbour, but I looked out of the window. The tide was going out. We were five rungs down, so I tied it up in a plastic bag and put it in a bucket on the back deck, hoping the seagulls wouldn't like Tim's spare ribs. *Josie Grace* behind us was still unloading.

'Will you be taking it to be auctioned at Newlyn?' I shouted.

'No, it's bait,' someone replied in the dusk.

I went back inside and bullied Tim into going to bed.

'Go on, love, don't worry. I'll check the ropes before I join you, but I need to type up the log, so I'll be a couple of hours.'

He fell into bed and was soon snoring again.

It was coming up to midnight by the time I was finished. The flashlight was on the step in the wheelhouse and I shone it on our ropes. They looked dangerously taut. I remembered what Dame Edith Kevins from Falmouth had said about boats being 'hung up' on harbour walls. Rushing to the bow I managed to loosen two ropes. Back in the wheelhouse I kicked off my fluffy slippers and searched for my trainers. They were under the camping sofa. An empty can of Coke began to roll from beneath the metal frame. The boat was beginning to list. I picked up the can, threw it into the bin and grabbed a knife. We keep several in the wheelhouse for emergencies. I stood on the gunwale and looked up, hoping to see someone on *Josie Grace*, but they must have all gone to bed.

'Oh my God!' Quivering, I hiccupped with panic. I climbed the ladder with my heart in my throat. The first few rungs were covered in slippery, slimy, stinking seaweed. Up and up and up I went, not daring to look down. After what seemed like an age I crawled on to the quay on my hands and knees. A keen wind was blowing. Tim had tied the rope against the top of the ladder. The knife was still in my teeth and I was tempted to cut it, but thought I should try and undo it first. My hands were trembling but I felt the rope give a little and quickly untied one of Tim's extra special knots, thinking how lucky I was to have had all these years to practise doing so. I quickly let out more slack. I knew if I didn't get back on board straight away I would be up the top there till the morning, so I made myself climb back down the ladder, trying to stop my mounting hysteria. I began to talk to myself as I used to when the kids were learning how to walk. 'You can do it, one step, one step.' *The Princess Matilda* was sitting on the mud – I smelt it before I saw it – as I stepped backwards on to the deck. I kicked off my trainers, locked the doors and went below. I drank neat gin out of the bottle and shook for two hours. It was 2am before I went to bed.

Tim woke me up four hours later.

'I've just been out to check the ropes. We're on the bottom.'

'Yes I know,' was my reply, 'and I'm not going to spend another night here!'

I told him what I had done.

'But that ladder is 25 feet high!'

He looked startled. I could hardly believe it myself.

Tim took out his maps. 'All right darlin', we are almost home and dry. Swansea's about 28 miles away. They've got a big marina, give them a call. See if they can give us an overnight mooring and if the weather's OK we'll push on to Cardiff.'

I was happy to hear this. It was still early so I left a message on Swansea Marina's answering machine. Tim, meanwhile, was putting our route into the satnav. At last I felt we were almost there, and the weather was looking good. I looked at the AA map book. Cardiff was just up the road from Swansea.

Our Geordie twitcher cameraman, Phil, had flown down from Manchester to Bristol the night before. I sent him a text at 7am, telling him we planned to leave. He wandered down to the quay after breakfast.

'Look at the bags under my eyes. I'm not going up that ladder again, so we're going to Swansea,' I said.

Just then my phone rang. It was Swansea Marina; they said they didn't have room for us.

Tim had just put our course into the autopilot. He swears a lot when he does this. And then his phone rang. I saw his agent's number.

'*Harry Potter* want me on standby!' he said when he hung up.

'You are not leaving me here in Ilfracombe! Surely they should know if they need you to film.'

Tim looked at his charts and the *Reeds*. I went below; I could hear the kettle whistling. Phil followed me down the steps to the galley.

'Wanna cuppa, Phil?'

He nodded and said, 'So if Tim's on standby they might need him in the morning?'

Phil directs films so he knows the business.

I felt overwhelmed. Tim's job has always taken top priority in our lives. He found out he had cancer and finished his day's filming before he went to hospital. And actors don't get paternity leave; he went to work one hour after Rafe was born. I even did an availability check with his agent before I arranged my mother's funeral. We can't plan ahead.

Phil trailed me up the steps to the wheelhouse and quietly said, 'I don't want to add to your problems, but Paul booked a helicopter to come over at 12 to shoot aerial shots of you going up the channel.'

'Well he might have just spent a lot of money for nothing at all. I don't even know what time high tide is, and we have to leave before the harbour dries, and Tim's still working on that!'

Timothy had his charts all over the floor. He was on the phone, so we both waited for him to finish.

'Right, we're going to Watchet in Somerset,' he said. 'I've booked us a place in the marina.'

'Watchet, I love the sound of that,' I said with relief.

Tim pinched my arse a little bit too hard.

'Watchet! That hurt.'

Then he chased me down the steps into the saloon and we embraced and yelled in unison, 'WATCHET!'

'So if I have to work in the morning they'll have to send a car to pick me up at 3am,' he said after we said 'Watchet' another ten times.

We left Ilfracombe at noon just as a helicopter came over. In all the rush we had quite forgotten about Paul's plans. He wasn't actually on the chopper; it was a specialist firm. 'What's Tim doing?' Phil asked as he re-emerged from the saloon when the helicopter left.

'Hopefully dropping the anchor,' I replied. 'We have a few hours to wait for the tide to take us up the channel.' All of a sudden I felt exhausted. 'Why is it every morning on this boat seems like three days at the moment?' I asked as I wearily waited to hear the hum of the anchor motor lowering down the chain. 'Is it working?' I shouted to my husband through the open door.

'I think so,' came Tim's reply.

I heard the anchor splash. 'Hallelujah!'

I turned off *The Princess Matilda*'s engine as soon as I realised we were holding fast. Tim was still on the bow, so Phil and I joined him.

'The great thing about making mistakes is that it's the only way I learn,' Tim said to Phil. 'Rick who fixed our anchor in Padstow said there was something missing from the end of the anchor chain. It's called the "bitter end", which is a piece of rope that goes down in the anchor box in the forward hold. Say for instance a storm is coming and our anchor gets stuck, I may have to cut the rope, hence, "to the bitter end".'

I climbed on top of the boat to unfurl our tangled Devonshire courtesy ensign. It was a beautiful day; it hardly fluttered in the breeze. The golden syrup rays of the sun lay like oil on the smooth surface of the sea. I watched Tim walking along the gunwale. He had a long piece of rope in his hands. He was demonstrating to Phil how Pete, the old sea dog, had measured out the rope for the spare anchor.

'He did this,' Tim said, moving as if he was working out with gym equipment – the kind where you stretch bands of thick pink elastic behind your head, hoping they won't snap and slice off your ear.

'Do you know what that is?' Tim asked, demonstrating with his length of rope. 'A man's arm's length from hand to hand outstretched is roughly a fathom.'

He looked up at me expectantly. Tim always says I am his hardest audience. I pretended to look the other way; I knew what was coming.

'I couldn't fathom what he was talking about!'

Phil laughed and so did I.

We had nothing to do but read and enjoy the scenery after that. Ilfracombe is built on a series of cliffs. The most famous, Hillsborough Hill, is known locally as the sleeping elephant. I looked but couldn't see it myself. I lay on the roof and read a book.

Chapter Thirty-Seven
The Severn Estuary

Ilfracombe to Watchet: 30 nautical miles

'Come on Shane,' Tim shouted. 'It's time to go, we're going to push the tide for a while.'

I joined him in the wheelhouse and showed him the book I had been looking at on the roof. 'It says the Severn Estuary is the greatest tidal waterway in Britain, and it runs into the Bristol Channel, and has the second highest tidal rise in the whole world. Can we not just miss it out?' I said.

'If we had got here earlier in the year we could have cut straight across the estuary to Milford Haven,' Tim said. 'But we're going to be hugging the coast up the channel from 'combe past the Exmouth National Park. It will take us about six hours to get to Watchet; we're going to take our time. We don't want to get there too early as we have to wait for the tide to get us into the harbour – it dries out. Rick and Pete said Watchet is a fucker to get into. The tide can pull you on to the rocks.'

'Oh we'll be fine, Tim, but sometimes I wish we didn't have to worry about getting from A to B.'

The rugged cliffs and rolling hills were covered in forest. Every now and again green pasture broke up the thick deciduous trees. Someone hundreds of years ago would have cut down the timber. Now sheep grazed on the rich grass that appeared to hang by magic above the high cliffs. Some of the fields looked as if they were in danger of slipping over the hillside and into the sea. We saw no other boats as we wended our way up the Bristol Channel. The sea was smooth at first, smooth enough to allow me to sit on the bow, away from the engine. I sent Phil up there for his cigarette break. Once the tide turned it was a different matter. The speed of the flooding tide was running against a stiff breeze so it kicked up breaking waves. In the space of a few minutes the breeze became a wind and the wind began to gust.

'Reading the tide is a science,' Tim said to Phil as he helped him into the wheelhouse.

'Howay man, how could it have changed so quickly?' Phil asked, wiping the sea-spray from his face with the bottom of his jacket. 'I hated science at school!'

'So did I,' Tim said solemnly. 'I just hope my calculations are right.'

For some time we had seen what looked like multi-peaked meringues in the distance. The forest and cliffs had given way to yellow sand. Fortunately the meringues were on the shore, but I instinctively knew the wind against the fast-incoming tide would soon cause us problems.

'I've got a feeling that's Butlins at Minehead. We should be in Watchet in about 40 minutes,' Tim said as he peered through the binoculars.

The Princess Matilda was picking up even more speed as the surging tide took her up the channel. The sun was already setting behind us. I knew we only had about 30 minutes of daylight left. I went below and put on our navigation lights. We had never entered a port in the dark before. On the other side of the channel we could see the gaudy, glittering lights of Barry Island funfair in Wales. When I came back up the steps Tim was on the phone.

'Looks like I'll have a lie-in then. They don't need me on the set tomorrow! Now all I have to worry about is getting us into Watchet.'

The sea had become extremely choppy and had turned an ugly-looking grey, but the sunset behind us was purple. None of us were in the mood to wax lyrical about the sky. We were all literally on edge. Not one of us spoke for a while as we were intent on keeping on our feet. The bow of *The Princess Matilda* ploughed through and over the undulating sea. Her nose dipped and her stern rose and the wheelhouse was drenched, but at least we were facing the waves. But then my heart sank as I realised what was going to happen next.

'That's Watchet Harbour over there,' Tim said. 'But we're here far too soon. I'm going to have to keep turning around until I'm sure there will be enough water to get us into the outer harbour. Can you see the lights?'

It was hard to make them out as a rolling, white, twisting wall of sea grabbed hold of us. *The Princess Matilda* recoiled and bucked like a horse in a rodeo show. I could just about make out the red and green warning lights. One on each side of the entrance to the harbour. They seemed to be impossibly close together. Tim must have turned *The Princess Matilda* around half a dozen times. And each time he did so, the incoming waves hit us along the whole 54-foot length of our boat. Suddenly we shuddered as a breaking wave caught us and threw *The Princess Matilda* into a whirlpool of heaving, angry sea. It felt like we were about to be sucked into a vortex but then we were tossed up and out. *The Princess Matilda* groaned like a wallowing pig. It was getting quite dark.

*

The doctor had tried to break the news to me slowly.

'Just tell me!'

'OK, we have an unlicensed antibiotic. This means there are no guarantees.'

'And if you don't use it or it fails then he will die!'

'It's not looking good. He's been on prolonged anti-fungal treatment for 40 days...'

'If I have to sign the release form for the unlicensed stuff, give me the pen please.'

*

'This is going to be the toughest challenge I've ever faced,' Tim said as he now steered *The Princess Matilda* towards the flashing red and green lights. 'The entrance is only about 20 feet wide.'

And we're 15, I thought to myself. I hung on to the top of the doorframe above the steps. I know Tim's technique for getting into tidal locks and, frankly, I knew this was going to be a difficult thing he was attempting. But I trusted him one thousand per cent.

'Come on, Tim!' I said quietly.

What was going to stand us in good stead was the practice Tim had had on the Medway, getting into us into Chatham lock. That was always tricky, and so was Limehouse on the Thames. I could sense Phil becoming nervous. I could almost hear what he was thinking: 'What the fuck am I doing on this boat that is about to hit a sea wall...?'

Like some kind of maniac, Tim headed for the starboard wall. He had to over-compensate for the speed of the tide. At the very last second he pushed the boat into reverse and fought with the wheel. *The Princess Matilda* spun around and we all hung on for dear life as we headed back into the angry unforgiving sea.

'I'm going to have to do the approach again,' he said. 'Brace yourselves!'

*

This morning when I woke up I willed my energy out through my solar plexus. I sat for 30 minutes, focused on you, imagining you as you used to be. I slowed down my breathing and every breath I took, I gave to you, sending my breath through the ether to your room in UCLH. I could see the room very clearly. I was in the room, my lungs became your lungs and I breathed for you. I breathed for you. I kept my mind focused even while making the kids their breakfast and sorting out their quarrels. I was still in UCLH breathing, breathing … I drove to the hospital, concentrating, breathing, breathing and chanting, very quietly at first. 'You will get well you will get well you will get well' and by the time I was crossing over Waterloo Bridge I was growling. I was angry and my anger turned to rage. I was not going to let this thing happen. I would not let you die. I wanted to stamp on the filthy, filthy thing growing inside you, to smother it with my fury. I sat in the car just underneath your room. I knew you would be unconscious. I played a track from Crash Test Dummies, one very personal to us, and I cranked it up so it boomed out of the speakers. I opened all of the car windows. It boomed out louder and louder. You are a sick man but I had to wake you up. Wherever you were in your pain-ridden, morphine netherworld, I had to grab you, reel you in. When the track ended, I knew you would be awake.

'Hello my love,' you said weakly. 'Will you help me up, I want to go to the bathroom.'

'I'll call a nurse to help.'

But you already had swung your legs out of the bed and attempted to stand. I grabbed hold of you and you shuffled slowly to the bathroom. You were pushing the mobile drug pump before you, using it like a walking stick. I managed to get you by the sink, and then you began to silently cry and, for the first time in front of you, I did too. I held you up and we both wept.

'They are starting you on a new antibiotic today my darling and I just know it's going to work.'

'You will stick with me to the bitter end won't you?'

'You know I will.'

*

Once more, Tim headed *The Princess Matilda* towards the gloomy dark harbour wall, but this time he accelerated. For a moment my life flashed before my eyes. I was sure we were going to crash and be smashed to pieces. I shut my eyes and thought what a wonderful life we had had. Then I opened them and realised Tim had navigated us into the safety of the slack water. We were out of the swell of the Bristol Channel and were sliding into the shelter of the outer harbour. We were safe. Tim and I both cheered.

'Well done my darling,' I said, throwing my arms around him.

'We ain't out of the fire yet,' he said. But I could tell he was pleased.

Tim called the harbour master on the radio but there was no reply. I knew we couldn't get into the inner harbour until the green light came on to show it was safe to enter. We hung around for what seemed like hours, then the light changed to green and then back to red. Tim and I were getting tetchy with each other, so I went below to check on my baked potatoes. I am always hungry after dicing with death. Fortunately, I had prepared dinner when it was still a millpond.

Tim shouted for me, 'Quick, Shane, the light's on green!'

I rushed to get the fenders dropped down; the flashlight was already on the bow. We entered the narrow, dark opening of the marina. I felt the stern hit the tidal flap wall, but I knew it wouldn't be serious: *The Princess Matilda* has taken harder knocks than that. Our allocated mooring was just ahead and, as usual, Tim turned around so I had to change the fenders to the other side. But no matter; I was so relieved to once again be in a marina with pontoons instead of a beastly ladder.

We said goodnight to Phil, then Tim and I had dinner and collapsed into bed. In just nine days we had completed over 150 nautical miles.

Chapter Thirty-Eight
The Final Voyage

Watchet to Wales: 19 nautical miles

The next morning I phoned Miriam Jones. I knew she was in Cardiff, staying with her mother. I told her we would not fly the Welsh Dragon unless she joined us. She said she wouldn't miss it for the world. After I hung up I got a text from Steph, Tim's agent. 'YOU HAD BETTER GET TIM TO LEAVESDEN STUDIOS BY MONDAY MORNING!'

So we had a whole weekend.

A chap called George came to *The Princess Matilda* while Tim was in the shower.

'That's my crane over there,' he said, pointing to an ancient-looking contraption on the other side of the harbour. 'I'm going to be lifting a boat out of the water soon. Do you think your husband would like a go? It is Timothy you are married to, isn't it?'

'It was this morning when I woke up,' I replied.

Tim joined me in the wheelhouse just in time to see George lift a little boat.

'He says do you want a go?' I explained.

'Of course I do, come on!'

Phil was hanging around the harbour as Tim and I walked over. He looked quite bedraggled. Tim walked ahead and I stayed back to speak with Phil.

'I slept in my clothes,' he complained. 'It was a filthy dirty hotel I was put up in. I'm not spending another night there, the production co-coordinator's going to find me somewhere else to stay tonight.'

'That's a shame, and all the places Paul has stayed in have been marvellous.'

'Well Watchet's not Padstow!' he replied grumpily.

'Have you met George yet? Tim's going to drive the crane. I had a good chat with him earlier on. He used to be a unit driver when they were filming *Return of the Native* around here. Apparently he drove Catherine Zeta-Jones. "If you see her," he said, "ask her if she remembers me. She used to sit opposite me and have her dinner. She'd look at me and say, 'George, I want to marry you and have your babies!' and then she'd laugh and say, 'See, George, that's what you call acting!'"' 'Yes, I've spoken to him,' Phil said, laughing now as he rolled a cigarette. 'He also works on the local radio and goes surfing. He's a bit of an all rounder.'

We watched as Tim shook hands with George. I thought it best to keep out of the way of my husband driving 40 tons of heavy machinery. He was quite good at it. When he and George had finished playing, we all walked down to look at the sea.

'You did a brilliant job last night, getting us in here,' Phil said.

'Even if you did take a lump out of my wall, Timothy,' said George with a twinkle in his eye. 'But don't feel bad, you're not the only one to have done that. It's hard in the dark and there's an odd flow that comes out of here when the tidal flap is lowered. How long are you going to stay with us here in Watchet? We have plenty of room if you want to winter here.'

'That's very kind of you, George,' Tim replied. 'But when we left Weymouth in April, I had it in my mind we'd get to Cardiff and the weather is set fair, so we're going to leave tomorrow.'

'You'll have Saturday night in Wales then,' George said.

He joined us for a drink later that evening. He wanted to say goodbye as he was going to drive through the night to spend the weekend surfing in Cornwall.

'What a grand man he is,' we both said as we waved him goodbye.

I went shopping the following morning and kept getting texts from Miriam. Cardiff may only be a few miles by sea, but to get to Watchet on public transport was more complicated. She eventually got to us as Tim was on the fuel barge, filling up. I gave Miriam her life jacket and we sat on the bow together as we left the outer harbour.

'I can't believe this weather,' Miriam said.

'No, nor me. The Bristol Channel is a mirror.'

'How do you feel about going to Wales again after all these years?' she asked me.

'Strange, very strange. To misquote Dickens, Wales was the best of times and the worst of times. One day I shall tell you all about it … I married my first husband 37 years ago today in a little Welsh town. He's been dead now for 33 years.'

'You must've been so young.'

'I was also lighter. Come on, let's put the kettle on then you can sit and chat with Tim while I spring clean. I want *The Princess Matilda* to be spick and span when we get to Cardiff.'

'Have you booked *Matilda* in for the winter?' Miriam asked me as we walked down the gunwale to the wheelhouse.

'I've booked a flight from Cardiff to London for Tim. I told the marina we only need a couple of nights. I'll break the news to them slowly.'

I was a whirling dervish, polishing and scrubbing. Miriam kept coming down to see what I was doing.

'I must say, Shane, in all the years I've known you, I've not seen you be so domestic. It's so out of character. Now, is it too early to have a glass of champagne?'

'No!' I replied. 'We'll drink it out of a paper cup, then no one will know, and I'm all finished down here, so will you help me hang up some bunting and put up the Welsh flag? See, I think *The Princess Matilda*'s got a heart. That's what I think. Tim was amazing getting into that harbour the other night. But *The Princess Matilda* is extraordinary. She was just, like, really solid and safe so she's going to get a present. It's a celebration.'

Miriam and I climbed on to the roof with our paper cups and unfurled the bunting. It fluttered in the breeze. *The Princess Matilda* looked beautiful. We were approaching the outer harbour of the Cardiff Bay Barrage and I felt exhilarated and happy. Just the other side of the lock was our final destination.

*

You walked all the way to the nurses' station. It took about ten minutes. All the domestics came out of the kitchen and gave you a round of applause. I've seen visitors come and go on this ward and patients emerging from isolation rooms like bald chrysalises, weak, unsure on their feet, shuffling up the corridor. You did it today. Panos gave us the results of the latest bone marrow biopsy. Two per cent cells. You are in complete remission and your immune system is kicking in. We can't believe this yet. I phone everyone: Sylvia, Jenny, Miriam and Jimmy, Frankie, Brenda and Mike. 'Tim's in remission, his counts are coming back.' We live one day at a time. This is all we can do, not think about the future, just the moment...

*

Miriam and I joined Tim in the wheelhouse and I hung around his neck. Tim picked me up and spun me around.

'We did it, we fucking did it darlin'!' He tickled me and dug his fingers into my ribs.

'Stop it!' I said impatiently as we waited for the green light so we could get into the lock. I looked up as we entered; the high wall rose up and up, and above the steel barriers were people. We all waved.

'Is this really Wales?' I yelled.

Behind us a large yellow RIB pulled up. It was full of little girls. We waved to them and once again Tim and I embraced.

'Well done my darling,' I said quietly in his ear.

He kissed me and saw the little girls staring at him.

'Are you having fun?' Tim asked them as he turned off our engine.

'Yes it's my birthday and you're in *Harry Potter*!' one of them said.

Another added, 'We like your boat, she's so pretty.'

Miriam and I went up to the front of the boat to tie up.

We sat on the bow of *The Princess Matilda*, holding the thick, black, plaited rope against the pontoon as the turbulent water level rose and lifted us up the lock. I looked back towards the wheelhouse. Tim waved to me and we both gazed at the many flapping Welsh flags. I could see he was laughing. It made me want to cry.

'I will die laughing and crying with the love of life,' he had once said to me.

Miriam topped up my paper cup with champagne. A siren sounded and we watched everyone move away from the heavy-lifting Cardiff Barrage bridge.

'Go back and stand with Tim, I can manage on my own up here,' Miriam said.

High above our boat, hydraulics lifted the road bridge into the air. I joined Tim and we saw the silver-slated Welsh Assembly ahead. To the right was a white weatherboard church. The warning light on the lock turned from red to green. Tim and I held hands as he put *The Princess Matilda* into gear. She moved majestically out of the pen, into the freshwater lagoon. I swear I felt *Matilda* tremble. But that may have been my imagination, because just at that moment the RIB trip boat followed us out. All the little girls were waving and shouting to us.

Croeso i Gymru!

Acknowledgements

I would like to acknowledge the help and support given to me by my agent Laetitia Rutherford who kept saying, 'Paint a picture!'

Jake Lingwood my editor who knew Wales was another country, and all the team at Ebury.

And the fisherfolk, old sea dogs and finally the volunteers and crews of the Royal National Lifeboat Institution.